*Immanence and Transcendence:*

*The Theater of Jean Rotrou*

*1609 - 1650*

**P**eux-tu n'adorer pas ce sexe précieux,
Ce charmeur innocent des âmes et des yeux,
Ce sexe en qui le ciel admire ses ouvrages,
A qui souvent, lui-même, il offre ses hommages,
Et qui força jadis tant de divinité
A venir dans ses mains rendre leurs libertés?
Peux-tu, le cœur libre et plein de tant de glaces,
Voir ces trônes vivants des vertus et des grâces?
Et vois-tu que le ciel, sur ce bas élément,
Se soit fait de soi-même un portrait plus charmant?

CLORINDE (III.1)


**I**l n'est si haut crédit que le temps ne consomme,
Puisque l'homme est mortel et qu'il provient de l'homme;
Ce qui nous vient de Dieu, seul exempt de la mort,
Est seul indépendant et du temps et du sort.

BÉLISSAIRE (v.2)

# Immanence and Transcendence

The Theater of Jean Rotrou

1609-1650

By Robert J. Nelson

Ohio State University Press

Copyright © 1969
by the Ohio State University Press
All Rights Reserved

Standard Book Number 8142-0009-5
Library of Congress Catalogue Card Number 76-79846

*For*

ANDREW PAUL AND ALEXANDRA

# Table of Contents

|  |  |  |
|---|---|---|
| | Preface | ix |
| | Acknowledgments | xiv |
| INTRODUCTION. | Rotrou's Theater: "Dieu Caché, Dieu Visible" | 3 |
| I | Immanence and Transcendence in *Le Véritable Saint Genest* | 19 |
| II | The Temptation to Total Immanence | 39 |
| III | The Temptation to Total Transcendence | 91 |
| IV | Nostalgia for Immanence | 131 |
| V | Last Things . . . First Things . . . | 179 |
| APPENDIX A. | Rotrou in Legend and Criticism: A Brief Summary of Positions | 189 |
| APPENDIX B. | *Sacrement* and *Sacrilège*: A Brief Etymological and Historical Review | 191 |
| | Notes | 199 |
| | Bibliography | 227 |
| | Index | 239 |

# *Preface*

Jean Rotrou (1609–1650) is France's neglected classic. Generations of critics have recognized his merits but have done so in a tangential manner. He has been called the "mentor of Corneille," but, as in a famous judgment by Voltaire, the mentor is said to have become only the pupil's own pupil.[1] He has been celebrated as the precursor of Racine in classical tragedy and of Molière in classical comedy. That Rotrou can be linked to all three of France's great classical dramatists has been in part responsible for the respectful neglect of his long canon (thirty-five extant plays surviving from a production presumed by some to be many times as great). For a tradition prizing generic purity, Rotrou has been too easily drawn to all dramatic genres, especially to the genre that is the despair of classical purists: tragicomedy.

In recent times, critics have attempted to correct centuries of neglect. By stressing certain plays or isolated aspects of his total work, various critics have reminded us of Rotrou's intrinsic worth. They have also related him more independently but no less favorably to his great contemporaries. The provocative existentialist study of eight plays in Jacqueline Van Baelen's *Rotrou: le héros tragique et la révolte* has fruitfully expanded the range of critical attention beyond the trilogy in which Rotrou's tragedy has been too long circumscribed (*Le Véritable Saint Genest, Venceslas, Cosroès*). Again, stressing Rotrou's technical inventiveness more than most critics, Harold C. Knutson has analyzed still another genre in Rotrou in his *The Ironic Game: A Study of Rotrou's Comic Theater*. The brilliant, ambitious study by Francesco Orlando, *Rotrou: Dalla Tragicommedia alla tragedia*, extends the franchise of the "serious" to

PREFACE

Rotrou's tragicomedies as well as to his tragedies. Finally, over the last decade, in a number of incisive studies, Jacques Morel has perceptively linked theme and dramaturgy as he situates Rotrou in the development of French thought and especially of French classical tragedy. His assiduous study of the playwright has just culminated in the publication of his doctoral dissertation *Jean Rotrou: dramaturge de l'ambiguité*, which appeared even as the manuscript of this book was being read for the Ohio State University Press. I have thus been unable to integrate here specific insights from M. Morel's superb book. However, having had an opportunity to read the latter while my own was in press, I believe it correct to say that our studies are different in approach but complementary in results. Each concludes that Rotrou's vision is unitary throughout the canon, particularly with respect to the major themes that Morel studies in the early part of his study.

Like Hubert Gillot's study of Rotrou's "théâtre de l'imagination" somewhat earlier in this century, these recent studies do much to correct the stinting evaluation of Rotrou passed on from one generation to the next since Voltaire's somewhat offhand remarks. This restoration has also been stimulated by the more general re-evaluation of French classical literature over the past three decades. The studies of Orlando and Knutson owe much, for example, to recent interest in the relation of the baroque to the classical.[2] Mlle Van Baelen profits from the perspectives of phenomenological criticisms as these have been brought to bear on French literature of the seventeenth as well as other centuries.

My own study profits, I trust, from this general re-evaluation as well as from the particular studies of Rotrou in the various aspects indicated. Attempting a comprehensive re-evaluation of the dramatist here, I have been drawn more to those studies that first seek to situate the dramatist in his own times. It has seemed to me that by understanding Rotrou first in that perspective, we can then see in what way he may be related to the literature of later times—not only our own but of the nineteenth century in particular, when, as Jules Alciatore, J. Jarry, Emile

PREFACE

Deschanel, and others have shown, romantics like Stendhal found much in common with "Corneille's mentor."

To the extent, then, that my scholarly research and critical imagination have made it possible, I have turned to Rotrou in his own setting. This is the perfervid philosophical and religious atmosphere of the first half of the seventeenth century. In that setting Jean Rotrou grew to manhood and wrote the long canon containing that fine play on an actor converted while acting. *Le Véritable Saint Genest* is considered the most impressive example of his genius and one of the most expressive signs of an enduring religious outlook. This vision endures, in fact, as the explicit expression of ultimate truth *per omnia secula seculorum* for one-sixth of the world's population at this very moment. I have, to some extent, explored aspects of this "eternal philosophy" both before and since Rotrou's time. However, my professional conscience has guided me in this exploration. I have tried to avoid the tone of the breviary, concerning myself with earlier and later forms of this philosophy only to show its relevance to seventeenth-century French drama, notably to Rotrou's theater of immanence and transcendence.

I am not concerned with establishing an exact influence of orthodox theology on Rotrou. There is a philosophical consonance between Rotrou's vision and that of certain of his contemporary co-religionists, particularly the Jesuits in their opposition to the Jansenists. But any attempt to establish this connection with precision is subject to caution on two counts. First, too little is known about Rotrou's early life and education. His biographers (Abbé Dom Liron, Henri Chardon, Thomas Frederick Crane) know only that at about the age of twelve, the future dramatist left Dreux to continue his studies at Paris and that in the great city he won the approval of his professors. Of the latter, the name of only one is known: Antoine de Bréda, professor of philosophy. M. de Bréda seems not to have impressed the well-known compilers of French ecclesiastical and religious history. My colleague, Professor Frank Paul Bowman, a savant of French ecclesiastical history, upon whose impressive resources I called in this matter, has also been unable to advance

PREFACE

our knowledge of M. de Bréda. I am grateful to Professor Bowman, and I trust he will not feel that his assiduous researches on my behalf have been pointless in view of the second caution I now raise in the matter of possible influences upon Rotrou. In general, the concept of influence should be used in the flexible spirit called for by Lionel Trilling in his famous essay, "The Sense of the Past":

> In its historical meaning, from which we take our present use, *influence* was a word intended to express a mystery. It means a flowing-in, but not as a tributary river flows into the mainstream at a certain observable point; historically the image is an astrological one and the meanings which the Oxford Dictionary gives all suggest "producing effects by *insensible* or *invisible* means"—"the infusion of any kind of divine, spiritual, moral, immaterial, or *secret* power or principle." Before the idea of influence we ought to be far more puzzled than we are; if we find it hard to be puzzled enough, we may contrive to induce the proper state of uncertainty by turning the word upon ourselves, asking, "What have been the influences that made me the person I am, and to whom would I entrust the task of truly discovering what they were?"[3]

With this caution in mind, I prefer to see a *consonance* of viewpoints between Rotrou and certain of his contemporaries, rather than an *influence* of those viewpoints upon him.

# Acknowledgments

Much of the work on this book was completed during a year in which the University of Pennsylvania granted me leave from academic responsibilities. This leave and a fellowship from the John Simon Guggenheim Memorial Foundation (1967) sustained me and my family in that period. In terms of the concepts developed in this study, the support from the University and the Foundation was at once material and spiritual. However, I am sure that officials at both institutions will not be slighted if I say that the spiritual support had to be far greater on the part of my wife and two children. Except for a brief period of research in France, they have been confronted over the past few years by a demanding scholar who converted their home into a "study" in which he researched, ruminated, wrote, and rewrote, at all hours of the day and night. It must have been hard to identify this creature with the husband and father they knew before this enterprise. Along with my gratitude, I owe them an apology.

I should also like to thank those institutions and individuals who aided me at other stages of this study. The American Philosophical Society awarded me a grant-in-aid (1964), enabling me to consult Rotrou holdings in libraries at Harvard University, Yale University, and Columbia University, and to purchase copies of original editions of Rotrou's plays. The American Council of Learned Societies also awarded me a grant-in-aid of research (1965) for travel to libraries in Paris, Rouen, and Dreux for editorial and critical study. I am grateful for this support, as I am to those colleagues who sponsored my requests to the Society, the Council, and the Guggenheim Foundation: Professors Jules Brody of Queens College (New York City),

## ACKNOWLEDGMENTS

Hugh M. Davidson of the Ohio State University, Nathan Edelman of Columbia University, Lawrence E. Harvey of Dartmouth College, John C. Lapp of Stanford University, Georges May and Henri M. Peyre of Yale University, and William J. Roach and Otto Springer of the University of Pennsylvania.

I want to express a special word of gratitude to a fellow scholar of Rotrou, Professor Jacques Morel of the Université de Lille. In personal conversations here and abroad, as well as in extensive correspondence, he has given to me, as I know he has to others, most generously of his rich store of knowledge of the dramatist and his period. As my allusions throughout this study show, his own scholarship on Rotrou has been invaluable to me. More than this, M. Morel's personal grace and professional generosity are ever-present signs that in consulting him, one is indeed consulting a "gentleman and a scholar."

Finally, to come, like Rotrou, to first things among the last, I wish to add a very special word of thanks to my wife. She has typed this book for me in both rough and definitive manuscripts. Her constancy and patience have helped through every stage. She and all those who have encouraged me in this effort have provided models of accuracy, judgment, and sensitivity that I trust they find reflected in the pages that follow.

R. J. N.

*Havertown, Pennsylvania*
*January, 1969*

*Immanence and Transcendence:*

*The Theater of Jean Rotrou*

*1609 - 1650*

INTRODUCTION

*Rotrou's Theater:*

*"Dieu Caché, Dieu Visible"*

MANY scholars of French Literature look on the seventeenth century as the "Age of Racine." Recently, Racine himself has come to be regarded as the dramatist of transcendence, in a specifically religious sense. According to Lucien Goldmann, Racine's is the theater of "Le Dieu Caché." In it the things of the world (physical attributes, a morality preoccupied with human aspirations and passions) are signs of man's dissociation from the Divine Ground of Being. In theological terms, the world is more sacrilege than sacrament.

Yet, this "sacrilegious current" is not unique or dominant in the century. Between the Edict of Nantes in 1598 and its revocation in 1685, a strong belief in "Le Dieu Visible"—an "immanentist current," so to speak—makes itself felt both in formal religious writing and in imaginative literature. Theologically, this literature views the world as a sacrament. To recall a famous literary dichotomy, it will undoubtedly occur to many that, as Racine is by tendency the dramatist of transcendence, so Corneille might be thought of as the dramatist of immanence.

An elaborate expression of both tendencies is to be found in a playwright to whom both Corneille and Racine turned at various moments of their careers: Jean Rotrou (1609-1650).[1] In comedies adapting models in Plautus, semi-pastoral plays adapting *L'Astrée*, philosophical dramas adapting models in Euripides and Sophocles and Seneca, political dramas adapting a wide variety of historical sources—in all these Rotrou develops conflict and resolution in virtually the same dramatic and ethical structures found in his most famous play, *Le Véritable Saint Genest*, the tale of a pagan actor converted while playing a convert. When the resolutions give us the world restored to its integrity, his plays express what might be called the "sacramental ethos." When these resolutions are not complete, their very incompleteness recalls those violations of the sacred known as sacrileges.

To forget that the sign of the sacred is only a sign is to profane it; to cherish the sign for itself is to commit sacrilege against what is signified. Many plays show this self-destructive emphasis on the sign itself. The quests in Rotrou's second, third, and fourth acts are often undertaken by the hero or heroine in the disguise of a pilgrim; the resulting mistaken identities and misalliances force many characters to condemn the world as a "sign" of malevolent determinism rather than divine providence. Confronted with the vicissitudes of fate, Rotrou's despairing heroes and heroines often feel compelled to withdraw from the world in stern self-reliance and reflective indifference. This Stoical spirit is to be found in such Christian apologists as Pierre Charron and Guillaume Du Vair in the closing years of the sixteenth century and the early years of the seventeenth. It had already been sounded in the theater by the religiously concerned Robert Garnier and others. Continuing these religiously based motifs, many of Rotrou's heroes cast brooding doubts on a world order in which all seems *dis*order or, at best, the senseless "order" of Fortune's wheel. Losing faith, these heroes call on their courage to salvage from destiny at least the quality of *généreux*.

As I said in my book on Corneille, during this period that term

> conveys far more than its English cognate "generous" or the parallel usage of the term in modern French: "kind," "bounteous," "charitable." In its seventeenth-century usage, *généreux* is closer to its etymological meaning: Latin gens, gentis, f. root Gen, *gigno*, that which belongs by birth or descent, a race or clan embracing several families united together by a common

name and by certain religious rites. Orig. only patrician, but, after the granting of the connubium between patricians and plebeians, also plebeian.[2]

Stoically responding to fickle fortune, Rotrou's heroes and heroines seek to be *généreux* in just these terms. Many of Rotrou's heroes are nobly born, and thus automatically behave as *généreux*. But I cannot say of Rotrou's *générosité* what I have said of Corneille's: "It is strictly its patrician sense that obtains in Corneille."[3] With its strict pairings on the basis of birth, rank, and station, *générosité* in Rotrou often finds itself at odds with pairings made by a unity higher than that of the patrician family: by Heaven and according to the tenets of what might be called the sacramental code of chaste desire. Conflicts between this desire and the fate of lovers mismatched in terms of *générosité* provoke Rotrou's heroes and heroines to their third- and fourth-act gestures of Stoical self-sufficiency or, at times, Neoplatonist transcendence.

But in the end these "pagan" positions yield to what is virtually a Christian resolution. Rotrou's fifth acts are filled with confessions on bended knee; with restorations to sanity after an illusory enchantment or madness in which a character thinks himself or others dead; with suicides stayed by such "resurrections"; with adjudications by king or father figure. These fifth acts thus manifest an eschatological structure. They sit atop the rest of the structure like scenes of the Last Judgment in the uppermost portion of religious paintings in parish churches. Yet, except for his play about the actor-martyr, most of Rotrou's plays are not literally about the Last Judgment or any other specific Christian motif or tale. Many are about enchanted kings and hapless princesses whose kingdoms are more like pastures than parishes. Others, based on ancient classical drama, are about mythological figures who invoke not the One True God but the "gods," doing so neither in terms of the Trinity nor of the intercessionary, incarnated Member of the Trinity. A few plays are about kingdoms of this world in which the prince hardly seems concerned with the will of God here on earth in the terms, say, of Augustine's City of God. Rotrou thus seems to continue that process known as "humanism."

Understood as the recovery of the past, Rotrou's theater is "humanistic." However, it is not humanistic in showing the secularization of this inheritance. To assume this is to ignore the real character of Rotrou's adaptation not only of the classical past but of courtly tradition, pastoral literature, and history. The spirit informing many of these adaptations has been called "Humanism" and is connected with the scholarly investigation of the past begun in the Renaissance and continuing in France well into the early years of the seventeenth century. We might designate the investigation as such under the rubric of small-*h* humanism to distinguish it from the widespread understanding of capital-*H* Humanism as a moral outlook appealing exclusively to man-made instead of God-made laws. This outlook is seen by some scholars to inform French thought not only in the early years of the seventeenth century but well into the "génération classique" itself. Indeed, in *Classicisme et baroque dans l'œuvre de Racine*, Philip Butler finds it appropriate to link the greatest French classic not to the Jansenists but to *libertins* of the early part of the century like François de La Mothe Le Vayer and Gabriel Naudé. In studying the past with a critical eye on their present, these Humanists seem to concentrate on man's fate in human rather than divine terms. They contribute to a "laïcisation de la vie" in this period, which Jean Dagens has probed so skillfully in his *Bérulle et les origines de la restauration catholique (1575-1611)*. Yet, as Dagens himself notes, the "laïcisation" is largely latent in the first part of the century. Its implied separation of the sacred and the profane is fully manifested only in the aesthetics and ethics of the great classical writers of the second half of the century. The first half of the century is characterized more by a "humanisme chrétien" whose "optimisme triomphal" is expressed in a harmony of "Humanistic" and religious outlooks.[4]

This optimism shines throughout the theater of Rotrou, even in its moments of extreme transcendental doubt on the values of this world. The harmony of the humanist and religious impulses finally emerges in so tragic a moment as *Iphigénie*, for example. Though presented with great sophistication, Iphigénie, like other figures the playwright derives from classical antiquity, sounds themes and strikes poses usually associated with Christian rather than pagan attitudes toward life. Taken from Seneca, Rotrou's Hercule is a dramatic *mise en évidence* of the analogies between the mythological and the Christian drawn by Florimond de Raemond a decade earlier in his *Histoire de l'hérésie*:

> . . . Vous croyez qu'un Hercule a brisé les portes d'Enfer, et pourquoi ne croyez-vous pas que Jésus l'eût pu faire? Vous dites la vie d'Hercule avoir été tout pénible, qu'il a dompté les plus terribles monstres de la terre: *notre Hercule chrétien* est descendu ici-bas pour détremper et dissoudre le venin de la mort en son sang et chasser le péché du monde. . . . De sorte qu'avec une merveilleuse Providence de Dieu, il se peut dire que la superstition des païens a été *une figure, un portrait, une idée et un dessin pour venir à la vraie Religion*, sans qu'il ait fallu tout changer et innover, chose pleine de péril et danger, mais expliquer avec un sens mystique et saint ce qu'ils entendaient philosophiquement et fabuleusement, pour combattre leur idolâtrie.[5]

In the context of such defenses of the pagan past, the Christian analogues of Rotrou's *Hercule mourant* stand out all the more clearly. Going to his glory at the end of the fourth act, he makes a last wish: that his rival for Iole be executed. But in the fifth act the ascended Hercule appears in a heavenly light and rescinds his unmerciful command, declaring it the act of a necessarily imperfect vision and ordering the marriage of Iole and Arcas. The "Christianization" of such motifs is pervasive in Rotrou.

That this is unhistorical in the work of a seventeenth-century playwright of classical tendencies must be reopened to question. Here, much depends on the way one reads cultural and literary history after the Edict of the Parlement of Paris of November 17, 1548, which proscribed "la Passion de Nostre Seigneur, ne aultres mystères sacrez," while permitting "aultres mystères profanes, honnestes et licites."[6] In time "mystères profanes" would seem a contradiction in terms; by the end of the seventeenth century, in fact, it will especially seem so to the highest French churchman of his time, Bossuet. In *L'Evolution de la tragédie religieuse classique en France*, Kosta Loukovitch recalls Corneille's self-consciousness in daring to present a religious play to the "lettrés" (*Polyeucte*).[7] In the century between the Edict and Corneille's famous play, subjects from the Christian religion were relegated to the private theater of school, convent, and study, and the public theater was, with few exceptions, secular. Humanism, particularly in the recovery of pagan mythology, is presumed to have abetted this tendency, with literary men as well as theologians agreed on the separation (often the two parties to the agreement were found in the same man). As Loukovitch sees it, Ronsard and other genuinely pious literary men unwittingly fostered the separation of the religious and the profane at the expense of true piety. They seemed unaware of what other contemporaries, especially certain theologians, feared: the recrudescence of paganism. Catholic and Protestant theologians uttered this warning, with the Council of Trent taking a particularly strong lead in the matter, as Loukovitch has shown.

And yet, among theologians as well as literary men, other voices were being heard. The "advance guards" of Trent itself, the Jesuits, were especially active in using the theater, both in profane and religious subjects, for educational and recreational needs. Toward the end of the sixteenth century, Jodelle's *Cléopâtre captive* or Garnier's *Marc Antoine* were played in a monastery for girls.[8] At the turn of the century, the literary theoretician Vauquelin de la Fresnaye proposed a literary conversion of pagan antiquity:

> He! quel plaisir serait-ce à cette heure de voir
> Nos poètes chrétiens, les façons recevoir
> Du tragique ancien? Et voir à nos mystères
> Les païens asservis sous les lois salutaires
> De nos saints et martyres?[9]

Vauquelin would not Christianize ancient subjects, of course; he prefers to have Christian subjects written in the dignified manner of antiquity. But he is convinced that, had Christ been known to the great writers of antiquity, they would have celebrated Him in the way modern Christians should. Here in this *fin de siècle* literary theoretician is the spirit of a reconciliation between antiquity and Christianity of the kind found in the Hercule of Florimond de Raemond and of Rotrou, a third of a century later. Within that third of a century at least some of the *libertins*, finally attacked by Pascal and others, felt it possible to forge a Christian epicureanism. Pierre Gassendi (1592-1655), whom many consider the fountainhead of *libertinage*, was and remained a Catholic priest.[10] Even while Jansenius and Saint Cyran were shaping the positions that would inform Bossuet's much later strictures on the theater, other pious clerics found it possible to reconcile Word and World with an "optimisme catholique." Contrasting this spirit to the "sévérité protestante" in the period 1580-1625, René Bady finds its best representative in Le Père Richeome, the author of a Christian treatise on death:

> Certes le P. Richeome peut être dit optimiste. L'admiration, l'enthousiasme, *dont nous avons déjà vu plusieurs auteurs témoigner à l'égard de l'homme considéré comme le chef-d'œuvre de la création*, atteignent chez lui à leur comble. A son tour il loue la beauté du corps humain et montre la convenance symbolique qui existe, selon lui, entre toutes les parties et les différentes facultés de l'âme.[11]

Death is not real to this exegete of the theology of salvation. But life is no less real to this same cleric, for whom "en la face reluit spécialement l'image de l'âme."[12] This concept of the human face as analogue of the beatific vision is one that recurs frequently in Rotrou. The dramatist gives artistic expression to a liberal, ecumenical theology represented by several contemporary prelates. Their influence has been seen by a learned historian as one of the causes for reformist movements like Jansenism, L'Oratoire, and the "cabale des dévots." Within the church itself, writes Alfred Rébelliau, several prelates, "doctes et beaux esprits, fils de la Renaissance, séduits par les succès de Pierre Charron et de Saint François de Sales, s'ingéniaient à 'humaniser' la théologie, l'apologétique et la controverse, ou bien, à l'exemple de l'oratorien Baronius et des jésuites Bellarmin et Sirmond, s'enforçaient dans l'érudition ecclésiastique."[13]

Throughout the century others protest the ready reconciliation of the natural order and its Author. Nor are the protesters all Protestants. True, like many of his Catholic contemporaries, the dramatist himself often defines *Sacrement* in the limited sense reported by Furetière in his famous dictionary toward the end of the century: "*Sacrement*, se prend quelquefois absolument pour le mariage."[14] But in the very years that Rotrou's company of fictional characters were compromising the divine and human orders by limiting "le sacrement" in this sense, La Compagnie du Saint Sacrement was applying its own uncompromising spirituality to the human order. As Rébelliau has shown, this secret society of both lay and ecclesiastical membership, active from 1627 to 1666, devoted itself to acts of "amour et charité" in the name of sacramental faith. For this "company" *le sacrement* was the Holy Eucharist, and the Society's spiritual sacramentalism can be grasped in the very fact of its secrecy.[15] Under certain conditions not even the Eucharist itself was to be visible, according to one of its precepts.[16] Whether from piety or caution, the stamp of such devout thought left its mark on the classical writers of the second half of the century. Pointing to Racine's pious renunciation of *Bérénice*, Bossuet comes close to proscribing the theater itself. And though at some remove from the "dévots," Boileau found himself at quite a remove in his *Art poétique* from the conciliatory proposals of Vauquelin three-quarters of a century earlier: "[Et] fabuleux Chrestiens, n'allons point dans nos songes/ Du Dieu de vérité, faire un Dieu de mensonges."[17]

We continue to be affected by this classical bias. Even philosophical critics who protest the separation of art and life have been ready to accept the post-Reformational separation of art and the "*other* life." Our critical autonomy from religious frames of reference for literature is post-Reformational. Platonism, Aristotelianism, Stoicism, Marxism, Existentialism, Freudianism, all have seemed legitimate references for elucidating the literature of seventeenth-century France. But many students of the period hesitate to adopt a religious reference. It is as if Pascal, Racine, and other writers of the period wrote anywhere but within the religious context of their own times. It is as if, in returning to the mythological religion of antiquity resuscitated by "humanism," dramatists were attempting to rekindle the fires of paganism. If so, they were not alone. As the Pascal of *Les Lettres provinciales* knew, their pagan spirit was easily matched by that of theologians of more than one order. I make this observation not to take sides with Pascal and his cosectarians but to show that in "Christianizing" Hercule and the Menaechmi, for example, Rotrou finds himself at one with some of *his* religious cosectarians who speak from realms other than art. Pascal and his partisans might find that Rotrou overstates, in both time and space, the catholicity of the Christian view that this world is a part of God's goodness. But these "catholic" viewers might also find that Pascal in *his* views understates Christianity itself: the religion of mercy that redeems fallen man.

These humanist universals as retrieved in a Christian context enable us to understand Rotrou's theater. Not that these universals cut him off from antiquity. His plural gods look in two directions. Rotrou uses the plural *dieux* instead of *Dieu* because of the growing pressure of the *bienséances* that proscribed the use of the singular even in a subject where the setting is presumably Christian.[18] To us the convention seems empty; we read the detour sign as if it directed us away from, instead of toward, something. But it directs us toward Rotrou's religious present, first of all. Between the Edict of 1548 and Bossuet's *Maximes* of 1694, many of the greatest playwrights turned directly to the Judeo-Christian tradition: Garnier (*Les Juifves*); Corneille (*Polyeucte, Théodore*); Rotrou (*Le Véritable Saint Genest*); Racine (*Esther, Athalie*). Rotrou also turns specifically, but less programmatically, to the dramatic integration of the

Christian God in other "secular" plays: *Bélissaire* and *La Sœur*. Parlementary edicts, sacerdotal strictures, and secular *bienséances* do not divide the artistic sensibility. In his entire theater Rotrou is often profoundly preoccupied with the relation between the human and divine. At times the playwright exceeds the doctrinal bounds of the sacramental theology whose premises inform his work both explicitly and implicitly. But in this and other excesses, he only shows the internal tension of that theology itself. His plural gods look back to Christian as well as to pagan antiquity. In his theater the concepts of sacrament and sacrilege show the continuity as well as the disparity between Christianity and the classical heritage retrieved by humanism.

This continuity is especially difficult to grasp in what Gabriel Vahanian calls our "Post-Christian era of the death of God." According to Vahanian, we are past the Christian era when "not only theologically and philosophically, but culturally as well, the reality of God was taken for granted and was the starting point of both reflection and action."[19] One may not agree with Vahanian that "every culture rises from a 'substratum of religiosity'."[20] However, as the historian Pierre Chaunu has maintained, seventeenth-century culture certainly remained profoundly religious. "Le XVII$^e$ siècle, comme tous les grands siècles," he writes, "est fondamentalement théologique. . . . Tout le siècle cherche Dieu."[21] The fundamentally theological character of the century gives a special resonance to what we have come to think of as "merely literary" or "dramatic" motifs and "poetic" conceits. Given the century's religious substratum, in Rotrou terms like *grâce, indulgence, pénitence, sacrilège, charmes, pieux office, divin visage, célestes attraits*, etc., and motifs like the ascension into Heaven (Hercule and Iphigénie), *résurrection* (in too many plays to mention here), *descentes aux enfers* (*L'Hypocondriaque* and *L'Innocente Infidélité*) take added force from specifically theological uses of them in the period. In particular, the tension between *sales* (or *lascifs*) *désirs* and *chastes désirs* in almost every Rotrou play is "dramatic" in a virtually Christian sense. Now, for Christians who turn to the history of the early church for guidelines, this means a special enmity for "la concupiscence de la chair."[22] In Rotrou's time, within the Roman Catholic church itself such Christians were to be found chiefly among the Jansenists. Because Pascal's greatest works, *Les Lettres provinciales* and *Les Pensées*, were written in the mid-1650's, many literary scholars tend to situate Jansenism in the second half of the century. Yet, Jansenius himself, Saint Cyran, Arnauld, and the Pascal of the "affaire de Saint Ange" were active in the period of Rotrou's career (1630-1650).

Sacramentalism, then, provides a basic philosophic framework for studying Rotrou's theater. This does not mean that Rotrou's work is a catechetical application of the decrees of the Council of Trent or of the doctrines of sacramental theology. Many plays of the first half of his career, in particular, exceed the most liberal interpretation of these sources. Thus, in *Hercule mourant* and *Les Sosies*, the playwright might be said to overstep the bounds. But this excess is best understood in light of both the literary and religious modes of the plays. From a literary point of view, the plays are "serious"—*Les Sosies*, in particular, is hardly the satirical play Molière made of the same motif. From a religious point of view, support for the immanentist theses of both plays can be found within the religious community of Rotrou's time (a point I have already anticipated in the case of *Hercule mourant*). We may thus wonder if Rotrou really does overstep the bounds. Similarly, at his most transcendental moments—for example, *Bélissaire* and *Le Véritable Saint Genest*—Rotrou clings to the immanentist verities of his early theater. This, too, is in keeping with a literary-religious tradition that accommodated the things of this life with those of the afterlife.

Through the framework of sacramental theology, we can probe more profoundly into the theater of Rotrou—its ideological position, psychological mood, and artistic practice. In a purely religious context, that framework was being severely challenged from within by an otherworldly emphasis and from without by a very worldly emphasis. In a purely literary context, the framework was being challenged by a classicizing tendency. However, in Rotrou's time these challenges themselves point to the continuing vitality of the accommodation between the religious and literary traditions. For the dramatist and many of his greatest contemporaries, the virtually Christian motifs I study in detail in this book were accepted intuitively, as it were. This is not to deny in these artists a keen sense of this world in all its naturalness. However, it is to remind us that for them, the natural was what might be called "incarnational" rather than "naturalistic." They viewed the natural in light of the heritage bequeathed by Christ and continued in the works of St. Augustine, St. Thomas Aquinas, and St. Francis de Sales.

As unobtrusively, as pertinently, as respectfully as possible, I have drawn on this religious heritage to illuminate the theater of Jean Rotrou. In the same spirit, I have also drawn on his theater to illuminate the heritage itself.

Both illuminations emerge from a long series of plays that (1) are uneven in quality and (2) show a definite change of emphasis, if not of fundamental idea, with respect to the key motifs of immanence and transcendence. I have, therefore, selected only certain plays for extensive analysis, giving brief commentary on the others in the notes. I have also divided the plays according to major religious tendencies as follows (title in capital letters indicates that the play is the subject of extended analysis):

I. Le Véritable Saint Genest

II. *L'Hypocondriaque*, La Bague de l'oubli, *Les Ménechmes, La Céliane, La Diane*, La Pélerine amoureuse, *Amélie, La Célimène*, Le Filandre, *L'Heureuse Constance, Les Occasions perdues, La Doristée*, Hercule Mourant, *L'Heureux Naufrage*, L'Innocente Infidélité, *Clorinde*,

*Florimonde, La Belle Alphrède, Agésilan de Colchos, Les Deux Pucelles,* LES SOSIES

III. CRISANTE, ANTIGONE, *Laure persécutée, Les Captifs,* IPHIGÉNIE, *Clarice,* BÉLISSAIRE.

IV. *Célie,* LA SŒUR, *Dom Bernard de Cabrère,* VENCESLAS, COSROÈS, *Dom Lope de Cardone*

For plays analyzed at length, I have provided a résumé of the plot in a footnote at the outset of the analysis. (The reference indexes in the text followed by R alert the reader that the note contains the résumé.) Those familiar with Rotrou scholarship will see that, except for *Le Véritable Saint Genest, Crisante,* and *La Sœur,* I have followed the chronology established by Lancaster.[23] (The order in Viollet-le-Duc's edition of the complete theater is extremely erroneous, according to Lancaster.) The changes in position, especially for *Le Véritable Saint Genest,* should be explained here, since they bear in general on any approach to all of Rotrou and, in particular, on the approach I have adopted.

Any scholar attempting a comprehensive interpretation of Rotrou's entire theater must confront the "respectful neglect" of most of the plays. Moreover, even within the trio of plays for which he is best known, *Le Véritable Saint Genest* is set apart for many scholars. It is a "sacred" play, whereas *Venceslas* and *Cosroès* are "profane." This distinction seems invalid, reflecting, as I have indicated, certain preconceptions of our "post-Christian era." Furthermore, in specifically religious terms, though the play on the converted actor is transcendentalist in tendency, it does show Rotrou clinging to the immanentist notions of his supposedly "profane" theater. Therefore, because of its probable familiarity to most of my readers, and because of its typical interplay of major themes, I have began with *Le Véritable Saint Genest.*

In discussing this play as well as all other plays, I have used

[15]

the terms the plays themselves provide in deriving religious concepts. Nevertheless, where especially appropriate, I have referred to the religious climate outside Rotrou's theater. Also, for readers interested in special aspects of the religious themes involved, I have included an appendix giving a brief etymological and historical review of such key notions as sacrament and sacrilege.

The changes in position of *Crisante* and *La Sœur* are also related to my study of themes. The changes are not intended as corrections of Lancaster's generally shrewd solutions of the problems in dating Rotrou's works. As I explain in greater detail at appropriate points, the changes are relatively slight from a historical point of view. However, thematically they are of some significance: the transcendentalist *Crisante* is surrounded in time by immanentist plays. With some reservations, a similar relation applies to *La Sœur*. This time, however, the comedy's immanentist tendency is at odds with the transcendentalist spirit of *Bélissaire* and *Le Véritable Saint Genest*, which precede it among the major plays I analyze at length. In varying degrees these thematic swings, from play to play, are to be found throughout Rotrou's theater. However, these minor swings are part of a more significant major swing. Rotrou's theater can be divided into three major moments: an early period of immanence, a later period of transcendence, and a final period of ambivalence in which we find the playwright yearning for the immanentist verities of his youth. Because *Crisante* seems to me to anticipate the theater of transcendence and *La Sœur* anticipates Rotrou's final ambivalence, I have discussed them in the appropriate, coherent context of plays that they anticipate.

For purposes of this study, I consider *Dom Lope de Cardone* Rotrou's last play. I do not discuss *L'Illustre Amazone*, attributed to him by some editors and critics. Nor have I discussed Rotrou's collaboration as one of Les Cinq Auteurs of *La Comédie des Tuileries* and *L'Aveugle de Smyrne*.[24] I have illustrated some themes through Rotrou's non-dramatic poetry, but have not been concerned with his verse as such here or in the plays. I have been somewhat more concerned with dramatic form. In this connection, I have profited especially from the work of Lancaster, Schérer, and Knutson.[25]

Rotrou is an important writer who has lived too long in the critical shadow of his great contemporaries. An effort to shed an "independent" light on all of his work is not without its risks. Some readers may feel that my choice of major plays should have been different. However, I trust all readers will find that the coherent vision I study in these plays will compel a long-overdue return to Rotrou.

CHAPTER ONE

*Immanence and Transcendence in*

LE VERITABLE SAINT GENEST

UNTIL he begins rehearsing his role, the pagan actor Genest is very much the professional man of the theater.[1R] His masters are a more pious lot. Valérie gives lessons in religious doctrine to her maid, Camille. The latter reproaches her mistress for believing in dreams, as if such belief were unworthy of one in whom Heaven had put "un si digne esprit dans un si digne corps" (I.1). Here is a pagan sacramentalism in which the beauty of Valérie shows the equilibrium of spirit and matter. But Camille's is also only a perfunctory piety, for dreams do not contradict Heaven's will. Valérie tells Camille: if Heaven wishes, "la voix d'un songe est celle d'un oracle." Yet, in the dream, Heaven's will contradicts the way things ought to be: how can she, a princess, be wed to a shepherd? Valérie finds an affront to herself and to Heaven's purposes in this alliance, so she will not be reassured by her maid's confidence in her father. He may raise people to dignity, as he had Valérie's mother; but he is himself subject to fate, "ce monarque insolent, à qui toute la terre/ Et tous ses souverains sont des jouets de verre." The world seems ruled by a force independent of the heavens, and the connections between the two ominously promise a highborn princess to a lowborn shepherd.

In her misgivings Valérie anticipates some of the terms with which Genest will forsake the world. I stress *some of the terms*, for Rotrou cannot fully surrender to the temptation to total transcendence here. Some of this ambivalence is apparent in the motif that now appears in this richly analogical first act.

Dioclétien confirms his daughter's dream by recalling the origins of her fiancé, Maximin. Dioclétien and Maximin are emphatic existentialists. Dioclétien himself is lowborn, a self-made man proud of any man who "élève sa bassesse,/ Se reproduit soi-même et forme sa noblesse" (I.3). He and Maximin find "le mérite dans l'homme et non pas dans le sang"; they choose "la personne, et non pas la naissance." These premises are obviously analogues of the destiny Genest will forge for himself. They provide a basis not for contrast but for reconciliation of the pagan piety of the co-emperors and the final Christian piety of Genest. Structurally, the play already provides in this motif those Jesuit premises that both martyrs pose as ways of reconciling the world and divine purpose. Both pieties are existentialist in their premises to a certain degree. It *could* be the purposes of the Christian God to regard history in the terms used by Dioclétien: "des grands cœurs la plus chère espérance" (I.3). Heaven *could* confirm Camille's insight into its workings, even if it is in a form the pagan maid never envisages: "Ainsi souvent le Ciel conduit tout à tel point/ Que ce qu'on craint arrive, et qu'il n'afflige point" (I.3). There *could* be more than a verbal coincidence between the *songe* by which Maximin attains high station and the *feinte* by which Genest attains Heaven. But the reconciliation of pagan and Christian piety is possible only if the materialist stresses of the pagan are invalidated within the spiritual stresses of the Christian. This is the lesson of play and inner play, of the martyrdom of Genest and of Adrien.

The lesson is drawn for and by each martyr in his own characteristic terms. Adrien's conversion is at once independent of, and closely related to, Genest's conversion. Here, whatever the difference in thematic stress between this play and others, Rotrou uses a dramatic structure we find in all his plays. Genest moves from reality through feigning to reality, a pattern we might conveniently designate as A-B-A.[2] As I shall show in some detail below, the first reality is at best imperfect, especially in light of the final reality. However, it seems important here to warn against the view of the dramatic structure of *Le Véritable*

*Saint Genest* as a Pirandellian pattern in which both the feigning and the final reality, art and faith, coalesce. One can understand the temptation to read an aesthetic of identification into this play about an actor converted while playing a convert.[3] However, to imply that the feigning and the conversion are one is to ignore Genest's specific denial of the theater qua theater. To fuse the feigned and the transcendental is to deny the reflective process whereby man uses his freedom to be, *in part*, responsible for his own salvation. Rotrou and Genest keep the aesthetic and the ethical separate.

The basic aesthetic of this play is imitational, but not merely in theory, as might be suggested by the discussion between Genest and his Décorateur just before the play begins. The Décorateur would have preferred more time in order to fool the spectator about what he is seeing. He knows that when you get too close to the stage you see that its perspective is false. Nature, as he puts it, is "nuisible à notre art." Orlando describes this illusionism as baroque and contrasts it to the "realistic" aesthetic of Genest, who here demands of his assistant " . . . un jour naturel au jugement des yeux" (II.1). For Orlando, Genest's aesthetic is in keeping with his earlier preference of ancient over modern authors. Yet, says the critic, "nella concretezza di tutto il resto del testo la tematica barocca domina invece sovrana."[4] However, we may wonder which of the two aesthetics does prevail in the play. Apart from the illusionism of the staging, the depiction of Adrien's martyrdom could not be more "imitational" and "classical." True, Genest himself tells us, "Je feins moins Adrien, que je ne le deviens" (II.4). But this is well before his conversion. When conversion has occurred, he says, "Adrien a parlé, Genest parle à son tour" (IV.6). The use of the same verb stresses that Genest is imitating Adrien; he is acting *like* Adrien, following his example.

In the end Genest rejects the aesthetic of metamorphosis for the aesthetic of imitation. Here, *becoming* is naturalistic in an Aristotelian sense. Final stages of a process, spiritual or physical, actualize a potential form; final form realizes (makes real) inner form. Plays or games show the final form a datum of reality could achieve. Play-acting and other feignings become occasions not only for reflecting reality but for reflecting *on* reality. Illusion provides an occasion to follow an example if it is judged good by the spectator or not to follow it if judged bad by him. We have this process here in Rotrou's thirty-first play as in his first play.[5]

The play about the martyrdom of Adrien is a reflection of reality upon which Genest reflects. Some find that the play within a play here is too long.[6] (In this light the middle acts of all of Rotrou's plays are too long.) "The Martyrdom of Adrien" occupies the B portion of Rotrou's structure: Acts II, III, and most of IV. The A portions are those initial and final moments in which the pious pagans damn Christians for their sacrilegious piety. Initially, Genest and all of the actors are among these pious pagans, and they remain there throughout the playing of the "The Martyrdom of Adrien." They are both actors and spectators, a motif that is rendered explicitly before, during, and after the play. For example, as the actors go off to prepare the play, Maximin says that he will be " . . . spectateur/ En la même action dont je serai l'acteur" (I.5). The differences between Rotrou and his models in Lope de Vega and Desfontaines here are instructive. In Lope's *Lo Fingido Verdadero* the fusion of planes occurs not only in the play about the persecuted Christians but in the previous secular play put on by Ginés and the actors. In Lope, Ginés is in love with the actress Marcella, but she is in love with another actor, Octavio. In the secular play they first put on, Ginés arranges to play a part in which he can make love to Marcella while he abuses Octavio. The fusion of illusion and reality during the performance is frequent. Again, when Ginés does put on the play about the persecuted Christians, he has already been converted during the rehearsal. When he goes on stage, he plays himself quite literally.

As for Desfontaines' *L'Illustre Comédien*, his Genest is not so perfunctory as Rotrou's in scoffing at Christians. Desfontaines' actor is actually more like the Adrien whom we meet in Rotrou's inner play. Planes of reality dissolve—or, there is only one plane of reality. We do not need theatrical props to put on a play, says the actor. He even rejects the subject of martyrs who were also actors. He can come closer to reality with the subject of his own family in which, to his shame, his father and sister converted to "la loi prophane" of Christianity! In the inner play of Desfontaines, Genest pretends to receive baptism to ensure his inheritance, but his sacrilegious baptism has a real effect: when Genest as the character in the inner play returns from baptism, he has been in fact converted by it. Feigning becomes transcendence in Desfontaines' actor. A sacrament has apparently been efficacious *ex opere operato* in a way that would make the most liberal Catholic theologian blush. Coming to the baptismal waters in an improper disposition, Genest is nonetheless converted! The effect of grace is total, and Desfontaines' convert seems to have had nothing to do with it. The convert later speaks of an angel who had told him "qu'il ne venait si je le voulais croire/ Que pour me revêtir des rayons de sa gloire" (III.2). Orthodoxy is perhaps preserved in this recapitulation, but, both ethically and aesthetically, one is struck by the fusion of planes in Desfontaines' play. Displeased that Rotrou had not imitated *Polyeucte* by having a plethora of conversions at the end of his play about a converversion, Sainte-Beuve should have been pleased with Desfontaines.[7] Genest's off-stage mistress, Pamphilie (who plays herself in Desfontaines' play!) is converted. Dioclétien himself ends the play with a prayerful speech to the "chères ombres" of Genest and Pamphilie and with a repentance addressed to his own plural gods but of strongly Christian overtones. Desfontaines' emperor is at that halfway house between pagan and Christian piety in which we find Sévère at the end of Corneille's *Polyeucte*.

When one considers Rotrou's models, one is tempted to believe that Rotrou used the epithet *véritable* in his title precisely to point to the orthodox truth-saying of his actor.[8] The truth that Rotrou's actor pronounces in his conversion is his own as well as God's. It is the same truth for both, to be sure; but if Genest's dignity as a free man under God is to be preserved, it *must* be his as well as God's! This co-operative relation is one of the key lessons he learns as an actor who reflects Adrien, and as a spectator who reflects on Adrien. If his conversion is to be meaningful even in God's eyes, it must come through a human response to God's call. The actor in the Divine Comedy must be as free in his choice of role as Genest shows himself to be in putting on "Human Comedies."

This point comes out especially well in a portion of the "rehearsal scenes" that Jacques Schérer has discovered and restored to the play.[9] Even in the version of the scene as it is widely known, Genest and Marcelle have radically different attitudes toward their profession. She complains about the distractions of her admirers in the audience, but on stage she acts in a way to encourage these importunities. The stage simply gives her the chance to be herself, and this self is conceived in strictly materialistic terms. When she rehearses Natalie's pious joy, Marcelle impresses Genest by her artistic prowess as much as she does her stagedoor suitors by her personal charms. The gist of this brief scene is thus to dramatize the discrepancy between the piety of Natalie and the frivolous impiety of the actress portraying her.

In the portions of the scene republished by Schérer, these aesthetic and ethical premises are spelled out more clearly. Her role, the actress tells Genest, "me trouble, et j'aurai de la peine/ A feindre à votre gré cette amour surhumaine." How, she asks with indignation and bewilderment, can she portray in a touching manner "une femme crédule/ Qui mieux qu'un bel époux préfère un sot trépas?" Obviously, Marcelle's conception of the actor's art denies the objective theses of Diderot's actor. "Comment juger, sentir . . . " asks Marcelle, as romantic on stage in her aesthetics as she is off stage in her no doubt easy-going ethics. "Mais par analogie," answers the director of the troupe, and he asks his colleague if she has never loved anything preferable to life itself. His aesthetic is imitationist and reflective: life provides models for art, and art reflects the model of life. Such subtle perspectives elude the actress; she complains that were she to suffer death for such a love, she would nevertheless still find it ridiculous to savor that death "comme autant de délices," in the manner of Christians. "Il faut être Chrétien . . . ," replies Genest. "Non, il faut être fou . . . ," retorts Marcelle. They are now talking not about acting but about the reality that, in Genest's view, good acting would reflect "par analogie." Not surprisingly, with his objective aesthetic, the director must curb Marcelle as she puts herself in Caesar's shoes in expressing violent hostility to the Christian sect. "C'est sagement pensé, grave législateur," he tells her with gentle irony, "Mais restons comédiens aujourd'hui."

The imperative is in the first person. Backstage, Genest is a *comédien,* an actor for whom art and life are separate. This is true when, rehearsing his lines alone, he considers the effect of the lines upon him as a man. He pulls himself up short when it appears that he is *becoming* rather than *imitating* Adrien. He considers that habit might be responsible for this confusion of planes, but he then dismisses this on the grounds that here "des verités sans fard" go beyond habit and "la force de l'art." Moreover, it seems "que Christ me propose une gloire éternelle/ Contre qui ma défense est vaine et criminelle." Christ *proposes* that which seems just, but He does so in the words of a play on which Genest reflects. In its rehearsal the play has already taken on the sacramental character of its actual production: an occasion of grace with which Genest *may* co-operate for his own salvation. In the concept of resistance as vain and criminal, we see the compulsive inclination of higher reason, the conception of sanity and rationality that characterizes even the conception of freedom in that arch-rationalist of Rotrou's time, Descartes![10] But for the moment, in the actor's recall to the *raison raisonnante*—"Mais où va ma pensée?"—we have a corrective stress on human agency in the act of salvation. This co-operative relation between two free agents, God and man, is stated from the divine side as well: "Ton salut," the mysterious voice from on high tells the actor, "ne dépend que d'un peu de courage,/ Et Dieu t'y prêtera la main" (II.4). God's hand and man's courage: as we shall see throughout Rotrou, *courage* is a public faculty. *Cœur* in Rotrou is an instrument of knowledge within what Pascal would call the order of *esprit,* not an instrument of knowledge constituting its own order. These ethical reflections tell us, then, exactly what Genest's aesthetic observations have told us. What we see in "Martyrdom of Adrien" is not a single action fusing two planes but two actions in which a potential martyr considers the example of an actual martyr.

While on stage, Rotrou's actor can be a far more attentive spectator than either Lope's or Desfontaines'. Rotrou does not link the actor and his on-stage wife in an off-stage amorous relationship. Rotrou avoids the slightest possibility of having his actor's conversion attributed to an unrequited love, but he does portray the love relationship between a martyr and "mistress": Adrien and Natalie (played by Marcelle) do love each other, and one does have a part in the other's conversion. But as Deschanel showed some time ago,[11] the terms of the relationship here come from Father Cellot's Latin play about the martyr Adrian. Thanks to Natalie's secret Christianity, says Adrien, he has come, in part, to the Christian faith: "Enfin je reconnais . . . que je dois mon salut au saint nœud qui nous lie" (III.5). Here, momentarily, Rotrou seems to overstep orthodox sacramental theology on matrimony. Marrying Natalie when he was a pagan and when he thought her one, Adrien hardly brought the proper disposition to his marriage—a desire for its benefits of grace. But the orthodoxy is nonetheless quite clear: the benefit accrues to Adrien because it was sought by the baptized Natalie. *Ex opere operato,* and through the proper disposition of his wife, Adrien can claim that he owes his salvation to holy matrimony.[12] Moreover, Adrien was a pious pagan. He was thus eligible for salvation according to the liberal theology associated in Rotrou's day with the Jesuits and St. Francis de Sales.

The overt conditions of Adrien's conversion as well as the terms in which he expresses his new faith give further parallels with St. Francis' conception of "la vie dévote." Adrien was moved by God's grace, but *his* part in the act of salvation was due to a reflection on the soldierly courage of the Christians whom he persecuted as one of Maximin's loyal officers.

> Ne délibère plus, Adrien, il est temps
> De suivre avec ardeur ces fameux *combattants*:
> Si la *gloire* te plait, l'occasion est belle;
> La Querelle du ciel à ce *combat* t'appelle.
>
> (II.7; italics added)

These are the first words of the inner play, already heard in the rehearsal scene. As a soldier, Adrien knows the horror of death as well as Marcelle does; but unlike the actress, he was struck by the martyrs' acceptance of it as "des délices," by their "vigueur" and "vertu." The etymological overtones of "vertu" are pertinent in this soldier's praise of the Christians: *vir, virtus*, Latin for man and manly courage. Through this example their manly persecutor is brought to imitate them. The inner play provides a sustained lesson in *générosité* as it appears in Corneille. Adrien is a believer in *générosité* under whichever gods or God he serves.

This is not to say that his newfound Christian piety is a matter of indifference to him. Corneille's Polyeucte can be suspected of seeking to go to Heaven to replace God. And some of this emphatic self-assertion may characterize Rotrou's Adrien (viz., his defiance of Maximin in particular). Nevertheless, Rotrou's soldier-convert thinks considerably more of Heaven than he does of himself, and he seems more aware of Heaven's role in his conversion. One cannot say of Adrien what Pauline says of her husband: "Polyeucte est Chrétien, parce qu'il l'a voulu" (III.3). Note that God is disturbingly absent from this formulation. But for Adrien, "La grâce dont le ciel a touché mes esprits / M'a bien persuadé, mais ne m'a point surpris" (II.8). The forces are in delicate *im*balance in which man has had a sufficient, but not the capital, role. Adrien has not been surprised; he has had time to reflect on whether to co-operate with Heaven. He reconciles divine persuasion and human freedom. He also attempts to reconcile his pagan piety and his newfound Christian piety. When he is brought before Maximin, he does not, like Polyeucte, aggressively and egotistically goad his royal captor into granting him his martyrdom:

> Pour croire un Dieu, Seigneur, la liberté de croire
> Est-elle en votre estime une action si noire,
> Si digne de l'excès où vous vous emportez,
> Et se peut-il souffrir de moindres libertés?
> Si jusques à ce jour vous avez cru ma vie
> Inaccessible même aux assauts de l'envie,
> Et si les plus censeurs ne me reprochent rien
> Qui m'a fait si coupable, en me faisant chrétien?
> Christ réprouve la fraude, ordonne la franchise,
> Condamne la richesse injustement acquise,
> D'une illicite amour défend l'acte indécent,
> Et de tremper ses mains dans le sang innocent:
> Trouvez-vous en ces lois aucune ombre de crime,
> Rien de honteux aux siens, et rien d'illégitime?
>
> (III.2)

The moral law is for all men an expression of natural law. Even instances of positive law—here, the proscription of adultery—show that the natural law in question is being interpreted according to the "liberal" strain of sacramental theology.

Now, however, the stress has shifted from the material to the spiritual, from the tendency to view God as immanent to that of viewing him as transcendent. Maximin is horrified at his officer's right to "choisir des dieux." He has not understood that Adrien's choice was a co-operative one in which an *essentialistic* ethic of benevolent determinism has co-operated with an *existential* human freedom. Just as gravely, Maximin denies the reconciliation that his officer proposes between the old and the new law. He does so, in Adrien's view, because he exalts matter over spirit: "Je cherche le salut, qu'on ne peut espérer/ De ces dieux de métal qu'on vous voit adorer." In a doctrine connected with the Jesuits of Rotrou's day, Adrien had appealed for reconciliation, since there was much in common in both faiths. Under this "dispensation" certain religious practices could be regarded as valid forms of worship so long as such "accidents" of matter and event were regarded for their signifying value. But his appeal having failed, Adrien abandons any attempt at reconciling this ancient worship of matter and the new worship of spirit. When Maximin threatens him with death, the emperor only underscores the incompatibility of his materialist faith with the spiritual faith of the prospective martyr. The latter replies: "Nos corps étant péris, nous espérons qu'ailleurs/ Le Dieu que nous servons nous les rendra meilleurs." Even here, note that there will, after all, be that reconciliation of matter and spirit for which Adrien had at first appealed in this world! Rotrou finds it hard to yield to transcendence completely.

Thus, when converted, Adrien finds it hard to forsake completely the habits of thought in which he grew up as a *généreux*. True, his wife can now be only his sister, he tells her. In this we see the connection not only between Rotrou and his model in Cellot but also between married love here and in other plays, for example, the spiritual love of the "femme et sœur" who is the heroine of *La Sœur*. But when this "sister" reveals herself to be a Christian and seeks to announce her faith as publicly as the husband she now calls "frère," he tells her that she must go on as before, even if it means that in the eschatological fulfilment she is to enjoy only a "second rang" (III.5). There are ranks in Heaven even as there are ranks among officers and classes on earth. The notion jars somewhat in the context of the earlier existential pride of the self-made emperor and, more seriously in this context, with the "democracy" of souls informing the Christian ethic. On the other hand, in counseling continuing secrecy to his wife, Adrien breaks one of the most important "laws" of *générosité* as it operates elsewhere in Rotrou: the imperative to deal with others openly. In view of what she regards as her husband's apostasy at a later point, Natalie herself is indignant at her own earlier secrecy. Here, we find one of the sharpest points of difference between Genest and Adrien as converts: the converted actor will refuse the counsel to secrecy or hypocrisy from Marcelle because he is bound to declare his profession of faith openly (V.2).

Natalie resolves to declare her own faith publicly after his death, like various women martyrs whom she evokes as examples to her own courage. Analogy and example, in life and in play, through life and through play. In no other play of Rotrou is this "objective" principle applied so rigorously in both ethics and aesthetics. The play about Adrien is interrupted at a number of points by off-stage events or comments by the royal spectators. This structural device emphasizes the differences between art and life. As Natalie leaves the stage after this litany of resolution, Genest steps out of his role to come forward and ask the emperor to quiet the crowd, which is spoiling the emperor's pleasure by confusing the actors with "ce désordre extrême." The actor and man of the theater in Genest seems to have the upper hand over the spectator and man of the world. This does not mean that Genest as a man is not listening to the "lesson" of the part he plays. The disorder of which he complains is in part his, since he wants to listen attentively to that part. But Genest's professional concern here does show that he is not yet converted. If he were, he would in all conscience be obliged to discontinue this sacrilegious mockery of Christians. These are the very grounds to which he will resort when he does discontinue! But for now he is still a man of the theater, one who, in Christian terms, is "taking instruction" through the *example* of Adrien. The contrast between the "two" men and their different loyalties is heightened further by the emperor's ironical retort that the beauty of the actresses is responsible for all this disorder! From their side of the footlights, the spectators abuse the principle of objective aesthetics as much as some of the actors. They come to see Marcelle as Marcelle, and she offers herself to them chiefly in that "role"; they do not heed the play.

Genest, the actor, is the only spectator to heed the play; he alone has respected its autonomous character. We cannot say of Rotrou's actor that he is converted by a *feigned* baptism. Genest does reflect on the grace of baptism (of blood) that Anthisme describes, but his own true baptism occurs separately from the feigned one:

>           Adrien,
> regardant le Ciel, et *rêvant un peu longtemps*,
>              dit enfin

> Ha! *Lentule!* en l'ardeur dont mon âme est pressée,
> Il faut lever le masque et t'ouvrir ma pensée;
> Le Dieu que j'ai haï m'inspire son amour;
> Adrien a parlé, Genest parle à son tour.
>
> (IV.5; italics added)

It is a *real* soul that God has inspired. The stage direction shows us the wordless ending of the play and in the next moment Genest's use of his fellow actor's off-stage name confirms the sense of the long reflection by "Adrien." Genest has understood that the play has been an occasion for him to come to a decision about God's call to him during the rehearsal. Having come to the sacrament in a proper disposition—his open-minded playing—the sacrament has been administered to him (by an angel, he tells us subsequently [IV.7]). Compelled by grace and by conscience, Genest stops playing this mockery of grace. True, throughout this scene and well into IV.7 (verses 1243 to 1372 in Crane's edition), Genest continues to use the language of the theater to express his new sense of reality, as if the human comedy and the divine comedy continued to be one. Yet, we must be careful not to see in Genest's theatrical metaphors his own fusion of feigning and transcendence. Having raised the mask in order to open his thought, as he says, he returns to the language of "mask" to make his listeners understand what has happened and, perhaps, to persuade them to follow his *example*. We are reminded of St. Francis de Sales once again: as Adrien was converted by a soldierly example and continued to express his new faith in a soldierly language, so Genest, converted by a theatrical example, continues to use a theatrical language in professing his new faith. Standing before the confounded co-emperors, Genest addresses not them but the heavens:

> Suprême Majesté, qui jettes dans les âmes,
> Avec deux gouttes d'eau, de si sensibles flammes,
> Achève tes bontés, représente avec moi
> Les saints progrès des cœurs convertis à ta foi!

And when the confused Lentule cries out, "Holà, qui tient la pièce," Genest tells him not to bother with *that* play, because

"Dedans cette *action*, où le Ciel s'intéresse,/ Un ange *tient la pièce*, un ange me *redresse*" (IV.7; italics added). And he persists in this theatrical language, the only one his auditors understand. But finally, he must use it only in order to abandon it in an extraordinary speech of fifty verses. He begins by assuming all the blame for what has happened:

> Ce n'est plus Adrien, c'est Genest qui s'exprime;
> Ce jeu n'est plus un jeu, mais une vérité
> Où par mon action je suis représenté,
> Où moi-même, l'objet et l'acteur de moi-même,
> Purgé de mes forfaits par l'eau de baptême,
> Qu'une céleste main m'a daigné conférer,
> Je professe une loi que je dois déclarer.
>
> (IV.7)

" . . . That I *must declare*." At this moment God's share in Genest's conversion is emphasized more than Genest's. "Par une incroyable et soudaine merveille/ Dont le pouvoir d'un Dieu peut seul être l'auteur," he goes on to say he has become one of those whom he had persecuted. Because an angel has led him into this port of salvation, he must give up the diversion of emperors and sing out other praises:

> Il est temps maintenant de réjouir les anges,
> Il est temps de prétendre à des prix immortels,
> Il est temps de passer du théâtre aux autels.
> Si je l'ai mérité, qu'on me mène au martyre:
> Mon rôle est achevé, je n'ai plus rien à dire.
>
> (IV.7)

Genest has a great deal more to say, in fact. However, he says it not as a man of the theater but as a Christian. The use of theatrical language is persistent throughout the rest of the play, but it is found on the lips of his persecutors. When his jailer uses a theatrical metaphor in addressing his prisoner, the latter uses a judicial metaphor! The unconverted continue to confound art and life; only in *their* view, given by one of them in the last words of the play, did Genest wish "D'une feinte en mourant faire une vérité" (V.7).

Genest knows better. He knows it would be sacrilegious now to regard feigning and truth as synonymous. In the first moments of his imprisonment, he places an even lower esteem than Adrien on the world he is about to leave. To him at this moment, God seems total transcendence, an immanence who has abandoned matter: "O fausse volupté du monde,/ Vaine promesse du trompeur," he says in lovely *stances* that contradict the exaltation of the world as sacrament heard so often in the early Rotrou. "Nos jours n'ont pas une heure sûre;/ Chaque instant use leur flambeau," he goes on, denying that time is rehabilitative. Time is debilitative and meaningless, as he insists in a complex image of multiple reflections evoking the derision of Fortune to be heard in plays like *Bélissaire* and *La Sœur*:

> Chaque pas nous mène au tombeau
> Et l'art, imitant la nature,
> Bâtit d'une même figure
> Notre bière et notre berceau.
>
> (V.1)

The "round" of time, from cradle to coffin, is an implicit but no less striking image of the wheel of Fortune. The wheel is compared to a beloved object who has betrayed the lover, but now that object is not a member of the opposite sex. It is *art* and, through art, nature. The aesthetic of imitation could not express more dramatically God's seeming transcendence of the world Genest leaves and Rotrou's seeming transcendence in this moment of his own theater of immanence! Genest rejects *both* art and the nature it reflects for the sake of the truth that is opposed to them.

As with other heroes of Rotrou at similar points in their self-realization, Genest overstates the case. In the subsequent scenes of Act V where we see him for the last time, the converted actor pulls back from these transcendental premises. In his interview with Marcelle just after this eloquent soliloquy, Genest still maintains the distinction between art and life, but he does not see the two as necessarily opposed. Adrien began by positing the reconciliation of pagan and Christian piety and then ended with an emphatic denunciation of pagan piety. Genest reverses the process here: he begins with a disdain of the world but then instructs Marcelle in the potential compatibility of the old and new law. Marcelle has come to berate him as both foolish to give up the favor of the emperor and disloyal to his colleagues in remaining a Christian. (She plays Flavie to Genest's Adrien here in this play rich in mirror effects.) Genest here reminds us of the motif so constant in Rotrou: faith in Heaven is an act of reason. The convert tries to make Marcelle understand that the "récompense" of "notre art" pales in significance before that of Heaven:

> La faveur d'avoir eu des Césars pour témoins
> M'a trop acquis de gloire et trop payé mes soins.
> Nos vœux, nos passions, nos veilles et nos peines,
> Et tout le sang enfin qui coule de nos veines,
> *Sont pour eux des tributs de devoir et d'amour*
> *Où le Ciel nous oblige, en nous donnant le jour.*
>
> (V.2; italics added)

"Render unto Caesar the things that are Caesar's and to God the things that are God's."

The two realms are not incompatible. If they were, Rotrou's own play would be sinful—and, according to Jansenistic premises, *is* sinful. Jansenism logically leads to a view of art that is, ironically enough, in accord with the romantic aesthetic of identification between man and artist. But this Jansenist aesthetic is a pessimistic romanticism. The notion that the actor's art is something to which "le ciel nous oblige" would be a very instance of "la belle raison corrompue," the proof, in Pascal's terms, that "tout notre raisonnement se réduit à céder au sentiment."[13] Genest in these moments does not believe this is necessarily so. He gave up playing Adrien because he was playing a martyr in derision. The society in which he finds himself is committed to the derision of Christians. He must, therefore, suffer martyrdom. But in a different society, tolerant of Christianity, the theater as such is not condemned by the objective aesthetics of Genest (and Rotrou).

Look to the intention, the disposition of spirit that one brings to the playing of a sacramental drama. The depiction of sacrilege can be instructive. According to the orthodox theology informing this play, only an errant Jansenism will regard the theater as a *dis*grace rather than an occasion of grace. The linkage with Protestant suspicion of the sacraments is clear. For extreme Protestant thought, the things of this world are not occasions of grace. The latter is the arbitrary gift of God, an intervention into history of God's will, saving man at the cost of his own will. But for Genest and Rotrou, pagan believers continue to believe in "ces dieux de métal et de pièrre" *at their own risk*:

> Ta grâce peut, Seigneur, détourner ce présage.
> Mais, hélas! tous l'ayant, tous n'en ont pas l'usage;
> De tant de conviés bien peu suivent tes pas,
> Et, pour être appelés, tous ne répondent pas.
>
> (V.2)

Here, in keeping with his reconciliation of the old law and the new law, Genest reconciles divine foreordinance and human freedom. "Many are called but few are chosen"—or, to view the phenomenon from the human side with Genest here: "*All* are called, but few *choose*."[14]

In validating man's will, Genest not only restores man's freedom but, once again, stresses reflective reason. Throughout Rotrou's theater, early and late, reason surrenders to an irresistible "inclination." Confronted with the evidence of Heaven's will, usually in the form of a beautiful woman, the "believer" surrenders immediately. In such instances the stress on the causative effect of "sacramental beauty" ties in quite well with the

Tridentine emphasis on the doctrine of *ex opere operato*. Given Protestant emphasis on the validity of the sacraments *ex opere operantis* at the time, Trent's emphasis on the causative rather than the signifying aspect of the sacraments is understandable.[15] Again, the stress on physical causality in the sacraments continues the long-standing Catholic emphasis on the presence of the Creator in His creation. Both within and without the church, however, it was feared that this emphasis only led to materialism, a fear whose extreme consequences are seen in Rotrou's *Les Sosies*. Genest's *stances* at the beginning of Act V do correct this materialism, at times sounding doctrines of God's transcendence as extreme as any to be heard in Rotrou's theater. However, as the subsequent scenes with Marcelle show, it is Genest's persecutors who make the relation of God to the world a question of kind rather than of degree. Their materialism will not allow for a spiritual god, whereas Genest's spirituality regards the world as a necessary step in the soul's journey to God. Were Genest to persist in his utter dismissal of art and nature, he would have to condemn the divine direction manifested in the dramatic occasion of his own conversion. Human art is not limited to the imitation of a nature judged absolutely incorrigible in Heaven's eyes.

Nevertheless, in the resolution, matter and spirit are not in equilibrium. In his very last words before going to his death, Genest restates the image of the natural world as a "round" of time, meaningless in comparison to the eternal world to which his soul is about to be transcended. To complain about dying is to complain about being a man, says Genest. At the very moment man arrives on earth, "il part pour le retour,/ Et commence de perdre en recevant le jour" (V.2). These final words of the former actor show that the A portions of the drama of pagan piety are the B portion of the drama of Christian piety in this play. From the Christian as well as the pagan point of view, an A-B-A structure is apparent in this play. The "return" of which Genest speaks in his last moment recalls the Christian tenet, "Dust thou art and to dust thou shalt return." In that tenet, as in the image Genest uses to evoke it, the pronoun only refers to the corporeal part of man. His soul makes a different "round-trip": from God through life and back to God. Given the stress on man's freedom in this play, given the disparity of belief between the converted Genest and the others, the generality of this proposition may seem in doubt. Yet, though every man may not end the journey *"in* God," he must spend its penultimate stage *before* God in the eschatological judgment. In their last words, both Adrien and Genest show still another constant of Rotrou's theater: that of the resurrection unto life.

It is not a life in this world; the martyrs go beyond the world. They thus emphasize "le peu de valeur de la vie," says Van Baelen.[16] But it would be misleading to read "peu de valeur" as an absolute. The world is of little value, but that little is of crucial importance. Ultimate value can be achieved only by passing through the world; the world is the indispensable condition of "value-assertion." Adrien and Genest condemn pagan gods of stone and metal for the sake of the transcendental God. For Adrien, we remember, that God was not all pure Spirit. Like another "converted" pagan hero in Rotrou, Hercule, the soldier-martyr here looks forward to the resurrection of his body in even greater beauty after its mutilation for Christ. Genest's faith is considerably more spiritual. But however they view themselves in the next *life,* the martyrs here do choose that life and its values over this life and its "peu de valeur." As in every play he denominates "tragédie," Rotrou shows his "tragic" hero actually transcending tragedy. As Orlando has put it, in a combination of aesthetic as well as ethical insights, "il *Saint Genest* è una comedia de santo e non una tragedia: Alla mancanza di conflitto in senso aristotelico corrisponde il fatto che le morte non à in essa l'annullamento finale di un personaggio."[17] Death is the false datum of the Christian drama.[18]

In Rotrou's drama as in the sacramental theology of his co-religionists, there is undoubtedly more mystery than rationalists can tolerate and more reason than mystics can abide. By "rationalists" I do not necessarily mean unbelievers, for, in the seventeenth century, the argument between "rationalists" and "mystics" was really one *among believers.* Faith-with-reason and faith-without-reason: these are the terms of the intramural argument between liberal theologians and conservative theologians. Pascal's *Lettres provinciales* has consecrated this as an argument between "Pelagian Jesuits" and "Augustinian Jansenists." As Pascal shows, sometimes the mystic and the rationalist exist in the one person. In objecting to the Jesuit illogic of separating *sufficient* grace from *efficacious* grace, Pascal is as much the partisan of reason as he is of mystery. Both as empirical rationalist and "Augustinian" mystic, he objects to the Pelagian reliance on reason we have found in Genest's "tous l'ayant, tous ne répondent pas." For Pascal, one has only to look at the world to see that all do not respond; one has only to consider the relation of sinful man to the inscrutable God to find presumption in the claim that all have grace. At a very poor best, in such a view, Genest's extended playing of Adrien's martyrdom sinfully postpones the announcement of what has already happened. "Console-toi," Pascal recalls in his *Mystère de Jésus*, "tu ne me chercherais pas si tu ne m'avais trouvé." Grace comes unannounced, mysteriously, like those many "accidental" discoveries and rediscoveries of ultimate truth we find throughout Rotrou's theater. But the dramatist finds this truth expressed in both of the "concupiscences" suspected by Pascal: of the body and the mind. At his most transcendental moments, Rotrou remains on the hither side of Pascal's tenet about God's overwhelming responsibility in the act of salvation. "On ne croira jamais," writes Pascal, "d'une créance utile et de foi si Dieu n'incline le cœur et on croira dès qu'il l'inclinera."[19] Even in *Le Véritable Saint Genest* and other plays of a transcendental tendency, Rotrou shows too much ambivalence for such Jansenist views. An extreme Jansenist must look upon such ambivalence in that "worser" spirit Conor Cruise O'Brien finds in the young Karl Marx looking on his socialist confrères: " . . . For a 'worser,' the nearer a man's opinions are to one's own, assuming them not to be identical, the worse they are."[20] Less rigorous observers will feel that Rotrou remains dramatically and religiously "catholic" in both his theater of immanence and his theater of transcendence.

CHAPTER TWO

*The Temptation to Total Immanence*

THE hero of *Le Véritable Saint Genest* finds ultimate satisfaction in the afterlife—that is, in the life that begins after the death of what is religiously called "this life." Rotrou's early heroes find ultimate satisfaction more in this life than in the afterlife. Nevertheless, as in the transcendental play about the converted actor, in the immanentist plays of the early theater we find an A-B-A pattern of dramatic and ethical experience. There is a movement from a kind of sacramental reality into a virtually sacrilegious period and then a return to the first reality.

This broad frame of action is apparent, for example, in Rotrou's second play, *La Bague de l'oubli*, Comédie (1629).[1R] Yet, there is an interesting variation here: within the broad framework of the play there are several briefer examples of the same pattern. The framing play deals with Léonor and Léandre: the action of I.1 deals with these lovers in relation to the king, Léonor's brother, and the play ends with the resolution of the relation between the young lovers and the king. These are the A parts of the A-B-A structure. Within the B part (the story of the king's relation with Liliane) there are six points at which, through the effect of the ring on various characters, the action moves from reality to illusion to reality to illusion, etc. From I.1 till II.6, when Léandre manages to trick the king into putting on the ring for the first time, we are in reality. The rapid shifting between the two planes then occurs until the king throws the ring to the floor in IV.4; from this point on, except for a brief part of V.5, when the king has Fabrice put on the ring to verify its powers, we are in reality. However, a different "illusion," the king's pretended enchantment, occupies most of the last scene of the play.

In order to understand in what way the king offends, we need the first scene. There, the young lovers record their happiness in the name of chaste desire and their suffering according to *générosité*. Like the flowers and fountains all about him, Léandre loves Léonor for her "célestes attraits." But these perfect lovers are imperfectly matched: Léandre is lowborn, and his mistress, as he himself says here, deserves only a king. Chaste desire and *générosité* have gotten crossed. The virtuous but star-crossed lovers must resort to unusual means if Léandre is to be made worthy of this princess-born. Truly *généreux*, they refuse regicide. But extremes need not be considered, since Léandre knows an old man "que le ciel n'a fait naître/ Que pour vous faire Reine et pour me rendre maître" (I.1).

Before we meet this old man, we meet the king. We already know him as the enemy of the chaste love of the two young people. He himself is an unchaste lover. Like a later, famous Rotrou character, Ladislas (also the son of a king named Venceslas), this royal lover pursues his beloved illicitly. She who holds my heart, he tells his confident, will give me "Une heure de plaisir après ces maux soufferts,/ Eteindra tous mes feux et rompra tous mes fers:/ Voyons ce beau sujet de mes douces furies" (I.2). He hypocritically uses more pious formulas to describe his court to Liliane when she appears in the very next moment. However, Liliane reminds him that " . . . ces faveurs sont des crimes/ Que votre affection peut rendre légitimes". Here is a major tenet of chaste desire to be heard in Rotrou's entire theater of immanence: the physical as such is not to be condemned. It is to be fully licensed so long as there is, first of all, *true* love, that is, spiritual love. The law of first love is nicely illustrated in Léonor's fidelity to Léandre and her refusal to accept the political marriage with someone else that her brother has arranged. The corollary of loving spiritually first is illustrated in Liliane's refusal here to grant the king her favors.

Alfonce subordinates all to the pursuit of these favors. His politics serve his carnal desires: he arrests Liliane's father and Comte Tancrède (whom her father would have her wed) for treason. He will also arrest her, he tells her, so that he can keep her in the castle. By contrast, Liliane's father and the count emphasize the king's disgraceful character. The father is almost priggish in his moral purity, suspecting his own daughter of being "facile" as he broods " . . . que l'honnêteté/ S'accorde rarement avec la beauté" (I.4). The duke's misgivings remind us that though his daughter is more honest than he believes, her angelic beauty has paradoxically become the cause of a kind of sinful compulsion.

The sin must be absolved. The magician Alcandre provides this in the form of a ring with a magical inscription beneath its stone. Alcandre is also the name of the magician in Corneille's *L'Illusion comique*, a character as much playwright as magician. Rotrou's Alcandre is more like a priest than a magician: as Léandre brings out in I.1, he exists expressly in Heaven's name for the purpose of making Léonor a queen and Léandre a "master." When he appears in I.5, he confirms this prediction. Léandre promises him "un avantage" equal to his own; but with a kind of priestly purity, the magician replies that "pour tout prix de ma peine, aimez-moi seulement".

The religious construction of the motif becomes all the more striking in the resemblance between the occasion on which the ring is first put into use and certain religious practices. The king has carried through the first steps of his plan of seduction, the arrest of Liliane's father and her fiancé. Having promised his valet, Fabrice, two thousand ducats as a reward for his help, he orders that Liliane be brought to the palace. While he waits, he orders water to be brought so that he may wash. Léandre sees his opportunity: when the king slips off his ring of state to wash his hands, Léandre substitutes the duplicate ring. During this part of the action, the alexandrine verse shifts to an incantatory series of three quatrains in eight-foot lines.[2] The setting, the tone, the act of washing, are ceremonial.

Is it more magical than religious in spirit? Bronislaw Malinowski distinguishes between magic and religion on this very question of ceremony: "While in the magical act the underlying idea and aim is always clear, straightforward and definite, in the religious ceremony there is no purpose directed toward a subsequent event."[3] Léandre's purpose is so "clear, straightforward and definite" that the ritual here seems more magical than religious. Yet, the effect of the ring *for* Léandre is secondary in view of the effect of the ring *on* Alfonce. This is in keeping with the "creative" element Malinowski sees characteristic in religious rites as such: "The act establishes not only a social event in the life of the individual but also a spiritual metamorphosis, both associated with the biological event but transcending it in importance and significance."[4] Malinowski is discussing primitive religion and initiation ceremonies in particular. However, in the king's washing of his hands and putting-on of the magical ring, there are liturgical overtones of a virtually Christian character. The ablution is an occasion of absolution. Alfonce experiences a baptismal washing-away of old sins, and he receives a eucharistic object creating a spiritual metamorphosis in the recipient.

This effect is immediate. The king staggers under the impact of the change, then falls into a sleep-like state that he attributes to "l'Amour," which "ici . . . se venge." *Sleep-like,* but not sleep itself. The king continues to act, but in a transcended state comparable to the religious state of grace. He begins to act according to the highest spiritual and ethical imperatives. He orders that Alexandre, Liliane's father, and Tancrède, her fiancé, be released from prison, since they are innocent and dutiful subjects, not guilty of the ambition of which they have been accused. He condemns ambition and pride, "ce doux poison" that corrupts so many in this world. This reflection leads him to self-reproaches of a kind prevalent in French drama since the late sixteenth century; like the hero of Rotrou's first play in his hallucinated state, the king paradoxically attains a perception of the world extreme in its Neoplatonist demotion of the material and contingent. Such perception redounds to the advantage of the prisoners, of course; but it can only frustrate the hopes of those who are given to the material alone—like Fabrice, to whom the king refuses to pay two thousand ducats promised. Money is too much a thing of the world for this spiritually regenerated king.

So too is lust, as it proves. Liliane's *suivante*, Mélite, need not warn her mistress of the wicked intentions of the lustful king. The warnings are uttered in bawdy terms. "Vous seriez le premier qu'il tâcherait d'abattre," she warns Liliane, continuing:

> . . . je crains bien pour vous qu'enfin il ne dérobe
> Ce qui ne ferait pas étrécir votre robe;
> Que ce jeune Monarque à ces larcins instruit
> Ne vous ôte une fleur pour vous donner un fruit.
>
> (III.1)

Such "indiscreet" talk, as Liliane puts it, only dramatizes by contrast the spirituality of the king's new vision. When the cautious Liliane asks him about his real intentions in having imprisoned her, Alfonce can only wonder if she takes him for an "insensé." He urges her to address such "vains discours" to "un esprit blessé"; his own soul is too "saine" to be troubled by the suspicious probings of this "stranger." Liliane *is* a stranger to this changed king. He could never have loved her as she claims, since he has never seen her: "Quelle amour vos beautés aurait-elle fait naître/ En moi qui ne vous puis qu'à peine reconnaître?" (III.2). Through the divinely formed ring he wears, the king has been elevated to the truths of chaste desire. He has never really seen Liliane before because he has never really seen her spiritual beauty through her physical charms. He has only to remove the ring to revert to his former self, to the biblical *vieil homme* of pure carnality.

This actually happens when he gives the ring to Liliane as a "gage" to show the guards in releasing her father and Comte Tancrède. His old self shows clearly when he violently withdraws his amnesty to the prisoners and disdainfully takes the ring away from Liliane in the very breath with which he beseeches her to satisfy his desire:

Que mon désir est prompt et que la fin est lente!
Les fers de notre hymen pourront bien être forts,
Puisque le Ciel y met tant de temps et d'efforts.

(III.6)

The man she looks on is not a true lover according to chaste desire. Only after these verses and, as the stage directions indicate, "avec des contenances toutes changées" and with the ring back on his finger, is the king restored to what can be considered a state of grace.

In the words of the title of the play, this is a state of forgetting. One forgets "l'humaine nature," as Léandre puts it in IV.1; one rejoices in the susceptibility the "forgetful" king now shows to the entreaties of his sister and Léandre himself. Léandre thus reminds us that there are dangers as well as hopes in the state of utter innocence and pure virtue. In a world where others retain their "humaine nature," the utterly virtuous are easily victimized. Kings, in particular, are victimized by evil counselors. Already in this play we have in a somewhat minor emphasis a concept that is central in later plays of Rotrou: since a king, by definition, can do no wrong, his wrongs must be attributed to evil counselors. This is a corollary, obviously, to the notion of the king's two states of being in their relation to one another. When he is possessed of a carnal desire, the king is obviously not himself. In terms the historian Ernst Kantorovicz has studied so perceptively, the king is of two bodies, the vicious one being pure matter and the "true" one, the doer of virtuous deeds, a body informed with divine spirit. And so here, transformed by the ring, the king heeds the advice of his sister and her lover, having no reason to doubt their integrity. He would, in fact, derogate from *générosité* were he to entertain doubts about the good intentions of a sister who is a princess. Specifically here, the lovers urge the king to name Léandre the first among his ministers. They also urge him to execute Alexandre and Tancrède. However, in the state of innocence the king also continues to stress the utterly spiritual. Paradoxically, this stress leads to his final return to reality. Heeding Fabrice's ironical advice that gold is the root of all evil, the king invokes the heavens ("O Ciel! que ce discours met mon esprit en peine," [IV.4]) and casts away the gold chain and the diamond ring he wears. He had earlier fallen into a sinful emphasis on the material in his pursuit of Liliane's body, all the while hypocritically using the sacrosanct formulas of chaste desire. He now moves into extreme spirituality, casting away a material object of unknown spiritual power in the very name of that power.

The "grace" of the ring does its work, but then human reason must co-operate to do its part. Thus, the king here expresses true love for Liliane at the end of Act IV, having left his ring off for the last time while it still contained the inscription. This is surprising only if one is looking for a development of character in the causal terms of a psychology based on *vraisemblance*. In the terms of what might be called sacramental psychology, the king's behavior is consistent. This mysterious co-operation of grace with reason occurs at the end of Act IV. The fifth act provides plenty of time (1) to save the condemned prisoners from being executed; (2) to have a penitent Alfonce then propose to Liliane; and (3) playfully to rehabilitate his sister and her low-born lover. Reassurance is once again found in a fifth act tripartite in its eschatological "anti-climaxes": a recall from the dead that is like a resurrection; a declaration of love by the king that is like a confirmation; and a confession of guilt by both king and Léandre that is like an act of contrition.

In a certain sense, the king himself is "resurrected" in the fifth act. The old man being dead, the new man of true faith is risen to repent his misdeeds. More literally, however, Liliane's father is recalled from the death he is about to suffer on the king's orders. Before the order is rescinded, we hear the ethical implications of Christian theology in the duke's paradoxical thesis of life gained through death:

> Et plutôt bénissons la faveur de nos Dieux,
> Qui m'ôte de la terre et qui m'appelle aux Cieux;
> Il est vrai, justes Dieux, que souffrir mon supplice,
> C'est pour un juste effet; permettre une injustice,
> C'est vouloir par la mort, m'exempter de mourir.

(V.1)

*Natural death* points to an *eternal life* and to the justification of earthly existence, where just conduct has led to unjust punishment. The spirituality is not so extreme as the king's in casting away the gold. However, there is the same fusion of Neoplatonist and Christian theses. We also have a strong Providentialist strain as the duke predicts the king's "futur et juste châtiment".

Such punishment is not in the offing for any of the principals. Having discovered that the ring was responsible for his curious changes, the king is returned to true reality. But he is now guided by the insights gained in his "transcended" state. He decides to remove the inscription but to pretend to be still under its effect by wearing the ring. With only Fabrice alerted to his trick, the king invites Léonor to assume the throne because he himself is weary of rule. As Léonor's husband-to-be, Léandre becomes king. Alcandre's prediction comes true: Léonor becomes queen and Léandre, master. Now a "subject," Alfonce asks the new "king" to adjudicate a case he has heard of: the lowborn suitor of a princess enchants a king through a ruse, displacing the king's servitors and even inducing the enchanted monarch to order the execution of such loyal people. Exclaiming that they have been found out, Léonor panics at the example. Léandre is of cooler head and sterner stuff than his mistress. The new "king" replies in kind. He tells the story of a monarch who deceitfully promises to wed a pure beauty but concocts false charges against her father and his rival to get them out of the way and enjoy the beauty without marrying her.

The "kings" offer each other similar examples of unkingly behavior. They do so in an intercalated structure that resembles a play. *La Bague* thus looks forward to *Le Véritable Saint Genest*, but it also looks back to such a structure in the "feinte" and the "jeu" of *L'Hypocondriaque*. Rotrou's love of paradox shows itself especially strong here. We have a double pretense within a pretense within a pretense, a complicated relation best rendered schematically:

I. Outermost Frame of Reference: Rotrou's play, *La Bague*

II. Second Frame of Reference within I: the king's pretense about giving up throne

III. Third Frame of Reference within II: the king's "case" resembling Léandre's real behavior; Léandre's "case" resembling the king's real behavior.

The cases Alfonce and Léandre present for adjudication are like the real situations of Alfonce and Léandre in every detail. But the key word here is *like*. Once again, a feint, a play-like structure, is presented as both a reflection and an occasion for reflection.

The king creates a fiction resembling reality: in his fiction he speaks not of one Léandre, one Léonor, and one Alfonce but of "un vassal infidèle . . . la sœur d'un Prince. . . ." Because of the previous scene with Fabrice, we know that he is the author of a fiction within a fiction. Léandre quickly catches on. He momentarily interrupts the king's fiction with its "lie like the truth," but only to return to it with his own "lie like the truth." He then appeals to the king on behalf of his client, the monarch who would seduce a mistress and murder her father:

> Sire, vous dépouillant de toute passion,
> Qu'auriez-vous estimé de semblable action?
> Pour moi, je n'y vois point d'excuses légitimes
> Si ce n'est que l'amour est auteur de ces crimes.
>
> (V.8)

Like Genest's "Ha! Lentule," his apostrophe ("Sire") announces that he is no longer acting. He is no longer the "king" Alfonce had made him and whom he pretended to be in giving his own example. When Léandre addresses Alfonce in this way, he once again becomes the subject; the play has ended. Its spectators, including the king who recently was also an actor, now reflect on the meaning of the play. The play is an occasion for action in the plane of true reality.

The king returns to the true reality from which he had fallen as the play begins. The virtual sacrilege of his behavior lies in his failure to live up to the tenets of chaste desire. The king's derogation from this code is rendered implicitly and explicitly in the dramatic structure of the first two scenes. The king's sister behaves one way, the king another. The dramatic evidence is rendered explicitly in the very first scene in which we meet the king: usually the repository of higher virtue, he is at this moment a slave to love in its carnal meaning, whereas his comic valet, Fabrice, typically the repository of such low desires as lust, is above such vice. Again, the king has heard his sister say that in Léandre "c'est la Vertu que j'aime." He shows himself aware that his own soul had at one time known such motivation:

> Si d'autres sentiments m'avaient l'âme blessée,
> De si sages discours confondraient ma pensée;
> J'accuserais à tort un vertueux amour,
> Dont l'objet... Mais Fabrice est déjà de retour.
>
> (I.6)

In the "development" of the king, Rotrou shows us the *re*-sacramentalization of the universe of the play. This motif is also apparent in the A parts of the A-B-A pattern of the over-all plot, especially in the story of Léandre and Léonor. Having begun with the sincere desire to achieve their ends in Heaven's name and with no harm to the king, they fall into a disgraceful deception of the king. They even lead him to order an execution they know to be unjustified. The imaginative recourse to the *double* pretense at the end of the play is both dramatically and doctrinally necessary if the play is to be the "comedy" Rotrou called it.

Now, in spite of its designation as *comédie* and in spite of the presence of Fabrice, *La Bague de l'oubli* is "tragic" in both its basic *données* and many of its developments: a sacrilegious king; false imprisonment for purposes of seduction; unjust arrest ordered by a king both when he can and cannot know better; the misuse of power by a vassal and his royal mistress, sister of the king; and so on. As so many of Rotrou's nineteenth-century critics have noted, in tone and subject matter there are very few of Rotrou's comedies that do not veer into the "tragic" very rapidly. *La Bague* is a case in point. Nevertheless, the rubric *comédie* is thematically just. The play moves toward a "comic" resolution of the tragic dilemmas it poses, and it does so within "this life." At early moments it may seem that there can be no happy ending to the lives of these or any other human beings; however, a happy solution *is* realized within this life. This comes out strikingly in the different ending Rotrou provided from his model in *La Bague*.[5] In the French play, the offending vassal and his mistress are not punished by the denial of life in all its pleasures, including the pleasures of each other. No lonely exile for Léandre and no abstemious "old-maidenhood" for Léonor. Instead, though their king banishes them, it is as a couple whose marriage he blesses. He gives them a kingdom, Saragoce, where Léonor will be a queen and Léandre a master, not only in pretense but in reality, thanks to the Divine Will. This is only as predicted in the heaven-sent Alcandre's prophecy.[6]

In *La Pélerine amoureuse*, Tragi-comédie (1632-33), Rotrou re-emphasizes the spiritual with an even stronger religious accent than in *La Bague de l'oubli*.[7R] Lucidor is a faithless lover who repents his infidelity to Angélique in the very moment that he reflects on a new object, Célie, in the first scene of the play. "Un secret repentir" draws him back to his first love. Still later, when his valet reminds him that the new mistress is quite well-to-do, the repentant hero rejects such materialistic precepts. "Une femme enrichit et la maîtresse baise," the valet argues, observing further that even for the average wife, "un ami plus parfait est l'objet qui l'enflamme," and if husbands possess the body, "d'autres possèdent l'âme" (II.2). In Filidan's sly proddings of his master, we have a half-mocking, half-serious reminder of courtly love.[8] In Rotrou's Filidan the mocking tone cautions against giving too spiritual an emphasis to the "courtesy" of the friend the wife finds outside of marriage. However, Filidan does look on love and marriage in the "courtly" terms summarized by C. S. Lewis as follows: "Conjugal affection cannot be 'love' because there is in it an element of duty or necessity: a wife in loving her husband is not exercising her free choice in the reward of merit, and her love therefore cannot increase his *probitas*."⁹ Lucidor also rejects not only the unlicensed carnality ("la maîtresse baise") but also the excessive spirituality Filidan describes in separating the body and soul of a married woman:

> Le respect, Filidan, qu'on doit à ce mystère
> Doit retirer nos cœurs des autels de Cythère,
> Rendre dessus les sens les esprits absolus
> Et nourrir la vertu chez les plus dissolus.
> C'est là qu'un long martyre accompagne les vices,
> Et que la continence établit les délices,
> Que le désordre règne en des cœurs criminels,
> Et qu'on nourrit chez soi ses bourreaux éternels.
> Mille fois le Soleil est pâli des carnages
> Que l'infidélité produit en des ménages,
> Et ce malheur qui suit un hymen vicieux
> N'épargnait pas jadis les fils mêmes des Dieux:
> Alcide eût tout vaincu, s'il eût vaincu la flamme
> Qui contre ses beaux jours fit attenter sa femme
> Et n'eût pas rendu l'âme étouffé du poison,
> Si l'amour n'eût premier étouffé sa raison.
>
> (II.2)

Like Andreas, Lucidor stresses the spiritual character of love, but he puts spirituality under the seal of marriage and marriage under the seal of heaven. Célie *is* pregnant before the fact of marriage, but that pregnancy is legitimized by the doctrine of good intentions. Here as in similar illegitimate unions, physical relations symbolize spiritual relations and are further legitimized by various tenets of chaste desire (loving first spiritually and remaining faithful to one's first love). Good intentions and chaste desire consecrate the marriage of lovers. "Le sacrement" (marriage) ratifies an already valid union: lovers are by definition husband and wife. In this figural view of physical union, as in Catholic doctrine, there is a sacramental basis to the indissolubility of marriage: the union of man and woman symbolizes the union of God and His church, and if one can dissolve marriage, one would thus be showing forth the dissolubility of the relation between the divine and the human.[10]

In Céliante and Lucidor, then, we have clear evidence of the religious and often specifically doctrinal character of *La Pélerine amoureuse*. It would be surprising if this were not most evident in the heroine. There is, of course, the personifying power of her name in religious terms: she is "Angélique." But is this power not apparent in the very title of the play? A pilgrim is a voyager on a religious mission. Angélique is greeted and consulted in this light by all those concerned with the "derangement" of Célie. Distraught by his daughter's seeming madness, Erasme welcomes the arrival of this "Pélerine, illustre de naissance" whose power to penetrate mysteries is due to her special "charité." The virtue is theological, we remember.[11] Thus, we are not surprised that this stranger " . . . au secours de Célie, un bon Astre destine" (II.6); that "on vante partout la science divine" of this pilgrim (III.3); that she is addressed in a series of epithets whose form and intonation suggest litanies to an intercessionary figure like the Virgin Mary: "Illustre Pélerine,/ Espoir des affligés, céleste Médecine" (III.8) and "Rare et pieuse fille, heureuse Pélerine,/ Jouis des longs honneurs que le Ciel te destine" (V.4). All those around her regard her as an irresistible image of beatific attraction: "Mais la voilà qui sort," says Filidan as he sees her for the first time, "Dieux! l'agrèable objet!/ Quel esprit peut tenir contre un si beau sujet?" (II.3). Little wonder that all consider and consult her as a distinctly sacred person.

All but herself. But this does not mean that she does not see herself in religious terms. Far from it: she regards herself as a virtually sacrilegious person. "Sommes nous Pélerins des Enfers ou des Cieux?" Clorimand had asked (III.2) as they arrived in Florence. Angélique answers his question with a blunt description of her mission as hell-bound, not heaven-sent:

> Que vous êtes déçu et qu'un prétexte honnête
> Vous cache, heureux veillard, une honteuse quête;
> Je ne visite point les temples de nos Dieux;
> Vers eux notre prière arrive de tous lieux.
> Je suis d'aveugles feux dont mon âme est atteinte,
> *Une profane ardeur prend le nom d'une sainte.*
>
> (III.2; italics added)

Later, she repeats this self-accusation: "Sous un prétexte saint, je suis, dans ce voyage,/ Les violents efforts d'une amoureuse rage" (II.3). Yet, as she goes on in this vein in an extraordinary speech of some seventy verses, we sense that she is "more sinned against than sinning." She is in quest of a lover whom she loved according to all the imperatives of chaste desire. He apparently betrayed her, so she now seeks him only in order "de lui reprocher ce honteux changement" (II.4). Like Clorimand, we are prepared to forgive her "hypocrisy" and, indeed, readier than he to regard this mission as a "pilgrimage." Far from being antonymous ("profane"), "amoureuse" is really synonymous with "religious" in her case. Her pretense only reflects what she is; her "role" only prefigures the "resurrection" from the dead that will occur when Lucidor sees her once again at the end of the play.

This ending does not depend directly on the feigning. True, Célie's pretense of madness does prevent something from happening: Lucidor gives her up. Yet, the conflict between Célie-Léandre and her father is resolved by fate: Filène's overhearing of the pregnancy of Célie and Filidan's eavesdropping on the daughter and the painter. Léandre then identifies himself as a Lucidor, and this identity is confirmed on the evidence of the name and the confession Céliante offers. What's in a name? Everything, in Rotrou. Names are consubstantial with Being, and with such essentials as truth-saying and proper station. Names have only to be mentioned, signals have only to be given, signs have only to be identified, for the truth to be ratified in the depths of the soul. Céliante says of Léandre—now Lucidor:

> C'est lui n'en doutons plus; que le Ciel m'est prospère
> Et qu'un secret instinct me fait voir clairement
> Ce bien que je retrouve en cet heureux moment.

(V.3)

Contingent events and things have been an occasion of grace and its secret powers.

The play has the air of a theorem, of a kind of Q.E.D. It is not surprising, therefore, that it should also contain an interesting sequence of artistic self-consciousness, but this time of a literary rather than a dramatic nature. There is no play-like structure here as in previous plays. Rather, in V.5 there is a discussion of poetry between Lucidor and Filidan, in which Filidan shows himself to be a poet. Those seeking autobiographical cues in Rotrou's plays might find this revealing. Not the master but the servant is the poet, as if Rotrou were projecting his own social situation as "poète à gages," provider of poetic pleasures for great men of the kind to whom he dedicates his works. As Lancaster and others have noted, the views of poetry and the poem illustrating them in this scene are rather unoriginal, casting Rotrou as a moderate leaning toward reaction in the aesthetic debate provoked by Malherbe and his adepts.[12] Filidan rejects "un mélange obscur de termes relevés," and frowns on a pompous dependence on mythological allusions. But if he is "modern" in prizing of the "natural," he is reactionary in asserting that dependence on the "natural" or "spontaneous" also applies to the method of poetic creation. He writes "sans beaucoup rêver," and he asserts that "Quand nature se tait, la science est muette,/ Le travail de cent ans ne peut faire un poète." The poem he recites to illustrate his views is addressed to "Diane." It is a fairly conventional piece in six stanzas of sixains in eight-foot lines, rhymed a-a-b-c-b-c, complimenting Diane in an ecstatic report of the benumbing effect of her "divin aspect" on the poet who worships her.

Undoubtedly, read out of context it seems to a twentieth-century reader "like many polite love poems of the period and, though correctly versified, makes to us neither an emotional nor imaginative appeal."[13] But the poem does fit nicely with the themes of the play. It begins:

> O rencontre agréable!
> Mort, horrible fléau des humains,
> Qui sur les célestes ouvrages
> Porte tes dangereuses mains
>
> (V.9)

Once again, the "convictions" are religious, only this time with strangely Manichean overtones. The spiritual force that oversees the universe is death. The "célestes ouvrages" that death menaces are human beauty and human love. In its benevolent form, the divine is totally immanent, and only its malevolent form, death, seems transcendental. Nor in the face of this evil transcendence does the poet appeal to some greater transcendence. Rather, in the last lines of the poem, he tells death: "Je puis faire, à ta honte, un généreux effort,/ Et par le fer, ou par la flamme,/ Avoir la mort, malgré la mort" (V.9). A spirit of stoical self-reliance, of atheism, informs these verses. This spirit is contradicted by the context in which the poem is read: the resurrection of the creature whose death the poem laments. The scene of literary criticism has, then, more than a critical or historical function in the context of the play.

It does nevertheless shed an interesting "critical" light on Rotrou himself, chiefly through the reactions of Lucidor to the poetic theories and performance of his valet-poet, Filidan. While Filidan is expounding his theories before reciting his poem, the master is somewhat bemused and skeptical about his valet's pretentions to poetry, teasing him about his claims to prowess in what Lucidor describes as the allied arts of poetry and making love. "Ton esprit, Filidan, se mêle de deux arts/ Où la sagesse est rare et court de grands hasards" (V.5). But once the valet has recited his poem, the master sincerely compliments his valet on his poetry: "Je trouve en cet écrit/ Des sujets, sans mentir, d'admirer ton esprit". He discusses both the virtues of Filidan's poem and his own fumblings along similar lines in a tone which shows that he has dropped his skepticism. He now requests a poem in honor of the dead mistress from this poet he had been gently mocking. This shift in mood is typical of Rotrou the dramatist. The early plays now succeed, now fail (or succeed only in part) in an effort to achieve what might be called the sacramental equilibrium of the material and the spiritual. After achieving this balance fairly well in *L'Hypocondriaque* and *La Bague,* Rotrou gives in, so to speak, to the materialist element in the next three plays, especially in *La Céliane*. In *La Pélerine amoureuse* he restores the equilibrium, depending on religious and virtually Christian spirituality in doing so.[14]

Though I do not intend to analyze them at length, I do think it valuable to consider one motif that emerges from the contrasting moods of Rotrou's next two plays. In *Amélie*, Tragicomédie (1633), Lancaster sees Rotrou reworking the elements of *La Pélerine amoureuse*.[15] The reworking is often bawdy. Thus the play stands in contrast to the spirituality of *La Célimène*, Comédie (1633). This spirituality is especially manifest in a motif that is obsessional in Rotrou: transvestitism and homosexual love. In showing members of the same sex falling in love with each other, especially women falling in love with women, Rotrou is, of course, pointing at the existence of this phenomenon in his own day. However, the homosexual love scenes also reflect the strong emphasis that certain plays put on one term of the recurrent conflict between flesh and spirit. A number of spiritualizing traditions—courtly love, Neoplatonism, Christianity—conflate in Rotrou and other early seventeenth-century writers. In these traditions woman is the repository of the Ideal, the symbol of the immaterial and the transcendent. Some see this conception as inevitable in the "battle of the sexes": women propound ideal conceptions of themselves in self-defense against the brutal physical power of men bent on physical satisfaction. In the light of this heritage, homosexual love reflects the intense sublimation of sexuality; it is a desexualization of love, an intense spiritualization of it.

Now, in its attempt to maintain the equilibrium of the spiritual and material, *La Célimène* has perhaps overstated the spiritual term of Rotrou's characteristic tension, even as plays like *Les Ménechmes* and *La Céliane* overstated the material. In this spiritual emphasis, *La Célimène* anticipates more the plays of Rotrou's late manner than those standing on either side of it. Nevertheless, Célimène does marry; she will find carnal as well as spiritual satisfactions in that state. We may thus take the play as relatively typical of its author's early theater and on this basis differentiate it from certain developments in French literature of the same moment.

Lancaster shrewdly points out that, though *La Célimène* is once again a Rotrou play without a specific model, its extraordinary plot is familiar to readers of Western European literature. He also suggests, however, that in essential features of both plot and characterization, it resembles the story of Diane in d'Urfé's novel *L'Astrée* (Part I, Book VI): the presence of one Filandre, verses of a poetic lover read while he sleeps, proof of sex by baring the breast, transvestism leading to seemingly homosexual love. Lancaster conjectures that Rotrou modified this principal source under the influence of the older tradition of European literature as well as under "that of pastoral plays with their woodland setting, their attempted enlèvements, foiled by faithful lovers, their symmetrically arranged characters."[16] As Marsan has also pointed out, the pastoral influence is certainly pronounced, although not so greatly as in the adaptation of *La Célimène* that Tristan L'Hermite wrote some twenty years later.[17]

Yet, in view of the metaphysic of the pastoral found by Jacques Ehrmann in *L'Astrée*, Rotrou's play might be seen rather as a critique of the pastoral. Contradicting a critical tradition that views *L'Astrée* as a series of platonic dialogues between practically disembodied lovers, Ehrmann shrewdly contends that:

> Par contre, l'amour sensuel est loin d'être absent de [*l'Astrée*]. Au plus pourrait-on dire que *l'Astrée* représente un *effort* pour spiritualiser l'amour. Et, comme dans tout effort, on remarque dans ce roman une tension entre deux tendances: l'amour instinctif et le point vers lequel on tend: l'amour spiritualisé. C'est précisément cette tension—plus que son point d'aboutissement—qui fait l'objet du roman. L'amour spiritualisé, qui donnera à la femme la liberté à laquelle elle aspire, n'est pas un acquis, c'est une conquête, avec ses victoires partielles et ses revers.[18]

Ehrmann sees this tension as a conflict between an "érotisme des corps" and an "érotisme des cœurs". Reflecting on both the length and the incompleteness of the novel, readers might well agree with Ehrmann that the whole point of the novel is in the conflict of these two eroticisms. The Neoplatonic premises of d'Urfé's metaphysic suggest that the tension is by definition unresolvable in *this* world. Only in a *transcendence* can this tension be resolved and, at that, only in favor of the "érotisme des cœurs". Speaking of the male partner's suffering under this tension, Ehrmann notes that the "érotisme des corps" and the fusion that results from it are forbidden him. The lover can rely only on, in the form of prayer, a solution that is always imperfect because words are inevitably tainted with illusion. Thus, Ehrmann concludes:

> Dans la pastorale (plus que dans toute autre forme de fiction) l'amour ne se *fait* pas, il se *parle*: il trouve ainsi existence autonome, il est au cœur des mots qui séparent l'homme et la femme. Il est un malentendu sur le chemin de la permanence.[19]

These propositions cannot apply to the early plays of Rotrou, even those derived from pastoral models. In the illusory or B developments of Rotrou's plays, as in d'Urfé, words are indeed never "complètement débarrassés de leur noyau d'illusion."[20] But in Rotrou these verbal illusions are dispelled by two irrecusable guarantees, standing, so to speak, one behind the other. There is, first of all, the guarantee of the other senses, especially the sense of sight. Visual appearances prevail over auditory "appearances"; the *seen* has ontological and ethical priority over the *heard* and especially the *overheard* of rumor or secondhand report. Thanks to divine ordination of all conventions—biological, social, philosophical—the word is made flesh "figurally." Divine ordination of the natural order and its conventions clears up misunderstandings that separate some men and women and join others. Such misunderstandings are temporary by definition. They are due to a temporary lack of awareness, an incomplete sense or a momentary confusion about what is essential. Eventually, the two eroticisms, of *corps* and of *cœur*, are reunited.

*Le Filandre*, Comédie (1633),[21R] is typical of all the plays studied thus far: it shows the familiar A-B-A structure. In the A portions, lovers are joined according to chaste desire; in the B portion of the play, lovers are separated and stoically contemplate exile or suicide; certain believers "sin," claiming that the very necessity of loving the beatific vision compels them to their sacrilege; and so on. Yet, the play also marks a shift in emphases in certain elements. It is the first of a long series of plays in which physical desire is an even more serious matter than in *La Bague de l'oubli*. The "sign," physical beauty, is prized in itself, while its spiritual significance is forgotten in moments of possession. Also, even in repentance, many of the sinners look back on these moments with considerable indulgence. In this series of plays, the theme of sacrilege becomes increasingly important. Confronted with the infidelity of friend, mistress, or lover, men and women are driven to doubt in Heaven's justice and to a purely human reliance on stoical courage. In certain plays here, the familiar reconciliations of the fifth act occur as part of what amounts to a resacramentalized world. Nevertheless, the sufferings of the B portions of these dramas are rendered with an intensity that makes them seem less "illusory" than in previous dramas. This thematic shift is personified in the character who gives his name to *Le Filandre*. The play is presumed to have been drawn from a number of pastoral models, including, once again, *L'Astrée*. As with *La Célimène*, separated lovers are reconciled with the restoration of sacramental verities, violated here by the "philandering" of the eponymous hero. Again, excessive spiritual reactions to offenses against chaste desire are also corrected in the denouement.

The offenses are of two kinds. First, there are the real violations: the lies Filandre and Céphise tell about the other lovers or Céphise's robbery of the locks of hair of another's lover. Secondly, there are "illusory" violations: the unjust accusations the true lovers make to each other as a result of the lies told by Filandre and Céphise, or Nérée's destruction of her lover's lock of hair when she snatches it from Céphise after the robbery. In this disturbed universe, all sacred relationships are violated.

Céphise and Théane are "sœurs ennemies" just as Filandre and Célidor are "frères ennemis." So intense is the enmity between the brothers that they are barely constrained from a duel, which would violate "respect de nature" (IV.6). Again, prayers are offered more in malediction than propitiation:

> Dieux! vous laissez le jour à cette criminelle?
> Et vous n'avez ni mains ni supplices pour elle?
> Vous punissez le vice, arbitre des mortels
> Et vous souffrez Nérée *aux pieds de vos autels*?
>
> (II:7; italics added)

Thus Célidor speaks of his mistress, who has given her love to Filandre, or so he has been led to believe.

Yet, the cure for the pains inflicted is not chiefly prayer, whether of a minatory or propitiatory kind. It is, rather, withdrawal either through the stoical precept of *mépris* or through despairing suicide. Not surprisingly, the men usually seek the latter recourse, the women the former. After his mistress' first rejection of him, Célidor calls upon death to finish a life that is only odious to his mistress. The women are made of sterner stuff. Having learned from Filandre of Célidor's "treachery" Nérée condemns herself for having allowed her "lâche raison" to cherish servitude to this flighty spirit. Others might not be able to support this treachery:

> Mais j'ai l'esprit plus fort et partout cette rage
> Est capable de tout, sinon en mon courage;
> Un généreux dessein peut vaincre ces douleurs
> Et je suis préparée à de pires malheurs
>
> (II.2)

The appeal to *générosité* is not specifically linked to social station in this apolitical play, but the accents from Corneille are evident. Théane adopts a similar stance in her first reactions to Thimante's reported treachery. In lovely *stances* at the beginning of the third act, she laments the surrender of her "raison" and freedom to this treacherous lover. These *stances* are more than the ornamental verses the form usually proves to be in pastorals and tragicomedy of the period. Their seriousness here shows them to be much more in the spirit of those *stances-méditations* Jacques Morel has perceptively studied in the tragedy of the period.[22] We thus have further evidence of the "serious" or "tragic" mood of this comedy whose lack of comedy Lancaster has already noted.[23] But leaving the fatalistic tone of this meditation and returning to a "lâche amante" for suffering this way, she urges herself to sterner self-reliance:

> Ta raison peut dompter un dessein inutile,
> Puisque des maux naissants le remède est facile,
> Crains l'abord de Thimante, évite ses appas
> Le voilà, l'inconstant; fuis, cours, ne l'attend pas.

(III.1)

And when she meets Nérée, similarly betrayed, she urges: "Fuis, sans délibérer, un ingrat qui t'oublie;/ D'un généreux effort, romps le nœud qui vous lie". She also urges Nérée to rely on time and reason in such matters, for they work "métamorphoses" that show them to be "maîtres de l'amour qui l'est de toutes choses" (III.4). This stoical advice thus reverses certain premises of the sacramental universe concerning time and reason in early plays: that time is rehabilitative, one of the conditions in which the higher reason of divine love works things out to the benefit of all true lovers. But this is no time for such verities; Nérée's brother has been unfaithful, so it is a time for more stoical behavior.

Neither Théane nor Nérée is capable of persisting in this stoicism. In her encounter with Nérée, Théane is far from the pride of a *généreuse* and much closer to the very despair that drives her lover to attempt suicide. She concludes her stoical advice to Nérée by saying: "Mais j'offre du remède au point du trépas,/ Je donne des avis et je n'en use pas" (III.4). Nérée also haughtily rejects the faithless Célidor, giving him to Céphise as if he were nothing to her: "Aime ce beau vainqueur, tout coupable qu'il est"—but then she adds immediately, "Dieux! qu'il est malaisé d'oublier ce qui plaît" (III.5) The stoical perspectives of this play are canceled even as the Neoplatonist perspectives of La Célimène are canceled: by the restoration of the eternal verities.

The restorations occur in forms coming extremely close to the sacraments of the church. As the fifth act begins, Filandre and Céphise begin the rehabilitation that really constitutes the whole point of the act. The unraveling of the conspiracy had begun as far back as the end of Act III. There, Théane saw into the preposterous claims of Céphise that she, the least attractive of the three women, had won over both lovers of the other two women. Even the apparent suicide of Thimante at the beginning of the fourth act is related to the rehabilitation of Filandre and Céphise. The seeming death of Thimante is an occasion for these perfidious people to recognize the workings of the Divine. Their defeat leads them to acknowledge that, in Filandre's words, " . . . le Ciel, qui sait tout, a fait voir sa puissance"; that, in Céphise's words, misfortune always follows upon a "dessein vicieux," because, "Quelque adresse qu'on ait à causer ces ombrages,/ La vérité paraît et force tous nuages" (V.1). Truth will out. The Divinity makes itself manifest, showing Filandre the charms of Céphise and Céphise the charms of Filandre. But sacrilege can be rewarded only after it has repentantly acknowledged itself for what it is and has been forgiven. The occasion for this development is both Thimante's "death" and his "resurrection." Confronted by the vengeful Théane, Filandre admits his guilt. Anticipating the great criminals of Rotrou's theater of transcendence, Filandre shows the justice of Morel's observation that "les grands Saints et les grands criminels ont, dans ce théâtre, la même trempe."[24] We might say of Filandre that in his confession and contrition (made, in order, to Théane, Nérée, and Thimante) the criminal becomes a saint. The same is true of Céphise, who insists on sharing her newly chosen lover's guilt. Like Filandre, she describes herself as guilty of violating sacred objects and sacred relations.

Now, we remember that both she and Filandre had justified their perfidy in claiming they were driven to it by the irresistible beauty of those they loved. As Céphise puts it in suppressing her misgivings about betraying her sister: " . . . ô frivole pensée!/ Le Ciel me l'a permis, quand un Dieu m'a blessée,/ Aux esprits amoureux ces crimes sont remis" (I.3). Yet, after the fact, both she and Filandre forsake these doctrines of fatal necessity and of ends justifying means. They assume full responsibility for their "crimes." Thus, it may seem that the earlier submission to a fatal necessity was but a rationalization of a wilful love. The evidence of the play is against such an interpretation. Filandre and Céphise may be liars; they are not hypocrites. The sinner is not forbidden to worship, and when his worship leads him into violations of trust, the Divinity provides another "means" in which the sinner can be rejustified:

> Le sujet importun de mes malheurs passés,
> Et les crimes d'amour, *après la repentance*,
> Ne sont ni reprochés ni punis sans offence.
> Je vois cette beauté qui me tient sous ses lois,
> Disposée à donner ce pardon de sa voix.
>
> (V.8; italics added)

In sacramental theology, penance is the sacrament granting the remission of sins. As the decrees of the Council of Trent put it:

> . . . Penance has justly been called by holy Fathers a laborious kind of baptism. And this sacrament of Penance is, for those who have fallen after baptism, necessary unto salvation; as baptism itself is for those who have not as yet been regenerated.
>
> . . . . . . . . . . . . . . . .
>
> [But] the acts of the Penitent himself, to wit, contrition, confession, and satisfaction are as it were the matter of this sacrament. Which acts, inasmuch as they are, by God's institution, required in the penitent for the integrity of the sacrament and

for the full and perfect remission of sins, are for this reason called the parts of penance. But the thing signified indeed and the effect of this sacrament, as far as regards its force and efficacy, is reconciliation with God, which sometimes, in persons who are pious and who receive this sacrament with devotion, is wont to be followed by peace and serenity of conscience with exceeding consolation of spirit.[25]

There is striking consonance between these Tridentine decrees and the events of the last act of *Le Filandre*. On learning of Thimante's death, the conspirators are *contrite*; they immediately *confess* their crime to the afflicted survivors; they offer to make *satisfaction* in an expiatory death at the hands of these survivors; their penance leads to their forgiveness and *reconciliation* with the community of heaven-made lovers (one of whom has been saved or *resurrected* through what he himself calls the "pieux office" of his rescuers [V.7]); Filandre devotedly promises to dedicate his remaining days in "éternel hommage" of the Théane who forgives him. But this is a universe in which *things* are as sacred as the *spirit* of repentance. Filandre must, therefore, be restored to full community: he, too, will join in an "heureux mariage"—with Céphise.

The freedom that Théane cherished and momentarily regretted losing was a freedom not to do; the freedom that Filandre and Céphise attribute to themselves was a freedom to do wrong. Our modern conception of freedom, the opportunity to do right *or* wrong, is asserted only *retroactively*: in the guilt the conspirators assume *post facto*. Posited in this way, we may wonder if it is really like our modern conception of freedom. When sacrilege is shown in its worst effects (the presumed death of Thimante), it automatically triggers a repentance that is "divinely" instituted and that determines *just* behavior. Illuminated in his penance as to the unjust nature of his behavior, Filandre can now act only in a just fashion. He even implies that, similarly illuminated earlier, he would have behaved justly. Like the madness of earlier lovers, the crimes and sins of the conspirators in this play are abnormal and unnatural: "horreur de la nature," Nérée calls Filandre at one point (IV.5). Till he is sacramentally illuminated, Filandre is imperfect in his being. In the fullness of being, he "freely" co-operates with the Divine in attesting to the perfidy of his earlier behavior and "freely" repents that behavior. But once again, freedom is only the opportunity for a sane, natural, and normal surrender of the self to the workings of providential order. The events of the fifth act correct not only the illusory stoical precepts of the fooled lovers, Théane and Thimante, Nérée and Célidor; they also correct the imperfect faith of the foolish lovers, Filandre and Céphise.

The play lives up to its designation as a comedy, but, once again in Rotrou, thematically a comedy shows signs of being more of a tragicomedy than a play characterized by farcical humor, ridiculous lower-class types, or satirical thrusts at social conventions. As Lancaster has noted, there is relatively little of this kind of "comedy" in *Le Filandre*.[26] The "funniest" scene is that in which Célidor and Céphise laugh at each other for being unable to carry through on their threats of suicide (II.7). This scene actually jars with the serious tones and dire developments of a play in which rival brothers almost come to blows and an attempted suicide actually seems to succeed. But a benevolent determinism has provided for the reconciliation of the brothers and the resurrection of the suicide. The comedy is at once human and divine.

*Hercule mourant* (1634), the first play designated "tragédie" by Rotrou, presents a world in which the palace is "noirci" by philandering husbands and the temple desecrated by jealous wives.[27R] Yet, these are not new motifs for Rotrou. This first of his tragedies on a classical theme closely resembles the plays surrounding it in the canon, especially *La Doristée*. Given the uncertainty of dating the plays of this period, it may actually have preceded that play.[28] In her passionate rage against her husband, leading to actual physical attack after she has discovered her husband's plans for divorce, the wife in *La Doristée* is as "furieuse" as the wife who might have given the name "Déjanire furieuse" to this play. Déjanire's husband is in the line of the sacrilegious lover-husbands and king-figures Rotrou has depicted since *La Bague de l'oubli*. However, in his blatant lying, Hercule is much closer to more recent "infidèles" than he is to the king of the second play, whose "split" personality was due to a magical effect.[29] Again, like recent young people in similar situations, the beleaguered young lovers of *Hercule mourant*, Arcas and Iole, cast doubts on the justice, if not the existence, of Heaven. "O cruelle beauté! trompeuse! image veine!/ Que le Ciel m'a vendue au prix de tant de peine" (I.3), laments Iole when Hercule blames her beauty for driving him to lay waste to her land and murder her father. Beauty has become the occasion of sin.

It has done so not only in the beholder but in the beheld. Iole utters her blasphemous doubts on the goodness of Heaven throughout this play. At the height of her distress in the last act, she even ignores the assurance of her lover that Heaven finally avenges the "innocent malheureux" with its thunderbolts. When Philoctète executes his "pieux devoir" in the name of Hercule, Iole throws herself upon him crying, "O sacrifice impie! ô piété barbare!" and goes on in verses of haunting pathos to wonder:

> Sommes-nous abordés en un séjour sauvage
> Où l'on vive de sang, de crime et de carnage?
> Pourquoi, cruels, pourquoi jusqu'au palais noirci
> Hercule cherchait-il ce qu'il avait ici?
> Quel monstre plus sanglant, quel plus cruel Cerbère
> Que ses propres parents avait-il à défaire?
> Que voit-on en ces lieux que des objets d'horreur?
> Et qu'y respire-t-on que meurtre et fureur?
>
> (V.3)

Here the parents of the earlier plays have become worse than avaricious opponents of young love; they have become its murderous ravagers who license the indulgence of "sales désirs" in themselves and their offspring. Worse, one of the parents is a god who has become incarnate in a beloved son not to consecrate this world in a *grace*-ful sign of the divine benevolence but to desecrate it in a *disgrace*-ful sign of divine hostility.

Iole is not alone in casting doubt on divine order; so, too, do her enemies. Philoctète's reluctance in carrying out his master's wishes is only the last sign of doubt cast on the religious beliefs he shares with his master. Ironically enough, his hesitancy is weaker in its doubts than his master's and his family's. Iole tells us that faith fails because beauty *betrays*; Déjanire tells us that it fails because beauty *fades*: "Le temps, qui forme tout, change aussi toutes choses;/ Il flétrit les œillets, il efface les roses" (1.2). Time is no longer the context in which the Divine makes itself manifest in sacramental signs. Rather, it is an evil context in which the infuriated wife calls on objects of an antisacramental character. Déjanire at first reminds us of the stoical heroes of earlier plays with her appeal to her own courage here (" . . . et le cours de cet âge/ Qui m'ôte des attraits me laisse du courage" [I.2]). But she uses courage not to steel herself to adversity but to appeal to hidden forces of an antisacramental nature. The evil garment is soaked with the "sang d'un monstre affreux." Again, instead of being openly shown in a holy place where sacramental objects might normally be venerated, Déjanire has hidden the garment from view "sous le temple, un peu loin du palais,/ En un lieu que le jour ne visite jamais,/ Vaste, sombre et profond" (II.2). Her courage looks down, not up; her faith is not in Heaven but in Hell.

Hercule's faith, too, is a weak one. In the very first lines of the play, he appeals to his heavenly father to reward his piety and his accomplishments by taking him to the heavens. His patient rehearsal of his deeds has a sharp edge of indignation. In his questions about the jealous Junon, he verges on doubt that his heavenly father is powerful enough to carry out his son's plea. His determination to force the gates of Heaven in spite of its hostile queen and weak ruler borders on the sacrilegious, but he is too distracted by a different sacrilege to carry through on this resolve here. He thinks of Iole and casts doubts on his own integrity: "Et ce lâche à ce nom d'aise se sent ravir" (I.1). *Lâche*—which is to say, offender against the code of *générosité*, with its injunctions to respect oneself in choosing one's love. But his wife implies that one has a choice in the matter: she is furious with him because he loves a *captive* (II.2), loves out of place. The terms of her fury here are consistent with the concern for the self, the forgetting of Heaven we have noted in her decision to turn to the powers of Hell. The devil may be in her husband's flesh, but, in this motif of the lovely captive, that evil being is in her soul. This is not to say that Hercule's soul is completely absolved in the matter of his surrender to *sales désirs*. Still, his greater offense against true piety lies elsewhere: in his fierce pride as the very son of Heaven! Even in its most pious expressions, the faith of this demigod is at best perfunctory. Thanking his father for "guiding his arm" in recent victories, the sacrificer is more concerned with the adoration those victories have brought him. The prayer he utters on the occasion is respectful enough: it appeals for peace and fecundity on this earth and calls for blood to be shed only on altars henceforth. But it concludes with much self-gratulatory pride. Hercule seems to want to get to Heaven chiefly to displace an inefficient god there: "Et que le foudre enfin demeure après mes faits/ Dans les mains de mon père un inutile faix!" (III.1). Like his wife, Hercule thinks only of himself when speaking to the beyond.

If this is true before his fiery suffering, it is all the more so during it. His friend, Philoctète, sadly reflects that the son "porte le péché des amours de son père" (III.1). This is to accuse God himself of man's sin, a tragic perspective perhaps hinted at by Hercule also in his subsequent lament: "O Ciel! ô dieux cruels! ô sévère destin!/ O d'une belle vie honteuse et lâche fin!" (III.2). Yet, here as elsewhere in Rotrou, the Supreme Being is exculpated. In his goodness He is distinguished from a *destin* or fate on whom one puts all the blame for man's sin and suffering. But if the godhead itself is thus saved from guilt, Hercule is not to be thought of as moving toward an exemplary Christian humility or self-effacement. He regrets that a merely mortal woman is responsible for his defeat. (He presumably means Iole. Only later will he learn that it is Déjanire, a hint unwittingly given by him here as he wishes that he had been the booty of "un centaure affreux"). He would prefer in his pride that "la haine de Junon" had done him in, for "C'est une femme aussi, mais son être est céleste" (III.2). True, he pleads for instantaneous death to relieve his sufferings:

> D'un regard de pitié daigne percer la nue,
> Et sur ton fils mourant arrête un peu ta vue:
> Vois, Jupin, que je meurs, mais vois de quelle mort,
> Et donne du secours ou des pleurs à mon sort.
> J'ai toujours dû ma vie à ma seule défense,
> Et je n'ai point encor imploré ta puissance.

(IV.1)

The half-god, half-man seems more man than god here—humanized in a humiliation whose terms will be the paradoxical basis of his final divinization in the last act. Nevertheless, his humiliation here is that of the man who sees himself more worthy in his achievements than the very gods. He describes his plea as "cette lâche action," regretting that "aux prières en fin ce feu m'a fait résoudre" (IV.1).

Hercule's mother underscores this man-centered "theology." Alone after seeing her son in his humiliation, she describes herself as "infortunée." Like others in the play, she invokes the heavens only to make them seem man's creations: what, she asks, will become of her names, "mère d'un héros et d'amante d'un dieu." Seeing her son's mute relics beneath a tomb, she asks, "Quels si religieux priront à son autel/ Et quel ne dira pas qu'il était un mortel?" (IV.2). These doubts on her own "divine" self-importance drive her to attack Philoctète when he refuses to carry out her son's orders (V.2). Like Déjanire's, her faith seems stronger in the powers of Hell than in those of Heaven. Addressing the "fatales sœurs, reines des destinées", she wonders: "Que fait Alcmène ici quand Alcide n'est plus?/ Si le fils relevait d'un pouvoir si sévère,/ Quel aveugle destin en exempte la mère?" (V.2). She doubts Heaven and believes in hostile fate.

She is wrong to do so, as are all those who complain of their fate in this "séjour sauvage." They learn this from Hercule.

## TEMPTATION TO TOTAL IMMANENCE

Momentarily descending from the heavens to which he has been translated, he teaches them the lesson he himself has learned in the heavens:

> Admis dans le céleste rang,
> Je fais à la pitié céder la jalousie,
> Ma soif éteinte d'ambrosie
> Ne vous demande plus de sang.

(V.4)

This is the lesson toward which the whole plot has been moving. The introduction of the love between Arcas and Iole has completely restructured the *données* that Rotrou has taken from Seneca. As Lancaster has shrewdly observed: "Rotrou's chief invention is to give Iole a lover, Arcas, who has been imprisoned by Hercules and who is to be put to death if she will not yield to her captor. This invention gives rise to dramatic scenes between Hercule and Iole, Iole and Deïanira, Iole and Arcas."[30] In introducing the lover, Rotrou has also set the play squarely in those dramatic and thematic terms central to his vision in the comedies and tragicomedies already discussed.

For all the seemingly "inductive" nature of its dramaturgy, this first tragedy unfolds the terms of a pre-existent reality in the same way as Rotrou's previous tragicomedies. The structure is cast in the A-B-A pattern. Once again, a chaste love between legitimately linked young people becomes threatened in the fall from the twin codes of the sacramental universe by adherents who have an imperfect understanding of both. The love of Arcas and Iole is revealed in the first act, imperiled through the next three and part of the fifth, and finally restored in V.4. Iole's charge of sacrilege ("ô sacrifice impie! ô piété barbare") is vindicated; but so, too, is Arcas' confidence in Heaven, even if it is vindicated in terms that he does not quite see at the time. Heaven's mercy prevails.

This is not to say that Heaven's justice has been compromised. Déjanire dies after a debate with herself that we have already encountered. She rejects first the stoical pride of utter self-reliance: "Mais que veux-je du Ciel? Quoi! la femme d'Hercule/ Au chemin de la mort est timide, et recule!" She then rejects her attendant's doctrine of innocence by intention—"Celui ne pèche pas qui pèche sans dessein"—and blames herself exclusively: " . . . de cet accident mon bras seul est auteur". She goes on to exculpate Heaven as if it were the punitive ecclesiastical arm of a secular court of self-judgment: "Le juste bras du Ciel sur ma tête descend." But if Heaven is a just executioner, it is also a final court of appeals, and Déjanire asks for Heaven's pardon: "Pardon, mon crime, ô Ciel! n'est qu'un crime d'Amour" (III.4). And, as reported by Agis, her words just before death show her calling both on "généreux courage" and "innocence by intention" (IV.3).

The logic of this inner debate is no more satisfying than it has been in previous cases: Déjanire appeals both to her own sense of justice and Heaven's sense of mercy; she exculpates Heaven by the assumption of guilt, and she then exculpates herself by the doctrine of innocence by intention, which she had at first denied. Now, in the midst of her debate, she reproaches her own credulity for thinking that a garment of the unholy Nesse could be anything but harmful (III.4). Given the terms in which she herself speaks of the garment, as well as her later premonitions, she perhaps only rationalizes in accepting the thesis of innocence by intention. She spoke more truth in blaming herself, we would say. But on the basis of his themes thus far, we can also say that Rotrou wanted to resolve Déjanire's moral dilemma by exculpating her on two sacramental grounds: her repentance and her assertion of inner innocence. Though her suicide is nonetheless *sinful*, Catholic theology actually permits remission even of this sin because its perpetrator has lost the fullness of reason.[31] Déjanire's innocence in her crime does not thereby incriminate Heaven in that crime. Heaven only uses this innocent instrument to its own fundamentally innocent end of translating Hercule into Heaven.

Iole's beauty leads to Déjanire's jealousy which leads to Hercule's torment which leads to his assumption into Heaven which leads to his resurrection and re-intervention into the world.

## TEMPTATION TO TOTAL IMMANENCE

*The* world—the concepts of "this" world and "that" world are shown to be inappropriate by Hercule's descent from the heavens. His descent is a reintervention, for the first intervention occurred when he was conceived. Half-god and half-man, Hercule is the sacramental sign of the divine become humanly incarnate. In his life before his ascension, Hercule has mistakenly thought himself more divine than human. He has had to suffer, to be humanized before he can be divinized. Divinization is complete only when he recognizes that, like the anger of previous lovers in Rotrou, jealousy is an illusion obscuring insight into true reality. That he learns this lesson "dans le céleste rang" may suggest that it can be learned only there, that in this world of desecrated temples and blackened palaces such lessons are learned too late. But this Racinian perspective is denied by the very fact that the deified Hercule returns to this "séjour sauvage" in order to suspend the savage order he gave before his ascension. The Pascalian notion of a discontinuity between the orders of *cœur, esprit,* and *chair* may have its counterpart in Racine's theater. However, in Rotrou these orders (*pitié, amitié,* and *désir,* in his terms) are continuous: Hercule's pity cancels his former jealousy and its illicit grounds. Chastity is as much a part of *générosité* as *générosité* is of chaste desire in this play. Rotrou had already indicated this view of the death of Hercule in *La Pélerine amoureuse* when Lucidor rejected Filidan's sacrilegious advice to marry for money and take a mistress for pleasure:

> Alcide eût tout vaincu, s'il eût vaincu la flamme
> Qui contre ses beaux jours fit attenter sa femme,
> Et n'eût pas rendu l'âme, étouffé du poison,
> Si l'amour n'eût premier étouffé sa raison.
>
> (II.2)

Lucidor—and perhaps his creator—could not yet see that Hercule would render his life only to gain his soul.

The Christian formulation is appropriate here. As he takes leave of his jubilant worshipers, Hercule urges all the peoples of this place to build altars to him "Et qu'ils conservent la mémoire/ De la mort qui m'a fait un dieu" (V.4). Death has made him a god—not life, as he had originally insisted in his first complaints to his heavenly father. In Seneca's model the reappeared hero still talks in such terms, and he denies the sacramental immanence of the divine in the world of flesh:

> Non me gementis stagna Cocyti tenent nec puppis umbras furva transvexit meas; iam parce, mater, questibus; manes semel embrasque vidi. quidquid in nobis tui mortale fuerat, ignis evictus tulit; paterno caelo, pars data est flammis tua. proinde planctus pone, quos nato paret genetrix inerti. luctus in turpes est; virtus in astra tendit. in mortem timor.

In Seneca it is not so much the divine that has informed the human but the human that has joined, if not informed, the divine. But in Rotrou, the sanctified Hercule restores contact with the divine. The theses of Florimond de Raemond, Rotrou's contemporary and an orthodox Catholic historian of heresy whom I quoted in my Introduction, are especially relevant here: " . . . Il se peut dire que la superstition des païens a été une figure, un portrait, une idée et un dessin pour venir à la vraie Religion."[32] I remind the reader that one of the specific "pagan portraits" Raemond considers in this light is Hercule.

Rotrou's sanctified Hercule renews contact with the human and thus renews a spiritual contract that seemed missing at every turn of events in the action. He blesses the union of Arcas and Iole. Fulfilling his command to marry, they, too, will show the sacramental order of the world—just as those who will now build altars to his glory show that order in a more patently religious sense. *Hercule mourant* is an example of what Corneille calls "une tragédie heureuse."[33] The desecrated universe with which it began has been resacramentalized.[34]

Except perhaps for *Hercule mourant* and *La Pélerine amoureuse, L'Innocente Infidélité*, Tragi-comédie (1634 or 1635), is the most specifically religious in language and motifs of Rotrou's plays to date.[35R] In the struggle for possession of Félismond, "Le

Ciel" is forever on the lips of Evandre and Parthénie, and "Les Enfers" is forever on the lips of Hermante and Clariane. The fundamentally religious motif of the ring with spiritual power is central here as in *La Bague de l'oubli*, and the return to a "funeral scene," cast in an artistic or theatrical mode in *L'Hypocondriaque*, is here a specifically religious occasion, presided over by a priest.

Rotrou has significantly varied and deepened the meaning of these motifs and resolutions. The most obvious difference between the two plays about enchanted kings is in the actual effect of the rings. In Rotrou's second play, we had a ring of sacramental power. It signified and brought a kind of grace to its *wearer*; it made Alfonce forget his "fort instinct." In *L'Innocente Infidélité*, we also have a "bague d'oubli," but, worn by the chthonian Hermante, it has an evil effect on the *observer*, Félismond, making him forget that he has already overcome his "fort instinct." As the serene Parthénie brings out, this instinct is only the natural eroticism of youth. It will yield in time to the divinely sanctioned "pressant instinct" that leads her to love Félismond in spite of his passion for Hermante. The latter's ring is a serpentine object perfectly symbolic of the carnally evil wearer. It is virtually sacrilegious, a "counter-ring" to the matrimonial ring, and desecrates the sacramental rite (which, in fact, Hermante desecrates by her very appearance). The unnatural, sacrilegious object intervenes in—or, more exactly, countervenes —a divinely sanctioned natural process.

Of course, Parthénie's "natural faith," rather than Hermante's "natural power," eventually triumphs, doing so in dramatic and thematic terms familiar in Rotrou. But what gives the play special dramatic as well as thematic interest is the way in which the dramatist treats the theme of sacrilege. Lancaster has nicely observed that "the minor characters are unusually important: the avaricious and treacherous Clariane and the faithful attendants of the king and queen, who succeed in foiling the schemes of Hermante."[36] Knutson's insight into the use of polarized types is especially apt here. For Knutson, the effect is largely aesthetic, but the thematic effect is important too: Parthénie in her virtue is opposed by Hermante in her vice. As we have already seen, in Rotrou all is in a name; a name is a sign of value in rank and station. In *L'Innocente Infidélité* the warranty is given etymologically in the virginally virtuous Parthénie [παρθένος]. There is perhaps the same etymological personnification of her adversary: the name of this wicked *ambitieuse* might be a compound of Hermes, the scheming messenger of the gods, and *amante*, she who loves more through *amour* than *amitié*. Again, given the Spanish for sister, *hermana*, with which her name is cognate, perhaps Rotrou only means to show her as he has other sisters or sister-like mistresses—that is, rejected in the end. These interpretations of her name are perhaps etymologically fanciful, but they do point to the dramatic fate of Hermante. She is not paired with anyone at the end of the play. This is appropriate according to the "lois constitutives" of the sacramental universe that have been applied to, and illustrated by, other characters.

Hermante reminds us of Corneille's Cléopâtre in *Rodogune*, a play written almost a decade after Rotrou's. Like Cléopâtre, Hermante is true to her evil self. She is a consistent "sacrilège," excoriated as an "horreur de la nature" (V.3). But unlike earlier "perfides," she neither repents nor acknowledges Heaven's supremacy. Her evil aide, Clariane, surrenders, apparently in full contrition; she regrets her offense to Heaven's laws and calls for its punishment of her. We suspect that there is more attrition than contrition in Clariane's penance: she fears punishment more than she regrets the offense. However, as we know from Roman theology and from frequent examples in Rotrou, attrition is sacramentally valid. (Among Rotrou's strictly religious contemporaries, Richelieu as a theologian defended the validity of attrition and was, characteristically, opposed on the issue by Saint Cyran.)[37] True, at the moment of her exposure, Hermante seems penitent in her call upon the ruler of Heaven to destroy her: "Toi qui tournes les Cieux et qui soutiens la terre" is her apostrophe as she asks him to hide "à l'œil du jour cette horrible sorcière/ Dont les sales regards profanent la lumière" (V.4). Racine's Phèdre will speak in strikingly similar terms of herself:

## TEMPTATION TO TOTAL IMMANENCE

> Déjà je ne vois plus qu'à travers un nuage
> Et le ciel et l'époux que me présence outrage;
> Et la mort à mes yeux dérobant la clarté,
> Rend au jour, qu'ils souillaient, toute sa pureté.
>
> (V.7)

But Hermante calls on "Le Ciel" as only one of the demonic forces she wishes would destroy her. "Manes, Démons, damnés je vous invoque tous," her speech begins here. She speaks not in the "tristesse majestueuse" of Phèdre's tragic illumination but in the accents of "une amante ambitieuse et furieuse." She defies Heaven, for her faith is in Hell. When we last see her, it is "en une haute tour en prison, les fers aux mains et aux pieds." She leaves no doubt that her assumption of "guilt" is neither contritional nor attritional; she calls at once on the "ténébreux habitants du Royaume des Parques." When these fail to answer her in this profanation of prayer, she turns even lower:

> Que l'Enfer pour le moins s'ouvre aux vœux que je fais,
> Qu'il engloutisse tout, Roi, sorcière et Palais;
> Pour réparer un crime au Ciel épouvantable
> Confondez l'innocent avec le coupable,
> Faites pour mes forfaits souffrir tous les mortels,
> Renversez les Cités, les trônes, les autels
> Par la punition faites juger du crime,
> Que mon pays périsse et que l'Epire abîme.
>
> (V.5)

Her "prayer" goes unheeded. However, if the infernal powers ignore her, the heavenly ones do not now nor will they in the end of ends. The despairing Hermante wishes that her body were already "le butin des flammes." We are reminded of Bellarmin's description of eternal punishment: it will be more than the deprivation of the beatific vision, for "there will be very many punishments, I say, since each power of the mind and each bodily sense will have its own torture."[38] The concept is appropriately material in its sacramental stress. Signs of this premise had already been glimpsed in the punishments Evandre saw being prepared for Clariane. To be sure, he had reminded the evil seer that she would suffer the loss of the beatific vision: "Pleure, soupire, crie et déteste les Cieux,/ Leur lumière à jamais est morte pour tes yeux" (V.8). Again, Clariane hopes for "des tourments égaux à mes forfaits," and the destruction of her vile body by "corbeaux." Parthénie tells her that "l'effet suivra de près ce dessein légitime." On the other hand, the spiritual term is not denied. The conception of penance of earlier plays still holds: vice is its own punishment. In her final appearance, Hermante herself sounds it once again: "C'est trop, c'est trop, cruels, se venger d'un forfait,/ Et l'attente des maux punit plus que l'effet" (V.5). But the most dramatically apparent stress is the material one. Evandre had told Clariane that in the "affreux séjour" of her prison she was to punish herself with her own sins only as a *beginning* of the horrible "peine" he invited her to meditate on. And like Clariane, Hermante is in chains and in prison here. Her sufferings are as visible as the joys of Félismond and Parthénie. Hell is as real as Heaven.

The A-B-A structure applies in the familiar sense to Félismond's story: he is cured of his lust for Hermante when we first meet him; he is then enchanted back into his lust and finally disenchanted of that lust. But his enchantress does not see the illusoriness of her "manie" or "folie." Her mania is for power, not pleasure, and it endures: the last words we hear from her are not the complaint about vice being its own punishment but a stormy curse upon creation:

> Dieux, Enfers, Eléments, faites ma sépulture
> Dans le commun débris de toute la nature,
> Que le chaos renaisse et que tout soit confus,
> Dieux! tonnez, Cieux; tombez, Astres, ne luisez plus!

(V.5)

The chthonian Hermante, too, has gone through an A-B-A pattern: she began defeated in evil, triumphed in evil, and returned to defeat in evil. In her case the B developments of her story are not based on what Orlando calls a false datum. The datum of her evil is immanent and persistent in the universe.

In terms of the hard-headed realism that views experience as more ironic than irenic in its lessons, Hermante's consistency is the sign of a growing maturity in its author. One can understand Lancaster's enthusiasm for this play: in his compliments to its beauty and dramatic power, one senses his approval of its psychological and moral realism. Within the familiar framework of this still largely Romantic and quasi-pastoral setting, Rotrou accepts the problematic character of the universe. No deathbed confession for Hermante, who curses God and dies. But the reality to which she is restored in the final portion of her story is still one in which Evil has been vanquished. Her sacrilege is not triumphant. In being restored to his initial state of grace in the final A portion, Félismond is Heaven's king; he overcomes the reality of Hermante's enchanting evil. Already knowing the happy ending, Evandre had put it nicely when Hermante was led off to prison:

> L'Enfer n'a plus de droit, son pouvoir abattu
> Laisse du vice enfin triompher la vertu.
> Le Ciel marche à pas levés au châtiment des crimes,
> Sa Justice irritée ouvre tard ses abîmes,
> Mais quand son bras enfin s'applique au châtiment,
> Il répare le temps par l'excès du tourment.

(V.4)

In God's good time, the incorrigible temptress has been punished. In God's good time, the corrupted king has been redeemed by the love of a pure princess. Rotrou here gives us, without reservation, a royal redemption upon which he will look back with longing in his greatest play about a corrupt prince, *Venceslas*.

Amusing as *Les Sosies*, Comédie (1637), is, it resembles neither the rollicking comedy of Plautus nor the subtle satire of

Molière.[39R] In finally giving full dramatic vent to a theme that has obsessed him in comic and tragic moods, Rotrou does not draw the problematic moral and sociological perspectives that, with other qualities, make Molière's *Amphitryon* unique. For all Molière's "borrowing" from Rotrou here, it is a mistake to think of both dramatists as drawing the same lessons from their common subject. Viewed in this light, Rotrou draws the lesson rather poorly, whereas his imitator draws it superbly. However, interpreted in the perspective of Rotrou's own canon, the play once again offers a consistent vision rather than an imperfect realization of some other artist's vision.[40] Preoccupied with the twin motif in this subject from Plautus as in the last, *Les Ménechmes*, the playwright once again depicts the self according to virtually sacramental notions.

Mythologically, the twin theme is directly linked with the idea of the soul. Summarizing the work of many anthropologists, psychologists, and literary critics, Otto Rank links the twin theme to the larger theme of the double as this bears on the soul in myth and religion:

> Originally, the double was an identical self (shadow, reflection), promising personal survival in the *future*; later, the double retained together with the individual's life his personal past; ultimately he became an opposing self, appearing in the form of evil which represents the perishable and mortal part of the personality repudiated by the social self.

Both in *Beyond Psychology* (1939), from which this passage is taken[41] and, even more elaborately, in *Der Doppelgänger* (1914) (known to me in its French translation, *Don Juan: Une Etude sur le double*), Rank lists the last two of these three stages to civilized and specifically early Christian moments in the development of the double theme. In this religious connection, he notes, the double is explicitly linked with the idea of the devil: "Le diable, qui d'après la croyance de l'Eglise s'empare d'une âme coupable et la prive ainsi de l'immortalité, est donc un descendant direct de l'âme immortelle personnifiée qui, lentement, s'est transformé en un esprit mauvais."[42] This view of the self as split into a higher and a lower part, "good" and "bad," spirit and matter, is not specifically Christian; but its consonance with Christian concepts is striking, as Rank brings out in its history. He traces the theme of the double beyond its preliminary stage of shadow or reflection and into its sophisticated mythological and literary expression in the motif of twins. Both in primitive folklore as well as in sophisticated mythologies, Rank notes, the twin theme is linked to the founding of society, usually in the form of the city. In primitive forms the motif shows mother and twins being either slaughtered or driven off, and, in the latter case, founding the new city. Rank and others regard expulsion or quarantine (rather than death) as an advance toward civilized tolerance of the taboos associated with twin births. These taboos are linked with the fearful intrusion of the supernatural into the natural:

> For the twins through their unusual birth have evinced in a concrete manner the dualistic conception of the soul and thereby given proof of the immortality of certain individuals singled out by destiny.
> Among such specially endowed individuals, really deviates, the twin stands out as one who was capable of bringing with him into earthly existence his living double and thus had no need to procreate himself in any other form. By the same token, twins are considered self-created, not revived from the spirit of the dead, but generated through their own magic power, independent even of the mother.[43]

But the motherless twins can found a city, Rank goes on, only with one killing the other, with the higher self killing the lower self, the social self killing the antisocial self: " . . . In twin-mythology the typical motif of fratricide turns out to be a symbolic gesture on the part of the immortal self by which it rids itself of the mortal ego."[44] In Christian terms, the new man kills the old man, the spirit overcomes the flesh. The soul overcomes the "diable au corps" who, in the most pessimistic extensions of Christian psychology, is not only *in,* but consubstantial *with,* the flesh.

In *Les Sosies*, in fact, such pessimistic thought would contend, *le diable au corps* does indeed triumph, the lower self wins out over the higher self. Given the ontological premises of the play (a literal distinction between two realms, divine and human), we would expect the higher self to be located in the divinity and the lower self in the human. The reversal of this pattern is rendered in the human realm as strikingly as in the divine. Amphitryon and his wife represent the higher self. However, she is a more balanced person in this respect, showing her higher worth in the flesh as well as the spirit. Not that this Alcmène is the lively creature who complains about Jupiter's departure as we first meet her in Plautus. If anything, the wife in Rotrou's play is at first more spiritual. Her first words in this play are only a brief query when Jupiter departs. Her extended remarks when next we meet her show that, like the old Alcmène in *Hercule mourant*, she is melancholy, preoccupied with the apparent contradictions between human aspirations and the natural condition: "Par quel ordre fatal, ma chère Céphalie,/ Faut-il que la douleur aux voluptés s'allie." Nature's first law seems to be that "un plaisir s'achète avec usure"; it is a law of "maux . . . naturels," common to "grands comme aux petits, aux Rois comme aux bergers" (II.2). When her husband returns for a second visit in so short a time, her anxious reflections have as much to do with chaste desire as with *générosité*. "Ma chaste affection, lui serais-tu suspecte?/ Douterait-il, Hymen, combien je te respecte?" (II.3). However, this chaste wife also knows that, according to the sacramental ethos, chastity is not celibacy:

> Hier, à votre arrivée, avec quelle allégresse,
> Vous vins-je recevoir et vous fis-je caresse!
> Je craignis, justement, que ma civilité,
> Ne passât du devoir à l'importunité.

(II.3)

She is actually unjust here—too hard on herself, we know. Such "importunings" are the licensed extremes of legitimate marriage, not the licentious excesses her bewildered husband attributes to her. She expresses as much later. Querying her about the night before, distraught at the thought of what went on, the husband cries "comment, en même lit?" With more verve than elegance this time, Alcmène unblushingly counters with the sacramental law of licensed pleasure:

> Avec la liberté
> Qu'une pudique femme a de l'honnêteté,
> Et par la loi d'Hymen, immuable et sacrée,
> Qui m'y donne ma place et m'en permet l'entrée.
>
> (II.4)

Flesh and Word: Alcmène represents the sacramental equilibrium.

Her husband strives to maintain it, but he unbalances the terms of the equilibrium with a decidedly spiritual emphasis. In utter distress, he contends that a wife's deeds are the only measure of her integrity:

> S'agissant d'honneur, l'erreur même est un crime,
> Rien ne peut, que la mort, rétablir son estime,
> Entrons, rompons, brisons, secondez mon dessein,
> Surprenons, s'il se peut, l'adultère en son sein;
> Partout, l'honnêteté repose à porte ouverte,
> Cette porte fermée assure encore ma perte,
> Le vice seulement aime à se cacher,
> La femme qui s'enferme a dessein de pécher.
>
> (V.4)

As for earlier deceived lovers at the darkest moment of their deception, the world seems more sacrilege than sacrament. Here, the husband even denies that good intentions exculpate what would otherwise be misdeeds. Amphitryon speaks of the "partout" of other doors honestly open, but for him Alcmène's is the door to the whole world. We thus border on Jansenist notions of the world as a sacrilegious trap: beauty itself is a lure into sin. Such notions must be countered by the visible sign of the world's value. For Amphitryon this means the sign of his beautiful wife as a virtually sacramental object. This she is, in the news her servant brings forth.

The chaste Alcmène is possessed by the Ruler of Heaven for an exalted purpose. The B portion of this play does not depend on a false datum. Rotrou clearly dramatizes the distinction between his ontological realms, as Molière does not. For example, when Jupiter returns to the scene of his conquests after the husband has scolded his wife upon *his* return, Jupiter identifies himself in Rotrou. He does not in Molière. In Molière's *Amphitryon*, Sosie spots the image of the returning husband at the close of II.3:

Sosie

Amphitryon revient, qui me paraît content.

Scène IV: Jupiter, Cléanthis, Sosie

Jupiter, *à part*

Je viens prendre le temps de rapaiser Alcmène
De bannir les chagrins que son cœur vent garder,
Et donner à mes feux, dans ce soin qui m'amène,
Le doux plaisir de se raccommoder.

A *Cléanthis.*

Alcmène est là-haut, n'est-ce pas?

Cléanthis

Oui, pleine d'une inquiétude
Qui cherche de la solitude,
Et qui m'a défendu d'accompagner ses pas.

Jupiter

Quelque défense qu'elle ait faite,
Elle ne sera pas pour moi.

## TEMPTATION TO TOTAL IMMANENCE

Cléanthis

Son chagrin, à ce que je vois,
A fait une prompte retraite,

Scène V: Cléanthis, Sosie

Sosie

Que dis-tu, Clèanthis, de ce joyeux maintien,
Après son fracas effroyable?

Molière's reader knows what his spectator must wonder about. Whom has he *seen* and *heard* in this return: a repentant husband or the god in the husband's guise? In Rotrou's play the character begins his soliloquy here with "Je suis ce suborneur, ce faux Amphitryon" and ends it just prior to his encounter with Alcmène's servant: "Chassons pour quelque temps le trouble de ces lieux,/ Mais ne la détrompons que pour la tromper mieux" (III.1). Rotrou alerts us to his distinction between divine and human as if to stress all the more the surpassing value of the human. From a certain religious point of view, this is perhaps even more irreverent than Molière's sly, secular satire—for example, from the Jansenist point of view, whose premises Amphitryon touches on just before the fructifying burst of thunder. Rotrou's divinization of the union is at worst pride, the sin of the order of *esprit*; at best, it is lust, the sin of the order of *chair*. This point of view would regard even mythological depictions of divine subservience as "satirical" or "secular."

Molière's *Amphitryon* can be read in this Reformational or Protestant spirit more easily than Rotrou's *Les Sosies*. Not that Molière is Protestant, but his use of the gods is clearly metaphorical. Through them the playwright shows men as they are and would be. The separation between the divine and human in Molière is so total as to make it clear that the gods do not really exist. There is only man and his foibles—not the least of which is his projection of his foibles onto gods whom he creates. This, at least, is the lesson of his Sosie. As for his Amphitryon, the same point is made more paradoxically still: Molière's Jupiter expands a notion that is but passing in Rotrou. The husband is to blame for the pain Alcmène has endured, he tells her. "Juge," Rotrou's Jupiter tells Alcmène, " . . . si ton époux, ni ta fidélité/ Aux vœux d'un tel rival soustrairaient ta beauté" (III.2). Confronted with Alcmène's reproaches to him for wounding her "tendresse et [l']honneur," Molière's Jupiter tells his wife how right she is and goes on: "L'époux, Alcmène, a commis tout le mal;/ C'est l'époux qu'il vous faut regarder en coupable." Five times, in twenty verses, he contrasts this detestable "époux" with "l'amant qui n'a point de part à ce transport brutal" (II.7). The terms of contrast are strictly human: husband and lover in this play whose title is appropriately in the singular.

It is significant that Rotrou's play is plural in reference. The real Sosie and the "false" Sosie are evoked, just as, by analogy, the real Amphitryon and the "false" Amphitryon are evoked. In spite of the large role given the valets, human and divine, Rotrou's plural title might more appropriately have been *Les Amphitryons*, even as, for exactly the contrary emphasis, Molière's play might have been entitled in the singular: *Sosie*. Rotrou's valet is shown to be afraid of his own shadow. Even before his double identifies himself, his obscured presence provokes fear and doubt: "J'ignore qui je suis,/ En l'état malheureux où mes jours sont réduits;/ De peur le poil me dresse et le corps me tremble" (I.2). But there is more fear than doubt when he actually sees his double. Physically beaten, verbally harassed in the long, amusing confrontation with his double that follows, Sosie remains sure of his identity. For all the confounding resemblance, he no longer "ignores" himself:

> Mais cet étonnement fait-il que je m'ignore?
> Je me sens, je me vois, je suis moi-même encore;
> Et j'ai perdu l'esprit, si j'en suis en souci.
>
> (I.2)

## TEMPTATION TO TOTAL IMMANENCE

Remembering the synonymy of feeling and knowing in earlier lovers of Rotrou, we might also conclude that for Sosie, as well, to feel is to see is to know (or be, here). Sosie's first principle is Cartesian. The further implication is still more Rotrou's: to know is to love. In this case, undoubtedly, to love oneself—Sosie is not given a wife as he is in Molière.

The metaphysical difference between the two is even more profound than the social. Rotrou's Sosie is slyly concerned with his freedom from one end of the play to the other. This concern underlies what appear to be the gravest expressions of his identity, uttered when Mercure leaves him alone: "Où me suis-je perdu? . . . où me suis-je laissé? que suis-je devenu? . . . Moi-même je me fuis, moi-même je me chasse." But, returning to his master, he concludes with a clever hope that " . . . plût au Ciel aussi qu'il me pût méconnaître./ De cet malheur naîtrait ma liberté." Of course, Rotrou is no more revolutionary here than with other valets and *fanfarons* who have expressed similar hopes and despairs. Sosie remains in the identity he has been given by the Heaven to which he appeals here. Later, even when making what might be called an existentialist appeal, Sosie, like the Catholic whom Sartre advises in *L'Existentialisme est un humanisme*, decides to remain what he is.[45] Beaten by Mercure, he begins to know an existentialist doubt: "Et je commence enfin, non sans quelque raison,/ A douter qui je suis. . . . " But he dispels this doubt:

> Mais, quoi! qui suis-je donc? ha! cette ressemblance
> Tient à tort si longtemps mon esprit en balance;
> Convaincons l'imposture et conservons mon nom:
> Soyons double Sosie au double Amphitryon.
> Malheureux que je suis, par une loi commune,
> Cherchons le malheureux et suivons sa fortune.
>
> (V.1)

The "common law" is more purposeful than the hostile "fortune" with which he links it here. The structure of the play makes it clear that these existentialist assertions are the instruments of divine forces that submit Sosie and Amphitryon to their purposes.

The purposes are the enjoyment of the world as world. In this play Rotrou carries the materialist sacramentalism of earlier plays to its greatest extreme, to what an allegorical sacramentalism would consider the point of irreligion, to real paganism. The play forthrightly presents the King of Heaven as a slave to desire.

> Que tout charme défère à la beauté d'Alcmène,
> Qui rend un Dieu sensible à l'amoureuse peine,
> Qui l'attire du ciel en ce bas élément,
> Et qui réduit son maître à cet abaissement.
>
> (III.1)

Yet, the *abaissement* is not debasement. The doctrine of intentions assures all concerned that Jupiter follows divine, not base, desire. The "fruit" or actualization of this union will be the man-god Hercule. Jupiter's life-giving visitation is both an act and a gift of love. To brand it as "irreligion" is to forget that the basis of Jupiter's promise is Christian as well as pagan. The "thingness" of the world is justified by the Incarnation. There is no doubt, however, that the concept of Incarnation is far from the one we find in Cardinal de Bérulle, say.[46] Theologically, *Les Sosies* posits no transubstantiation of the material species into the spiritual. This is a virtual consubstantiation of sign and signified emphasizing the material to an extent even beyond that found by Auerbach in Augustine's "figuralism."

It seemed irreverent to the intensely spiritual Christians who were Rotrou's contemporaries. It might also seem an irrelevant literary conceit to the modern sensibility. For Rotrou, however, we know that the problematic is but an occasion through which the benevolence of the real either becomes manifest or provokes the human sufferer to awareness of the benevolent real. Like shipwreck in previous plays, so adultery in this play is a *malheur* become a *bonheur*. "Alcmène, par un sort à tout autre contraire," says her cuckold husband, "Peut entre ses honneurs conter un adultère" (V.4). Remembering Molière's play on the subject, this might seem naïve. Now, this sophisticated perspective is not entirely missing in Rotrou. "Cet honneur, ce me semble," says Sosie in the last speech of the play, "est un triste avantage/ On appelle cela lui sucrer le breuvage" (V.5). But this grumbling "realism" is not a denial of the power of the gods; it is a characterization of that power by a participant who has not been presented as the guarantor of value in the play.

Rotrou carries to logical consequences one of the stresses of the sacramental ethos found both in his earlier plays and the history of sacramental theology. The theme of the Incarnation, of the Divine Immanence, leads to the kind of reverence for life itself that we find in *Les Sosies*. The world is justified in its "thingness" and carnality.

In its thematic stresses as well as its subject matter, this comedy takes us back to Rotrou's first tragedy. The death of the hero in *Hercule mourant* is life-giving, just as the birth of the same figure is here. In Rank's terms, "the builder of the city" triumphs after all. Arcas and Iole, we remember, were urged to live in fruitful marriage by the ascended Hercule. The stress on human life in *Les Sosies* is still greater. The message the god from the clouds brings at the end is not a pity or *charité* correcting an earlier imperfect understanding of Justice. Jupiter here brings a promise of prowess. This suggests that, according to an allegorical sacramentalism as well as biological processes, *Les Sosies* should really have preceded *Hercule mourant*. There, the flesh became word. Here the word becomes flesh and acts as if it would be forever content to remain so. The dire predictions of Junon in the prologue are not realized within the structure of this play any more than they are in *Hercule mourant*. Because the prologue is based on the one spoken by Juno in Seneca's *Hercules furens*, it has seemed to some critics out of place here. But it fits perfectly into the tragicomic structure of this play. The movement from the dismaying prologue to the happy ending with its divine conception, annunciation, and birth miraculously takes place in a single night as long as three nights.

The material hedonism of the religion of this play flows logically from the quasi-pagan strain that both Michel and Auerbach have noted in the history of sacramental theology. Both scholars have linked this strain to Augustine.[47] It is somewhat ironical, perhaps, that, in terms of other Augustinian theses, this very "paganism" is found in the Roman church of Rotrou's day. Immanentist theses, sanctifying the pleasures of the flesh, are to be found, ironically enough, within the Compagnie du Saint Sacrement itself (only seven years after Rotrou's play) in the writings of one of its partly amusing and partly pathetic members, the Abbé Colas de Portmorand. Born in 1607, this ardent Christian cleric was at first an adept of Saint Cyran. But coming to denounce this Jansenist leader and his movement, the good abbé became a member of the Compagnie du Saint Sacrement to such an un-Jansenist degree as to embarrass his companions. He restated with perhaps even greater enthusiasm than Rotrou's pagan deities the placatory view of relations between the divine and human orders heard earlier in the century in Le Père Richeome. In 1644 the ardent abbé published a book on the exemplary figure of Saint Joseph in which he seemed concerned with justifying more the material sign in the sacrament of marriage than the spiritual element signified in the Eucharist revered by his companions. He was unable to believe that God had changed His mind since creating Eve in an act by definition good of itself. He thus concluded that "les premiers regards et agrémens des choses belles et bonnes sont innocens." The spirit of these pronouncements proved too much for the Compagnie. It duly announced to its branch at Marseille on October 21, 1644: "Nous avons esté contraintz de retrancher M. l'abbé de Pomoren de nostre Compagnie, de laquelle apparemment il n'eut jamais l'esprit."[48] But the expelled abbé only gave voice in the 1640's to immanentist notions prevalent in the century since Le Père Richeome three decades earlier, theses that Pascal later excoriated in his writings. Attenuated by such a materialistic, humanly indulgent theology, God's direction of the human condition might as well be non-existent; this is the complaint of the *Lettres provinciales.* For many Jansenists a materialistic atheism is the real term of the doctrine of inherent grace. Sanctifying the world and man, the doctrine leads them to wonder if it sees anything man has really to repent. The sacramental world itself becomes sacrilege.

These Jansenistic premises are denied in *Les Sosies*. Provoked at the use of his own name by his double during the "identity suit" before his captains, Amphitryon blurts out: "Qui suis fils de Dias," and his double retorts: "Qui suis mari d'Alcmène" (IV.4). The exchange is instructive as well as amusing. An honorable husband identifies himself as the son of his human father, and a divine lover identifies himself as the husband of human beauty. This is the measure of the immanentist extreme at which Rotrou arrives in *Les Sosies*.[49]

CHAPTER THREE

*The Temptation to Total Transcendence*

L ES SOSIES represents the high point of Rotrou's theater of immanence—or its low point, from the perspective of his transcendental coreligionists. They would find little satisfaction in its euhemerist premises. They would, however, find less to quarrel with in most of the plays Rotrou wrote in the forties, especially those I have arranged here between *Crisante* and *Dom Bernard de Carbrère*. I say "less to quarrel with," and the qualification is important. Even as he begins to stress the spiritual term of sacramental equilibrium, Rotrou finds it difficult to renounce completely the view of the world as a good thing, given its origin in the Divine Goodness. Though he is tempted to a totally transcendental interpretation of the Divinity, the dramatist clings to many of the premises of his theater of immanence in doing so.

Rotrou's second tragedy, *Crisante* (1635), belongs in a certain sense to the long series of plays, beginning with *Le Filandre*, in which a sacrilegious universe is ultimately resacramentalized.[1R] But its mood breaks with the idyllic serenities of the plays on either side of it. One way of reading its somber denouement even suggests that it belongs more in that theater of transcendence which makes up much of Rotrou's canon in the 1640's.[2]

These suggestions are sounded early in the play. In the haunting beauty of Crisante's introductory verses, Heaven's relation to man rather than man's to Heaven seems perfunctory:

> Ces murs que le porphyre et le marbre décore,
> Tous noirs, demeurent nus du bois qui fume encore;
> Ce reste est le débris du superbe Palais,
> Où régna si longtemps la justice, et la paix;
> Et ce qui fut Corinthe avant cette disgrâce,
> N'en garde que le nom et n'est plus que sa place;
> Sa fumée a caché le ciel à nos regards,
> Elle fut un bûcher, ardent de toutes parts.
>
> (I.2)

As in *Hercule mourant*, a worldly conqueror holds a chaste captive in a "palais noirci," a cloister desecrated by the conqueror's torches. The conqueror would now also desecrate the temple of the captive's body by the flame of his desire. Here are the first strong premonitions of the divine transcendence of Rotrou's late plays. Like many a Racinian captive, Rotrou's chaste captive is surrounded by counselors whose naïveté in some cases and shrewdness in others leave them less disturbed than their mistress by the rampant sacrilege that has hidden God from view. "Le Ciel peut rendre tout, comme il peut tout ôter. . . . Le Ciel, quoi qu'irrité, jamais ne nous laisse," Marcie tells the bereft queen, who fears the worst for herself. The queen's prayers ("Plaise à nos Dieux, hélas! que ma crainte soit vaine") are tinged more with fear than hope. Unlike her attendant, Orante, she sees in Cassie's very *générosité* the likelihood of more cowardice than honor: "de telles lâchetés un insolent fait gloire." Unlike the queen of *L'Innocente Infidélité*, she cannot excuse this "jeune cœur": the object of his lascivious "exploit glorieux" will be herself, not some diabolical Hermante. Heaven's name is more on the lips of the unthinkingly pious attendants than on those of the queen herself—or on those of her priggish husband. Even before he denies his wife's innocence, before she is violated, his perfunctory piety is evident. Antioche's first remarks would lead us to think he is a true Stoic of the ancient school:

> Heureux qui satisfait d'une basse fortune,
> Trouve la vanité des grandeurs importune,

## TEMPTATION TO TOTAL TRANSCENDENCE

> Qui sait à son besoin mesurer ses désirs,
> Et goûter du repos les solides plaisirs.
>
> (II.1)

This calm transcendence of fate seems to make Antioche different from the tense, prospective suicides we have met in earlier plays. Those psychological Stoics girded their loins with such impassioned *mépris* against fate that one suspects their real faith in the Stoical precept of *repos*. But as Antioche goes on even in this first speech (and increasingly throughout the play), one senses that he is more despairing and self-pitying than his earlier counterparts in Rotrou. His counselor Crates suggests that Heaven rather than fate is responsible for his misfortunes, thus punishing men for their crimes. Antioche pharisaically assents that "son [le Ciel] vouloir arrive et les Dieux soient bénis;/ Ainsi pour leurs sujets les Princes sont punis" (II.1). Priggish and self-pitying, this king is also sanctimonious. Little wonder that he turns on his sensitive wife after she is betrayed.

For all her despair, Crisante does show a certain kind of piety in slaying the impious Orante. True, Crisante shows no more faith in Heaven than that shrewd attendant; linking cruel fate to Heaven, she asks Orante: " . . . Qu'importe aux Dieux et ma vie et ma mort?" Determined to save her mistress' life, Orante then rationalizes as she had earlier with Cassie. She argues along lines similar to Crates' argument about suffering as the due of our sins: our punishments are the signs of Heaven's favor. Crisante penetrates to the immoral consequences of such a thesis: "On doit craindre les Dieux! alors qu'on leur est cher,/ Et depuis qu'on les craint, on ne saurait pécher!" For her, man is very much on his own. But this does not mean that Orante's sellout of honor is justified. Indeed, such a sellout is as offensive in Crisante's eyes as the most overt denial of the gods. Take your freedom, she says sarcastically in plunging her dagger into Orante, "en ta mort, *horreur de la nature*" (II.3; italics added). Crisante reveres honor more than life. Honor, not the Divine Will. The Divine Will seems to have abandoned her in the loss of her city; it abandons her in the advice of her attendants; it abandons her in her moment of greatest peril. "Le Ciel impunément a permis cet outrage" (III.4), Crisante tells her husband. This is all the more pathetic in view of the blessing from Heaven she asks for the "repentant" Cassie after he has prevented her suicide (II.4).

And yet, Crisante's way is Heaven's way. At first, her god-denying piety may be more profound than her enemies', her attendants', or her husband's. But it is still not profound enough. Like Cassie's, it must be put to a severe test. This test is not her husband's doubt, severe as that test is. A consideration of Rotrou's dramaturgy in this and other plays of the same period (1634-36) is instructive here: the "demonstration" of Crisante's integrity to her husband occurs in a fifth act that is related to an equally important "demonstration" in the first four acts. Crisante demonstrates to Antioche the illusoriness of a false datum: that his wife surrendered willingly to her violator.

A-B-A: the pattern is familiar. But within this A-B-A pattern (really more Antioche's than hers), Crisante herself goes through an A-B-A pattern whose B portion differs from her husband's. Violated by Cassie, she comes onstage a plaintive figure, far different from the fierce assassin of Orante:

> Il semble que je craigne et qu'encore je m'aime,
> Je possède ma mort et suis sourde à moi-même.
> Mon bras contre mon sein n'ose se hasarder,
> Quand je la vois venir, j'aime à la retarder;
> D'inutiles discours sont l'effort que j'essaie,
> Absente elle me plaît, présente elle m'effraie.

(III.1)

Quoting these lines, Mlle Van Baelen observes:

> ... Cette hésitation de la part de Crisante montre que l'honneur ne pèse pas aussi lourd que la vie dans la balance, et que, comme l'exprime Orante: 'Un jour que nous vivons vaut mieux qu'un an de gloire'. ... Crisante, dans un certain sens, est criminelle en n'ayant pas soutenu jusqu'au bout cette conception de l'honneur.[3]

True, but the play also makes us wonder whether this compromising doubt is to be attributed to Crisante at the moment of violation as well as in this aftermoment. Her insistence to her husband here that "Hommes, Dieux, Eléments, tout fut sourd à mon aide" seems justified, given Cassie's hypocrisy. As for the strength of her resolve before his hypocritical reassurances, the sequence of deeds and words as he comes upon the dead Orante is significant:

Crisante

N'ai-je pas en la main le secours qu'il me faut?
Porte, lâche, en ton sein ce fer chaud,
Ayant bien commencé, quil achève de même,
Et qu'un mal si lèger empêche un mal extrême.

Marcie

Ha Madame, calmez un courroux si pressant!
Quel effort tentez-vous contre un sein innocent?
Quel tyran est l'honneur, s'il perd ceux qui le suivent,
Et s'il faut que du jour les vertueux se privent?

(II.3)

Scene 4. Cassie, Crisante, Marcie

Crisante

O deffence importune,

Cassie *(lui arrachant le poignard)*

O dieux, à quel dessein. . . .

Crisante seems on the verge of plunging the dagger into her breast, but her hesitations here might be more than the occasion for rhetorical and thematic flourishes. A shrewd director or actress might find the basis for a subtle play of fear in this scene—less in the lines Mlle Van Baelen gives to support her similar interpretation than in the earlier lines of Crisante's appearance after the rape: "O mort, mon seul remède et mon dernier bonheur,/ Que me prévenais-tu celle de mon honneur" (III.1). Yet, whether before or after her violation, these doubts suggest that Crisante's development is independent of her husband's doubts. Through the crime, violated as well as violator learn the reality of evil. Each surrenders to the temptation to revere the sign more than the signified.

Like her violator, Crisante finds within herself the resources to carry through on a redemptive suicide. Perhaps because her piety had been greater than his at the beginning, her resolve comes more quickly and with a piety now truly respectful of the gods. Here editorial considerations are more relevant than in any play thus far. As Lancaster reports:

> ... The original MS. seems to have been in five acts, but the play was shortened for performance by the elimination of the end of III.4, all of III.5–IV.3 and the beginning of IV.4, with slight alterations made to prevent the omission from becoming apparent. Some printed copies keep the shortened form and have only four acts, numbered I, II, III, V; other copies replace the missing scenes on pages that seem to have been added after the others were printed, since they are not numbered. The editor of the Ed. of Paris, Desoer, 1820, reproduced at first only the shorter form, but finding the longer at the Bib. Nat., he added the missing scenes as a variant form at the end of his fourth volume.[4]

The alterations to which Lancaster refers are thematically more significant than his characterization ("slight") suggests. Crisante's ten despairing verses conclude here: "Ou si pareil forfait demeurait impuni,/ Gardez que des autels l'encens ne soit banni" (III.4 of shortened version). Mlle Van Baelen reads these verses as an indication that "les dieux ne jouent ici qu'un rôle tout à fait accessoire."[5] But in the original version, at this moment Crisante does not mention the gods. Her despair does not last so long as in the altered lines of the shortened version.

She recovers from her "cruel désespoir" in the fifth line of a twelve-verse speech with a recollection of her honor: "En plaignant mon honneur, je tâche mon estime". She then orders Marcie to assist her in the vengeance that on the morrow will satisfy her doubting husband.

Resolute and rational, her fear of death now seems what it should always have seemed to her: an illusion. She seeks out Manilie to ask for her violator's life in spite of the pleas of his lieutenants. "Que la loi de César, comme la loi divine,/ Des deux extrémités, à la douceur incline," pleads one of his lieutenants. He is seconded by another's more strictly human plea for Cassie "en faveur de nos pleurs." But an appeal in the name of divine justice, paradoxically uttered by a female captive, carries the day against these virtually Christian pleas for mercy paradoxically uttered by "chefs de guerre":

> Dieux, je laisse à vos soins embrasser ma dispute:
> L'innocence à vos traits n'est pas toujours en butte,
> La constance à la fin calme votre courroux,
> Vos caresses enfin succèdent à vos coups,
> Et vous ne trouvez pas nos peines légitimes,
> Jusques à conseiller l'impunité des crimes.
>
> (IV.5)

Is her appeal to the gods a debater's trick, a play on Manilie's Roman piety (compare Polyeucte's play on Felix's pagan piety in Corneille)? Perhaps. But the A-B-A pattern of Crisante's story, her own inner struggle, suggests that her invocation of the gods here shows a restored faith, one that appropriately carries the day. Her earlier imprecations against the hidden heaven have shown a testing of her faith. She and Cassie share this faith now even as they had momentarily lost it through the violation. Co-operating with the Divine Will in this retribution and repentance, she pleads Heaven's cause in the name of both human and divine justice. For the same cause, Cassie takes his own life.

This more profound piety also leads her to take her own life before her husband. His perfunctory faith has weakened even more when we see him again at the beginning of Act V. Repeating the familiar theme of Renaissance tragedy of fortune's particular enmity to kings, Antioche complains that "pour moi le sort, les Dieux et les hommes sont sourds." All Stoical reserve is gone. He borders on a conception of a punitive Heaven, Manichaean in overtone: the agent of his downfall was a lecherous woman who perhaps in this very moment sells his life to his enemies (V.1). In this moment, the hero is not Corneille's Auguste (*Cinna*); he cannot rise to the challenge of his attendant: "se vaincre est l'action la plus noble des rois" (V.2). Like Cassie and Crisante himself, his perfunctory piety must be deepened through suffering. To this end his wife appears, taking her own life as the final ransom effacing both her own and her husband's "soupçon." The terms of his redemptive remorse are familiar:

> Quel crime, quels soupçons ai-je conçus à tort?
> Par quel aveuglement ai-je causé ta mort?
> Le sang que tu répands avec tant d'abondance,
> Suffisamment enfin prouve ton innocence.
>
> (V.5)

These reflections suggest that Crisante's own hesitations about dying occurred *after* her violation. But more pertinent here is the motif of reconciliation through repentance of these lovers separated by their doubts on the meaning of worldly disasters.

Convinced of his wife's honor and piety, Antioche is restored to his own honor and piety. Like his wife, he is restored to his sense of himself as a person and to an understanding of his person in a larger moral context. This world is not the end-all and be-all of existence. Like *Hercule mourant, Crisante* is a tragicomedy. Like the great fire taking the life of the man-god (Hercule), or the Cross taking the life of the Man-God (Christ), the blades Cassie, Crisante, and finally, Antioche plunge into their bodies are virtually sacrilegious objects sacramentally cleansed by the pious intention of their "victims." Death is not an end but a means to an end—to a safe and sanctified other-life.

This conception emerges more in the death of Antioche than of his wife. Like her assassination of Orante, Crisante's self-assassination is of a piece with what one critic has called the "demonic heroism" of Horace, the first of the great tragic heroes Corneille drew from Roman history.[6] Here, like Horace, the queen rejects the demeaning advice of those who counsel the surrender of honor. In *Crisante* this counsel is not linked to charges of inhumanity uttered by a sister and a wife. Instead, it is proffered by an attendant whose role is more secondary than those of Corneille's Camille and Sabine. The counsel thus seems irrational. Moreover, according to the "lois constitutives" of the universe of the play as defended by Crisante herself, the action that Crisante takes against it seems rational and just. Supreme value is preserved in the final peripety.

However, to the extent that Crisante's suicide shows the same piety as Cassie's suicide, her husband's final reflections on Roman piety suggest that such piety is an evil. The dying Antioche is surrounded by counselors whose perfunctory piety does not prepare them for the "malheurs" of the royal suicides. "Mon cœur reste immobile," says Crates, crying over his expired master; "ma constance [est] abbatue," says Euphorbe, and in vain tries to render the last "devoir" to that master; "je ne le puis aussi," says Marcie, closing the play with an appeal for someone who can. But before he expires, Antioche is more than equal to the last rites to be pronounced over this world he leaves. In his deepened piety, he is glad to depart with his wife in the hope " . . . qu'un même destin à jamais nous assemble." Let Auguste triumph over "ces lieux" in all his fury and violence, let his insolence reign without punishment, for

> Notre sort s'est soustrait à son ambition;
> Crisante, sans danger est ma possession;
> Là-bas, d'aucun souci l'esprit ne se consomme,
> On s'y trouve à couvert des injures de Rome,
> On n'y relève point de l'Empire Latin,
> Et César quelque jour aura même destin.

(V.5)

Theologically, this Stoical disdain of the body violates the dogmatic injunction against self-slaughter. The Divinity being immanent in the world and, especially, in the image of man, to destroy that image is to desecrate the temple of the Lord himself. Again, self-slaughter of the kind here wrought by the king and queen is a sacrilege even according to an orthodoxy stressing the spirit rather than the body. Committed rationally, suicide shows the sin of pride. Now, Crisante's suicide might be forgiven under either stress as the product of a reason disordered by the violence done her by Cassie.[7] Her husband's is undertaken in a lucidity and rationality the equal of anyone's in Rotrou's fifth-act "illuminations." But if Antioche is to be damned for the sin of pride in this self-slaughter, it must be recognized that, like the material hedonism already seen in earlier plays, this "spiritual hedonism" grows logically out of orthodox sacramental theology itself.[8] Whatever the unorthodoxy of the suicide, Antioche is led to it not in despair but in hope. He looks forward to a world in which he will enjoy the "possession" of Crisante *and* be free of Rome's spiritual sacrilege. His vision of the afterlife is one in which the components of the sacramental union, flesh and spirit, will be once again fused. Even in his blackest play thus far, one clearly designated *tragédie*, Rotrou seems to get "beyond tragedy."

Nevertheless, to the extent that the "Empire Latin" is emblematic for this world, Rotrou posits in the final moments of *Crisante* the radically transcendental view of the plays of the 1640's: "Et César quelque jour aura même destin" (V.5). This final warning by Antioche repeats in strikingly similar terms the last verse of the converted actor in Rotrou's most famous play. Brought in judgment before Dioclétien, Genest announces that, happily, he is being tried in a still higher court under "un favorable juge" by whom " . . . *un jour César sera jugé*" (V.3; italics added). Now, in *Crisante*, Antioche has been converted, we might say, to a profound piety by the example of his wife even as Genest has been converted by the example of Adrien. The parallel in both situations and both final warnings suggests that, in its last moments at least, *Crisante* breaks radically with the immanentism of Rotrou's plays till the late 1630's. It repudiates, in its final moments, Manilie's boast in its early moments: "Tout succède à nos vœux et Rome est toujours Rome" (I.1). "Non," Antioche in effect tells the Roman general in his final warning, "Rome n'est pas toujours Rome."

*Antigone,* Tragédie (1637), is first about events occuring while Etéocle is king and then about events occuring while Créon is king.[9R] This structure has led some to criticize Rotrou for making an inconsistent assortment of material from various models. One of the most famous of these critics, Racine, found much to borrow in this play, but he objected that the author "avait réuni en une seule pièce deux actions différentes."[10] Lancaster has defended Rotrou against this criticism on two grounds. He notes that Racine is himself guilty of this "duplicité d'actions" in his third play, where a "similar shift from Andromaque to Hermione is found." Lancaster also argues that "Rotrou's tragedy is quite superior in characterization and dramatic interest to that of Racine and may be defended even for its unity. The theme chosen is the effect of the curse upon all the descendants of Cadmus that appear in the play, including Créon and his sons, as well as upon Jocasta and her children."[11]

As developed by Rotrou, the story of this curse centers on the misrule of young and old princes who violate the divine and human conventions of "natural law." In keeping with the dramaturgy of polarized types found in previous plays, this virtually sacrilegious theme is brought out both verbally and structurally. Sacrilegious figures are pitted against sacramental figures. However, no figure of either type is rigidly typical, and the playwright makes a subtle use of various figures of one tendency to dramatize the opposing tendency in another figure. Polynice is largely a sacramental figure, one more offended by, than offensive to, the largely sacrilegious Etéocle. Polynice marches with foreign troops against his own city, but this is an effort to repair his brother's greater sacrilege. The latter violated a *sworn* contract between them, entered into after the death of their father.

> . . . Qu'un traître viole avec impunité
> Le respect de l'accord entre nous arrêté,
> Et que j'observe après celui de la naissance,
> Une vertu si lâche excède ma puissance.
>
> (I.6)

Moreover, the law of contract has even deeper roots in nature than the law of primogeniture:

> La chose est résolue et la Nature même
> Souscrit à cet arrêt de ma fureur extrême;
> Outre qu'elle est muette où parle la raison,
> Elle ne s'entend pas avec la trahison:
> Au contraire, elle enseigne à repousser l'injure,
> Et condamne surtout la fraude et le parjure.
>
> (I.6)

Is this rationalization of a will to power? Perhaps—especially when linked to his reply to his mother, who invokes the "natural law" of love between kindred as a counter to her sons' fratricidal intentions. His eyes fixed in hate on his brother all the while, Polynice answers her:

> Ne désirez-vous point que je vous dissimule
> Ma sûreté dépend de n'être plus crédule;
> La nature n'a plus d'inviolables droits,
> De son propre intérêt chacun se fait des lois:
> Et l'épreuve m'apprend que du pur artifice,
> Nature son contraire aujourd'hui fait l'office:
> Votre parole, enfin, m'est suspecte en effet,
> Ma mère pourrait bien ce que mon frère a fait.
>
> (II.4)

But this is a sarcastic reply by a son who feels betrayed by almost everyone in his own city, including his family. Under the sarcasm of the beleaguered Polynice, there lies a nostalgia for absolutes revealing his true feelings. "Mais qu'un traître viole avec impunité/ Le respect de l'accord . . . "; "Non, non trop de justice à ce devoir m'engage" (I.6), Polynice proclaims in overcoming his father-in-law's opposition to the proposed fraternal duel. "Mon honneur plus que tout à ce devoir me presse:/ J'arme pour le bon droit, lui pour la trahison," he tells Antigone, "sœur, pieuse et sage fille," when she tries to dissuade him from the duel (II.2). *Justice, devoir, honneur, foi*—these are the values Polynice defends.

Were the context Racinian, we might suspect that these *are* unconscious "rationalizations." But in the context of the play, a number of dramatic motifs and explicit statements show that Polynice is a wronged rather than a wronging party. Most notably, he is the favorite brother of Antigone:

> Une étroite amitié de tous temps nous a joints
> Qui passe de bien loin cet instinct ordinaire
> Par qui la sœur s'attache aux intérêts du frère
> Et si la vérité se peut dire sans fard,
> Etéocle en mon cœur n'eut jamais tant de part.
>
> (I.4)

Here, Rotrou echoes the titillating abnormal sexual relations of earlier plays—this time in a relatively rare heterosexual but incestuous expression. Little wonder that Polynice's wife will tell her sister-in-law that she was jealous of her, for "Je paraissais sa sœur et vous sembliez sa femme." But as Antigone repeats in this very context, "L'amitié nous joignait bien plus que la nature" (III.7). *Amitié* has always been spiritual in Rotrou, and it is especially so in this play, where, if nature's language and man's language find themselves at odds with one another, it is man's contracts—his *word*—that takes precedence, whatever the relation. But the commitments must be spiritual, that is, fully in keeping with the higher reason expressive of, and implanted by, the Divinity. Etéocle violates this *faith* in the name of circumstantial or positive law. Etéocle warns Créon about his tendency to tyranny (II.4), but his own opportunism is no less overt. Clearly, he is wrong in violating a sacred contract with his brother because of the will of the people. Jocaste tries to make Polynice look like an "enfant prodigue" bringing an alien army against his father's house (II.4). The gambit cannot obscure the fact that Etéocle is the greater usurper and prodigal. There is no denying that Polynice's kingship would be more just than merciful, whereas Etéocle's throne is built on the sands of a violated oath and the quicksand of popular support. Again, Polynice is a faithful ally, a respectful son-in-law, a loving husband, and the first victor in the combat with Etéocle. These relations put him in a more favorable light than his opportunistic brother, monomaniacally bent on preserving power.

Polynice perhaps absorbs more than he sheds the sacred energy found in large degree in each of these relations. He seems more patriotic than pious. He renders unto Caesar the things that are Caesar's and seems only perfunctorily concerned with the things that are God's. Piety is a virtue for women with him: "Adieu vous que . . . le Ciel doua d'une vertu si rare," he tells his beloved wife (I.6); "pieuse et sage fille" is his apostrophe to his sister, Antigone (II.2). True, at his moment of victory as reported by Hémon, he thanked the gods for vindicating his cause. This is pride, not hypocrisy. Nevertheless, Polynice is no existentialist forger of purely human values; he is an essentialist espousing received values.

These values are public, those of house and family. If Rotrou's great contemporaries are to be invoked, the conception of character here recalls Corneille rather than Racine. As Philip Butler, a subtle critic of the later dramatist, has said of Rotrou's rebellious brother: "Le duel est [donc] la libre décision d'une âme altière, semblable à celle d'Horace punissant la sacrilège: 'Ma patience a la raison fait place.' "[12] At first glance, given Polynice's call to "passion," Butler's comparison seems inexact. Repudiating his mother's "inutiles avis," Rotrou's Polynice commands, "Parle, ma passion, les tiens seront suivis" (II.4). Here, passion does seem to prevail as it does in Racine: there is a surrender by reason to the violence of hate and personal ambition. As certain women have shown us (notably Salamacis in *L'Heureux Naufrage*), this Racinian tension has been a significant one for Rotrou. Yet, Butler's comparison of Polynice and Horace is exact: Polynice uses passion as the energy of his rational, just opposition to Etéocle's violation of the oath between them. The violation is as sacrilegious to the religiously patriotic Polynice as Camille's treason is to her religiously patriotic brother. The higher reason prevails in Rotrou's Polynice as well. In his adolescent anxiety, he is afraid not because his "self" confronts the abyss of absurdity but because it strives to achieve its entelechy. His "self" strives to become what it is destined to be in virtue of the received values of the world neither it nor any other man ever made. Imperfect as he is, Polynice has fuller *being*, greater *reality* than his brother Etéocle. The latter is a usurper: "Voyons s'il m'ôtera le nom que j'ai pris" (II.3). More than ever in Rotrou, all is in a name. To *take* a name with a view to keeping it is to confuse the planes of reality, to betray an ontological trust.

The brothers will go on hating each other beyond the grave, says the dying Polynice. The rest of the play suggests that in this statement, Polynice really shows himself imperfect in his being. Undoubtedly, this "deathbed lack of repentance" will have to be weighed by the gods against his intention before combat: to expiate the fault he was about to commit by taking his own life. Repentant before his fall, Polynice must seem a casuistical confessor, but confessor he is. In him the light of the higher reason works its way both independently and providentially. Nothing could demonstrate more tellingly the difference between Rotrou's vision and Racine's. Rotrou's brothers may hate each other beyond the grave; in Racine they have hated each other from the womb. Racine's Etéocle says:

> Nous étions ennemis dès la plus tendre enfance;
> Que dis-je? nous l'étions avant notre naissance.

> Triste et fatal effet d'un sang incestueux!
> Pendant qu'un même sein nous renfermait tous deux,
> Dans les flancs de ma mère une guerre intestine
> De nos divisions lui marqua l'origine
>
> (IV.1)

The brothers' mutual hatred in Racine is prenatal and prerational and thus irreparable; the brothers' mutual hatred in Rotrou is irrational but for that very reason *not* irreparable. In Racine the mutual hatred is "une guerre intestine," the norm of nature itself; in Rotrou it is "une peste," as Jocaste calls it, a break with the norm that after its paroxysm will find nature restored to her norms. Racine's is a desecrated universe beyond hope of resanctification; Rotrou's, a "dis-graced" universe in the process of being resanctified.

The relation between Etéocle and Polynice is paralleled in the relation between Créon and Antigone. She is obviously more pious than Polynice. Compared with the subtle portrait drawn by Sophocles, Rotrou's heroine seems monochromatic. Showing little of the ancient heroine's pathetic regret at her frustrated womanhood, Rotrou's Antigone is almost all piety. *Almost*, for she does show a momentary despair at fortune's special vindictiveness toward kings (III.1). She overcomes this despair only to behave with more pride than humility in carrying out the forbidden last rites. Her reproaches to her sister here seem arrogant (III.5). Finally, she *seems* to goad Créon into ordering her martyrdom (IV.3), just as Polyeucte goads Félix into a similar order in Corneille's famous play. I stress *seems*, for in another dramatic context, this behavior might point to tensions in the character's own conception of herself. Yet, we cannot believe in this context that Antigone "doth protest too much" her own piety. She is joined in that protestation by too many others. The theme of Antigone's piety is less an end than a means to the depiction of another theme: Créon's impiety and its detestation by almost all the voices he hears. Antigone's is only one of a chorus of voices and dramatic motifs, so to speak, putting Créon in the wrong as surely as a similar pattern put Polynice in the right in the first part of the action.

*Antigone* stands as a play whose spiritual sacramentalism corrects the materialistic imbalance of *Les Sosies*. Créon's sacrilege consists in his failure to respect the sacrament of the last rites. His position might be forgiven were his niece his only enemy. But his counselor Ephyte, his son Hémon, and the priest Tirésie, all add their calm appeals in the name of reason and justice. To this chorus Créon can only reply in a line of expressive power as sublime as the famous "Moi" of Corneille's *Médée*. When Ephyte seeks to excuse Hémon's opposition to his father, the following exchange takes place:

Ephyte: Mais, Sire, son amour?

Créon:                      Mais, Ephyte, ma haine?

(V.4)

Hatred here, like anger in earlier plays of Rotrou, is an emotion depriving one of being. It obfuscates the power of reason, makes one a prisoner of illusion. The king shows this deprivation in his subsequent attack on the high priest for avarice. This attack is not without satirical thrust on Rotrou's part. Nevertheless, the sanctity of this particular priest is no more in doubt than the piety of Antigone, the wisdom of Ephyte, and the good will of Hémon. Warned by the priest, Créon will retract his sacrilegious orders to refuse holy burial to Polynice and to execute the pious sister who would defy that order.

In his retraction Créon reminds us of two truths of a sacramental character. First, he is the real rebel and Antigone the defender of the existing order: "Le Prince pèche ici bien plus que le rebelle" (IV.3), says Antigone. Second, illuminated by the "sign" of the heavenly messenger, Tirésie, Créon repents his action. He does so because he is both compelled by necessity and fearful of the consequences for himself. His repentance is, sacramentally speaking, imperfect—more attrition than contrition. But it does restore his reason, showing him accepting responsibility for his crimes rather than attributing them to Heaven. His repentance also leads him to try to repair these crimes. In that reparation he would presumably restore the sacramental equilibrium. Respect for the dead Polynice would testify to the sacredness of *life*—would testify to the continuity between divine and human. As Morel has put it:

> Chez Rotrou, Antigone oppose, non plus loi à loi, mais personne à personne; la personne du roi à la personne de Dieu. Pour elle il n'y a plus hétérogénéïté des deux domaines, comme chez Sophocle; il n'y a pas non plus parallélisme entre les lois divines et les *vraies* lois humaines, comme chez Garnier; mais une hiérarchie spirituelle qui prolonge et parfait la hiérarchie sociale.[13]

The concept recalls Bellarmin's ladder, although by implication the de-emphasis on the human would perhaps be considerably reduced were Rotrou not bound by certain *données* of his subject.

*Antigone* veers into an excessively spiritual emphasis. The play is actually more Créon's than Antigone's. Its A-B-A structure revolves about the false datum of Ménécée's misapplied death. Reading the oracle's "dernier" to mean last in line of birth, Créon's son kills himself and thus leads to a series of illusory developments in a prolonged B part of the action. Créon sacrilegiously curses the gods for working out their wrath against the house of Œdipe through Créon and his house; Créon erroneously assumes that his son's interpretation of the oracle was the right one and that it really led to his own legitimate kingship; Créon attacks Antigone and her supporters as impious rebels; and so on. With Créon become king, we have two different conceptions of piety at odds with one another, as in *Crisante*: the profound and the perfunctory. However, with Créon's "conversion," it would seem as though the playwright wished to validate the piety of Créon's adversaries. This is a piety showing a sacramental equilibrium or, in Morel's terms, a continuity of the divine and human in a single order. Yet, when looked at in the very terms proposed by Lancaster—

of the effects of the curse upon the whole house of Cadmus—the play seems all B. Dramatically speaking, its A portions exist in the prerunning and postrunning times of the plot. Thematically speaking, these portions exist in the minds of the gods. Metaphysically speaking, this suggests that Heaven as a *good* lies *beyond* this world.

Antigone assumes piously what is never explained here: that her father's sin was innocent. She sympathizes with Créon over the loss of his son, but she berates him for failing to see that his reproaches to Œdipe were unjust in that her father's is an "innocent péché" (I.4). The reason for Œdipe's suffering is not given here, it just *is*. Now, Rotrou does not view human suffering in the neutral terms Kitto has attributed to Sophocles: the world is in a certain metaphysical and moral balance; Œdipe's "fault" impairs that balance; the world in its very processes removes that imperfection and thus redresses its balance.[14] Antigone shows that this is not the relation between divine and human in the universe of the play: "Les Dieux," she tells Créon,

> . . . sont maîtres des Rois, ils sont pieux, augustes.
> Tous leurs arrêts sont saints, toutes leurs loix sont justes:
> Ces esprits dépouillés de toutes passions
> Ne mêlent rien d'impure en leurs intentions,
> Au lieu que l'intérêt, la colère et la haine
> Président bien souvent à la justice humaine.
>
> (IV.3)

As Butler has already noted, Rotrou's conception is Christian and, according to that critic, inappropriate in a play in which hereditary curses affect the innocent.[15] (Antigone seems here to have forgotten her own assessment of her father's sin as innocent.) Butler suggests that Rotrou could not have chosen a worse subject for his particular non-tragic vision of the human condition: " . . . Son embarras, sa mauvaise humeur sont aussi visibles que ceux de Corneille aux prises dans *Œdipe*, avec un sujet contre lequel tout son génie se rebelle."[16] The observation is penetrating, but it stresses the negative unduly. Butler contends, "C'est Racine et non Rotrou qui écrit une tragédie de la prédestination."[17] But there is predestination in Rotrou: "Les Dieux ne sont pas Dieux," Ismène tells Créon, "si bientôt leur courroux/ Ne prend notre intérêt et n'éclate sur vous" (IV.4).The determinism is not tragic: suffering will come only to those who deserve it; the innocent will be eschatologically justified. In sum, Christian in its premises as these relate to the immediate conflict over sacramental burial rites, *Antigone* goes "beyond tragedy."

Niebuhr's famous phrase epitomizes the view of many Christian thinkers that Christianity is incompatible with the tragic view of life.[18] An opposing school would find Christianity triumphant through tragedy. However we regard the relation, in *Antigone*, the resolution points once again, in Rotrou, to the tension between flesh and spirit found in Christian theology. The pious tell the impious here that the earth could be a heaven if natural and divine laws were obeyed. Though impressed by such advice, the impious take it too late in this kingdom whose thrones are destined to be occupied by a series of sacrilegious kings (Etéocle, Créon) and where the innocent suffer inexplicably. Antigone does suggest that self-interest, hate, and anger preside often but not always. This presumably leaves room for resacramentalization of the world once the action is over. But the play ends with Créon looking forward to the fulfilment of the prophecy in which *he* will die as truly the last of the house of Cadmus. Unlike earlier plays, including the previous two tragedies, the eschatological moment here is somber in its suggestions of the way the world ends. The natural world is pure sacrilege here. Distinctions between "this" world and the "next" world apply to this play as they have to no other. The truly sacred reaches fulfilment out of this world, in the transcendent realm beyond death: "Allons, unis d'esprit," Hémon says to his prostrate mistress before he dies, "sans commerce de corps,/ Achever notre hymen en l'empire des morts" (V.9). Flesh is cut off from body. Christian overtones of the triumph of life in death undoubtedly inform this declaration of love and faith. But the moment in which it is pronounced suggests that the world is anything but a "sign of the sacred." Desecrated by the impious royal orders, Antigone's dead form seems to tell her lover that matter and spirit are not coterminous. The immanent divinity that rules this world is a fallen one. The infernal prison to which Hermante was condemned in *L'Innocente Infidélité* has burst its tower walls and spread to the ends of the kingdom of "this" world. With its heroine transcended to the "next" world, leaving her uncle with his tardy repentance, *Antigone* constitutes an important counter to the immanentist theses of most of the first half of Rotrou's theater.

Rotrou is more respectful of the classical model for *Iphigénie, Tragédie* (1640): Euripides' *Iphigenia in Aulis*.[19] Yet, the striking thematic departures between model and imitation suggest that the fundamental model for this play as for so many of his other "imitations" is Rotrou himself. Iphigénie gives her name to the play, but it might as easily have been named *Agamemnon*.[20R] The daughter does not appear until Act III, but the father has one of the longest roles in Rotrou's theater: he is on stage for three-fourths of the running time of the play, and even when he is off stage, he is as dramatically central as when he is present. I think it most useful, then, to explore the key motifs of the play as they are dramatically woven into the relations with other characters, first through the father, and then through the daughter.

The first of these relations is between Agamemnon as king and Agamemnon as father. The play begins with the father torn between "pitié" and "courage," between "nature" and "rang." As in other plays, *courage* is not the private value we think of in connection with the etymologically related concept of *cœur* in Pascal. Rather, it is the public value that Agamemnon defends in his role of "bon chef." Kings and generals live by this value, but fathers ("bon père" here) by another. When Agamemnon defends his "premier sentiment" for his daughter, we are reminded of earlier lovers who defended their first love. Chaste desire has always "sublimated" carnal relations between lovers in a way reminiscent of relations between the sexes within the family. The family has, of course, been the basic social unit of a great many of Rotrou's pastoral plays and tragicomedies. With rare exceptions, brothers have seldom been enemies or remained enemies if they were misled into being such. Again, male friends have treated each other as brothers, and female friends have called each other "sœur" both aloud and in their hearts. Through these connections, chaste desire becomes linked with the theme of natural love that preoccupies Rotrou throughout his canon, but especially in his theater of transcendence. At times, as I have suggested, the family unit has been reduced in scope, but only in order to increase the religious overtones of the unit. Thus, it is the holiness as well as the naturalness of the family that Agamemnon offends with his "*sacrilège* et barbare devoir" (IV.3; italics added). The terms are Clytemnestre's as she berates her husband, who has finally succumbed to Ulysse's persuasion.

Agamemnon has stood not for natural law but for *générosité* once again. He does so regretfully, for he is a far more complicated creature than Ménélas, Ulysse, and Calchas. As Mlle Van Baelen perceptively says, they constitute "une assemblée des personnages les plus déplaisants . . . faibles et violents . . . cupides et cyniques."[21] No doubt, Agamemnon has been the unctuous *ambitieux* described by Ménélas (II.2) and the ruthless assassin of the helpless whose earlier repentance Clytemnestre regards as hypocritical (IV.3). Yet, at the "limit case" of tragic challenges, Agamemnon shows himself less ready than even his victim to take her life for honor and glory. He goes along with Calchas' final demands for the sacrifice not out of respect for the priest's formulas but because of his daughter's reproaches. He must show himself the father of a *généreuse* as readily as she shows herself to be the daughter of a *généreux*.

Clytemnestre is a greater sinner than her husband against either of the basic codes of the sacramental universe. The mother here—like the mother in *Hercule mourant*—recalls that her child is destined for glorious martyrdom. When she warns her husband that her hand, too, can sin against the law of blood, her daughter recalls that this is to offend the Diane to whom she is devoted. "Hélas," says Clytemnestre, "je me souviens, sacrilège et profane,/ De vous avoir vouée aux autels de Diane" (IV.4). Like the attendant in *Crisante*, Clymnestre reproaches her daughter for her readiness to die for the sake of eternal renown: "Un an de vie en vaut cent de mémoire" (IV.6). (Luckily, she does not suffer the same fate.) Iphigénie must reproach her mother for dishonoring her martyrdom with such entreaties, like Hercule before the tearful Alcmène in Rotrou's first tragedy. Yet, again like Alcmène, Clytemnestre is unable to transcend her own selfish, human imperatives for this divine purpose. Different in its tenor, Clytemnestre's selfishness is no less compromising here. Alcmène sought the narcissistic glories of *générosité*, whereas Clytemnestre blindly adheres to maternal instinct. She accuses her child of cruelty in wishing to die for whatever cause.

In this sacrilege she is joined by the somewhat prissy Achille. Clytemnestre need not have resorted to a shrewd appeal to his self-interest in seeking his help. He is offended by the very fact that Agamemnon has used his name in a subterfuge. Evoking the doctrine of innocence by intention, he offers Clytemnestre his services and gives one of the most succinct statements in Rotrou of the concept of sacramental kingship according to the code of *générosité*:

> Ce n'est pas que rebelle au joug d'un Souverain,
> Je fasse vanité d'en secouer le frein:
> Mais je veux que ses lois comme ses mœurs soient bonnes,
> C'est par où se maintient le respect des couronnes.
>
> (III.6)

Clearly, the value system of this tragedy is neatly divided among sets of characters. The priest Calchas seems to regard the sacramental in strictly material terms; Ménélas and Ulysse seem ready to put the formulas of piety to strictly personal, human ends; Ulysse is a bizarre compound of the pompous and the unctuous. "Achille," that hero says of himself in a sarcastic thrust at Ulysse, "sans défense/ Vaut pour le moins Ulysse avec son éloquence" (V.3). "Eloquent" is an epithet used more than once to describe him, as if in a reminder that words have always been suspect in Rotrou. Falling away from their faith, Clytemnestre and Achille, too, seem to belong to the group of the perfunctorily pious represented by the Greek generals. Where, then, can true piety in this world lie but in Iphigénie and her father?

We can say this of her father only at the very end and, even then, only in that relativistic spirit in which Polynice was "more sacramental" than Etéocle in *Antigone*. The relation between Agamemnon and his brother is parallel in some ways. Ménélas is not too self-sufficient; he is more against than he is for things; he is a sanctimonious fool; and so on. But I do not wish to push this parallel too far, for ultimately Ménélas *is* regenerated in this more fully resacramentalized universe. Confronted with the prospect of Iphigénie's sacrifice, Ménélas no longer feigns pity for his brother and his niece. He actually is ready to forego the sacrifice (V.1). That he is restrained in this humane wish by Calchas' platitudes is really to the priest's discredit. Uncle and father feel what the priest cannot in his formulas. As the father tells Calchas: "Le Ciel sait mieux que vous combien il est contraire,/ D'ordonner en grand Prêtre et d'obéir en père" (V.1). But obey he does, for the father's faith is restored by the daughter's, even if his zeal is weak. "Le zèle défaillant," says the priest, "l'ouvrage est sans mérite" (V.1).

The theology must not be confused with Protestant insistence on sacramental validity *ex opere operantis*. The priest questions the sacrificer's *zeal*—the ardor one brings to a cause, not the cause itself. In Catholic sacramental theology, the efficacy of the sacrament depends on the disposition of the sacrificer, but efficacy does redound to the ill-disposed once he is properly disposed. The sacramental sacrifice is valid in spite of the perfunctory piety of the priest and the hypocritical piety of Ulysse. The latter complains that a girl alone defends the gods in their midst. Ulysse is wrong, for the father's zeal does increase

## TEMPTATION TO TOTAL TRANSCENDENCE

as the moment of actual sacrifice approaches. Interrupting the violent quarrel between Ulysse and Achille and regretting his own "différends" with the gods and with himself, the father asks the lover to stop irritating the heavens. To his daughter he promises: " . . . tu vivras malgré ce coup mortel,/ Ce ne te sera pas un tombeau qu'un autel" (V.3). His repentance and illumination are of crucial significance. He has freely come to co-operate with the divine will and is thus restored to full being and understanding. The motif of becalmed vessels aptly expresses the ethical relations between divine and human: Heaven proposes but Man disposes. Agamemnon had already partially regained his being through the *grace*-ful defense of his daughter. He had seen that his own earlier love for Helen before she married was as impure as hers for Paris; that his expedition to Troy was a *folie* just as grave. Now he sees that his very resistance to his daughter's sacrifice is also in error. At this moment he is almost equal to his daughter in divine insight.

She is not the psychologically complicated creature Euripides portrays in the model on which Rotrou drew. After the father's treachery has been revealed, Rotrou, like Euripides, has his heroine seek explanations from her father. "What can I have to do with Helen's love?" is the question Iphigenia poses in Euripides on this occasion. "Ai-je quelque intérêt aux affaires d'Hélène?" Rotrou's Iphigénie asks (IV.3). But Rotrou leaves the tears and recriminations of the original Iphigenia to the mother. His Iphigénie does not clasp her father's knees; nor plead with him, "Kill me not untimely! the sun is sweet!"; nor does she turn to anyone (the child-brother Orestes in the model) and urge, "Yet come and cry with me, kneel down and pray." Quite to the contrary:

> D'avoir recours aux pleurs, d'implorer votre grâce,
> Un si vil procédé sent trop son âme basse:
> C'est une lâcheté que le sang me défend,
> En cela connaissez que je suis votre enfant,
> Plus vous me témoignez de n'être plus mon père,

>  Plus je m'efforcerai d'éprouver le contraire,
>  Le sang qui sortira de ce sein innocent,
>  Prouvera malgré vous sa source en se versant.
>
>  (IV.3)

Iphigénie is equal to this occasion, as she is to whatever occasion, with appropriate piety. A virgin about to wed a mighty warrior, she has misgivings about the approaching wedding, but is nonetheless dutiful and loving to the father who has arranged it (II.1-2). Her dutifulness is one with her insistence on her rank; her dedication to Diane is one with her noble blood. Even before she seeks her father's explanation for his ignoble defense of an adulteress, she tells her tearful attendant that a fear of death would be "une lâche action" and that to die "est un tribut qu'on doit aux destinées." She *wills* her death because of her destiny. A redemptive sacrificial figure, Iphigénie sets an example of sacramental purity for all: her attendant, her lover, her mother, her father (and her uncle as well, though not by direct address).

She is at once a sacrifice of expiation and one of ordination. As a sacrifice of expiation, she assumes the impure character of all those about her. Henri Hubert and Marcel Mauss remind us that these sins or impurities are themselves sacred in character;[22] the profane is a religious category. In *Iphigénie* the domain of the impure sacred ranges from the adulterous sins of Hélène to the imperfect disposition with which the father begins the sacrifice (the "petit zèle" Calchas reproaches in him). Though not present before us, the adulterous Hélène is an important character, a sort of beauteous devil like Hermante in *L'Innocente Infidelité*. Describing her, Agamemnon gives one of the most paradoxical definitions of sacrilege in Rotrou's theater:

>  La beauté, ce tableau de l'essence divine,
>  Ce trésor de son sang est souvent sa ruine.
>  C'est un présent des Cieux à la vertu fatal,
>  Un bonheur malheureux, un bien source de mal.

## TEMPTATION TO TOTAL TRANSCENDENCE

> Et pour dire en deux mots mon sens de votre femme,
> Le visage en est beau, mais je doute de l'âme.
>
> (II.2)

In Hélène the premises of *Les Sosies* are reversed: physical beauty is not something toward which the gods themselves are irresistibly inclined; rather, it is a snare the gods place before men to lure them into sacrilege.

But not in all cases of beauty. There is Iphigénie. Her purity gives meaning to the impurity of others and vice versa. Rotrou's dramaturgy of polarized types serves him well in tragedy as well as in comedy: the sacrilegious physical beauty of Hélène is opposed by the sacramental spiritual beauty of Iphigénie. Iphigénie is physically beautiful, of course. Ironically, in Achille her physical beauty causes the very sacrilege that Agamemnon warns of in Hélène. However, Iphigénie must herself struggle against such offenses on all sides by insisting on her spirituality. As Hubert and Mauss have shown, the function of an expiatory sacrifice implies a "communal" function as well.[23] Iphigénie's sacrifice is an "ordination," as promised by her mother. In being dedicated to Diane, she expiates the sins of her family while realizing her own divine entelechy (symbolized by her virginity). She resacramentalizes the universe desecrated by others. "Ma flamme devient sainte et la profane cesse," Achille cries upon hearing the justification of the sacrifice from the goddess; "J'ai par mon zèle enfin satisfair à l'Oracle,/ Et de notre voyage il a levé l'obstacle," Agamemnon cries in the same moment (V.4). The sacrifice has been bloodless; his daughter has been spared from death by Diane. Her father had predicted this earlier in a figurative rather than literal spirit: "Je sais le respect de la Grèce,/ Son dessein me tient lieu de l'effet" (V.4).

Seldom has the doctrine of innocence by intention been stressed with such spiritual force. Whatever the intention of the generals at the outset, it has been purified by the *consistently* good intention of Iphigénie. In not being violated by a knife, her body symbolizes this spiritual purity. Yet, of even greater significance is the disappearance of that intact body. Iphigénie is disembodied before us. As the goddess says, material effects are not important here. Iphigénie does not suffer physically like Hercule. Instead, she is assumed directly into Heaven, and the explanation of all this comes not from the divinized person but from the goddess herself. Theologically, of course, Iphigénie is now one with the godhead. That she does not show this union in her own physical person only continues that emphasis on the spiritual which had characterized her even before her assumption.

The pure Iphigénie can resacramentalize this impure world only by leaving it. This is the reason for her presence in it. It cannot be said of Rotrou's play, as it has of his model, that the miraculous salvation of the victim is really an epilogue (perhaps tacked on by Euripides' son, according to some editors of the great classic).[24] The bloodless assumption into Heaven in Rotrou's play flows both thematically and dramatically from the *données* of his play. Once again, we have an A-B-A pattern. Agamemnon's lie about the marriage to Achille constitutes the false datum, and this false datum proves itself to be really "un mal source de bien." Iphigénie actualizes in the final portion of the play what was potential but no less real in the initial A portion: her unsullied consecration to the goddess Diane. And as in Rotrou's previous plays with the same pattern, the sufferings that all undergo in the B portion of the play prove to be mere illusions. This point is given fullest dramatic expression in the very fact that Iphigénie is not dispatched by the priest's sacrificial knife. This de-emphasis of the material borders on a devaluation of it. *Iphigénie* continues the marked shift in stress in Rotrou's theater since *Antigone*. Here the divinity seems present only on occasion; and perhaps rarely, if Agamemnon's misgivings about Hélène's beauty are generalized.

Yet, it would be a mistake to generalize those misgivings. In spite of the temptation to total transcendence, Rotrou's universe remains sacramental. The divinity may be disembodied, but it is not hidden. In principle throughout and in practice at the end, the material is de-emphasized but not denied. As in Thomistic theology, Iphigénie regards "orders" as more strictly necessary and higher than marriage. For all this spirituality, Iphigénie is not against the world and the flesh. "Si le décret des Dieux n'avait borné mon âge," she tells Achille, "Je leur demanderais cet heureux mariage" (IV.6). Each person has his role according to the decrees of a benevolent determinism. The "solution de continuité" obtains for this play as it has for others.

Rotrou's *Bélissaire*, Tragédie (1643), comes after the *Bélissaire* of Desfontaines, even as his *Le Véritable Saint Genest* comes after that author's play about the actor-martyr, *L'Illustre Comédien*.[25] Rotrou's play about the royally victimized soldier is closer to its Spanish source and so might well be called *Le Véritable Bélissaire*.[26R] Like the hero of Mira de Amescua's *El ejemplo mayor de la Desdicha* and unlike Desfontaines' eponymous hero, Rotrou's Bélissaire comes to an unhappy end in the world he serves so well. This is the grandiose world of the East Roman Empire in the middle of the sixth century after Christ. The connection with *Le Véritable Saint Genest* lies in more than a curious parallel of literary history; the allusion to Christ involves more than fixing the time of the play. Like the play about the actor-martyr, *Bélissaire* is a profoundly religious and specifically Christian play.

"Je suis Prince et Chrétien, de qui l'exemple importe" (III.5), says the Emperor Justinien in the midst of his remonstrances to his wife, whose perfidy he has at last understood. In believing in the religiously edifying and, here, adjudicatory function of his rank, this Christian ruler of the Eastern Empire does not differ from earlier rulers in the canon. Rotrou's rulers have always believed that: "Les Rois, comme rayons de la divine essence,/ En leur gouvernement imitent sa puissance" (III.6). At this moment in *Bélissaire*, the concept of sacramental kingship seems fully validated once again. We appear to be in the final A portion of a typical Rotrou play in which an innocent is the victim of fate or sacrilege. After a B portion full of deceits based on a false datum, the victim has been restored to the bliss he knew in the initial A portion. The false datum of this B portion is Antonie's unjust persecution of him unto death itself. The hero cannot know that this is only seeming, that he is the victim of a deeper, more abiding false datum: the enmity of the empress.

Her enmity is "false" according to another familiar notion: her jealousy is a *folie*, a deviation of natural reason. This comes out directly in the fifth act, with the empress' Heaven-directed confession of her guilt and Bélissaire's innocence. (V.6). Yet, well before that, in what appears to be the complete play of the first three acts, the notion appears in the emperor's sadly justified suspicions of his wife: "J'ai peine d'ouïr qu'un nom qui m'est si cher,/ D'un si lâche projet se soit voulu tâcher (II.12). The vindication of Bélissaire in the first three acts moves toward an equilibrium in which matter (political power, here) and spirit fuse. In the fusion the spiritual is obviously capital. The emperor can hardly believe a *name* to be guilty. In the contingent world of politics, a name points to an essence or being of which the physical person and political conduct are only temporal accidents, but nonetheless revealing. The empress' name is thus ironical; Théodore is hardly the gift of God her name signifies. She is a grand but disturbing figure. Earlier ferocious queens, like Déjanire, pale before the infernal power of this vengeful empress. Having loved and been denied by Bélissaire before she became empress, Théodore thinks of him now only with hate. Hatred is woven into the language of almost every scene, and in the profoundly expressive rhyme of "haine" and "reine," made by the empress herself, we sense that this realm is bound to be rendered asunder.

This "rendition" is Manichaean in overtone. During the reign of the historical Justinian, that heresy was still rather strong. We might thus be tempted to see in the palace of this dramatic Justinian some evidence of the Manichaean doctrine that the coterminous relation between the world and evil is represented by woman. Théodore is not, however, pure sensuality, as the Manichaeans regarded woman.[27] She is as spiritual as her adversary, driven by a lust for power equaled by no other woman in Rotrou thus far except perhaps Hermante of *L'Innocente Infidélité*. The comparison is especially instructive in a play where some might see a foreshadowing of Racine in this queen's use of *public* power for *private* ends. When we first meet this queen who loved Bélissaire before her marriage, she tells us that "ma haine est un effet d'une amour irrité,/ Dont il était indigne et qu'il a rebutée" (I.3). Accustomed to think of power and love in French classical tragedy in Racinian terms, the relation between Théodore and Bélissaire might remind some readers of that between Hermione and Pyrrhus, or Roxanne and Bajazet. As Lancaster has shown, the play is not without at least one Racinian pattern: the scenes after Théodore warns Antonie that she must not show her love correspond to those scenes in *Britannicus* in which Néron forbids Junie to acknowledge her love for the hero of Racine's play.[28] We may note another fairly familiar dramatic device that Racine will exploit in another play: the hero's betrayal literally by his own hand through a love letter to a mistress whom the jealous queen would deny the hero. (*Bajazet*).

Yet, unlike Néron and Roxanne, Théodore does not use the public *for the sake of* the private motive. She uses *both*. She is indignant in the quotation I have just given as much because her love has been for an "indigne" as because it has been "irritée." That is, Bélissaire insults her in two ways—both as a woman and as a queen. "Je suis femme et je hais," she goes on here, but then she adds: "Ne vois-tu pas qu'encor, pour comble de l'horreur . . . Il s'acquiert un pouvoir si près de l'insolence" (I.3). Later, in the very scene coming from the Spanish model and looking to Racine's *Britannicus*, she tells Antonie, "Qu'une Reine se venge *et* qu'une femme hait" (II.3; italics added). The conjunction co-ordinates but it does not fuse two separate motives. In her hatred of the lowly man she once loved, the queen is a double sacrilege—to both chaste desire and *générosité*. But, as Lancaster senses, there is more to the empress' motivation than the ill-repressed love that leads Hermione or Phèdre to their political masks. "Belisarius has a fine, but monotonous role," the historian writes, and "Theodora's extraordinary vindictiveness is insufficiently explained by the fact that she had once failed to win the general's love."[29] She is concerned with something more than *love*: she is concerned with her honor, with *générosité*, rather than chaste desire.

On the other hand, Bélissaire reverses the relations between the codes. He is the perfect example of the Christian paradox in its military version: a brave warrior, his chief virtue is not his courage but his charity. Christ-like, he pardons his persecutors and assassins. Threatened by a would-be assassin who sacrilegiously garbs himself as a *pilgrim*, he gives alms to the pilgrim and then, when he discovers the ruse, intercedes with the king on his behalf. Little wonder that the pardoned pilgrim calls his savior a "rare . . . divin homme" (I.6). From first to last, seldom has a hero been so regally if providentially determined in his behavior. "Le Ciel" is the key word coming from his lips and heart as frequently as "haine" comes from the lips and heart of his royal enemy. At the very beginning of the play, he stops his confidant's grandiloquent praise for his victories with the admonition "C'est en ôter le prix au Ciel, dont je la tiens" (I.1).

His sacred character and the specifically Christian character of the play come out at almost every moment, but nowhere so densely as with his third would-be assassin, Philippe, his rival for Antonie's love. A pious invoker of Heaven's favor upon his unknown rescuer (II.18), Philippe justifies the murder of the saintly Bélissaire on the grounds that "notre foi nous l'ordonne et qui s'engage aux Rois./ Se fait de leurs desseins inviolables lois" (III.2). He uses the queen's unholy rage to realize his own unholy love. While he reflects on this ignoble intention, Bélissaire appears, kissing the letter he has written to Antonie in hopes of restoring "une amour si parfaite et *sainte*" (italics added). The contrast between sacred and profane love could not be greater. Philippe kneels before the triumphant hero, as if in obeisance ("Incliné, sous couleur de lui baiser la main") but really to plunge a knife into "ce miracle animé par tant d'exploits insignes." This almost sacrilegious intention is checked at the sight of the ring he himself gave to his rescuer earlier.

> J'y proposais un mal et j'y *médite* un bien;
> Le dessein d'un affront à des vœux y fait place,
> J'y tentais un *outrage* et j'y cherche une *grâce*;
> Ma cruauté m'y rend et ma fureur s'y perd,
> Mon bras vous y menace et mon œil vous y sert;
> J'y *pèche* et m'y *repens*, je m'y *souille* et m'y *lave*,
> J'y viens votre ennemi, j'y deviens votre esclave.
>
> (III.2; italics added)

Once again, a ring has worked a sanctifying grace on a perfidious lover. But this time the ring is not invested with any special power, as in *La Bague de l'oubli*; instead, it is the "infidel's" own token of faith. Its grace inheres in the world of which it is a natural convention.

Bélissaire forgives Philippe as he forgave Léonse and Narsès. In the first three acts of this play, with their independent A-B-A pattern, Heaven does justify the hero's frequently reiterated faith in its *immanent* power: "Le Ciel en ma faveur fera crever l'envie" (I.2); "Le Ciel dessus les siens veille soigneusement" (II.7); " . . . J'espère au bon œil dont le Ciel me regarde,/ La bonne conscience est une sûre garde" (III.1). Thinking Bélissaire asleep, the emperor muses, addressing his words more to himself than to the tranquil figure:

> Quelque lieu d'où ton sang tire son origine,
> Tu dois être un rayon de l'essence divine,
> Puisque ce port céleste et ce divin aspect,
> Impriment à la fois l'amour et le respect.
>
> (III.4)

Vassal and emperor are both "rayons de l'essence divine," we remember. In the emperor's application of this key phrase both to himself and to his vassal, we see the spiritual expression of an identification on which the emperor insists throughout. Giving the vassal one of his royal rings, he says, "Tiens, avec celui-ci, comme un second moi-même,/ Prends dessus mes sujets un empire suprême" (I.6). These two are not really in a master-slave relationship.[30] They are "frères amis," both examples of a higher self, both emanations of the divine essence. In the long run, Theodore will convert them into "frères ennemis" precisely by accusing the lowborn one of *sales désirs*. However, before he fatally believes an ambiguous sign, the emperor now knows how to read the clear signs of Bélissaire's virtue and Théodore's treachery.

He learns of this treachery through a device that seems to anticipate the play-acting in *Le Veritable Saint Genest*. Yet, I think it misleading to see Bélissaire's relation to his "false dreamer" as analogous to Genest's relation to Adrien in the formal play. The ontological character of Bélissaire's feigning differs radically from all other intercalated structures in Rotrou: the "actor" really portrays himself in a "part" that does not reflect a true reality in another plane of being but presents a reality obscured within a single plane of being. The ontological unity of these "independent" planes of being is apparent in the psychology of the dream that the emperor gives here:

> Le songe est un tableau des passions humaines
> Qui dedans le repos représent nos peines;
> Un confident sans peur, un parleur peu discret,
> Qui des plus retentissants évente le secret.
>
> (III.4)

The unity of personality and of being is important. However ingenious this detour, in adopting it Bélissaire breaks the very codes by which he lives. According to chaste desire, virtue is its own reward, and *générosité* impels its adherents to give themselves always for what they are. The imperative to deal fairly and openly with all applies to vassals as well as kings.

Were the play to end at the end of Act III, Bélissaire's stratagem might be dismissed as an excusable casuistry of the kind we have seen in earlier plays. The concluding moment of Act III is filled with the familiar eschatological motifs of the semi-political plays of the first half of the theater. The ravages of sacrilege have proved illusory; grace has triumphed; an illuminated king makes an adjudicatory speech in which he condemns the vicious and elevates the virtuous to even higher material station; and so on. Placing the scepter the emperor offers him at the empress' feet, Bélissaire gives a supreme example of his Christian charity. He also provides an occasion for a *grace*-ful gesture to produce its sacramental effect on the worst "sacrilège" of this universe. (This is, in fact, what happens in the last act of Desfontaines' *Bélissaire*.) But even if Théodore is not converted, we have what has been seen in previous plays of Rotrou: the utterly sacrilegious figure has been either banished, exiled, or imprisoned without impairing the festive mood of the happy ending with its "heureux mariage" and long reign. The example of Hermante comes to mind, naturally. Though Théodore is an empress, imprisonment or exile would not be completely out of place in a plot ending with such lines as Narsès' "Quelle rage tiendrait contre tant de bonté" or Bélissaire's words closing Act III, "Arrête ici, Fortune, arrête ici ta roue" (III.7).

But in the lexicon of the play, Fortune is a woman. In a gloomy paradox, Fortune's wheel comes to a stop in the very persistence with which the woman Théodore holds out against such goodness through two more acts. The A-B-A structure of the first three acts proves itself part of the prolonged B portion of the larger structure of the play. In the latter the empress' rage is the "false datum." Her final confession shows it to be a folly, a deprivation of reason, a fall from grace. The consequences of this false datum are very real: Bélissaire is executed; emperor and empress are permanently separated as man and wife. The sinful rage of Théodore is relieved too late; it is a *real* datum of the B portion. But that portion is only a part of a larger structure in which both the initial A and final A portions define Théodore's rage as Heaven's way of bringing Bélissaire to his place of true rest. He will rest not in the arms of Antonie, as physical support of the throne of César, but in the arms of God, as spiritual support of His heavenly throne. In this play with a historical Christian setting, God is used in the singular, but His oneness with the plural gods of previous pagan or secular plays is clear in the relation between "Les Cieux" and "Fortune." There is a rift between them as in previous plays, with Heaven the source only of good and Fortune the source of evil or *misfortune*. But here the rift is not repaired. The fatal imperfection turns out to be a deprivation of reason inhering in the sinful just as pure grace inheres in the saintly.

In such a world pure grace cannot long abide, for "Fortune . . . est femme," an "instable Déesse" who raises the lowly not to their glory but to their "malheur" (V.10). Bélissaire is finally trapped by Théodore through her profanation of the tenets of chaste desire. She hypocritically claims that she would have earlier preferred his pretended love for her instead of his refusal because he considered himself of too low birth for her. She even claims to renounce all concerns of station for his sake now:

> Mais depuis vos bontés rétablissant vos lois;    un peu
> Achevez mes soupirs qui me coupez la voix,    bas
> Puisque vouloir forcer cette ardeur obstinée
> Est lutter vainement contre ma destinée,
> Témoignons-lui: Mais lâche! à quoi te résous-tu?
>
> (IV.2)

I give the original stage direction here, for in the most widely known edition of Rotrou to date, Viollet-le-Duc has mistaken the sense of this moment (and perhaps the whole scene) with his "à part" as Théodore turns in on herself.[31] The original says "*un peu* bas": that is, she is only pretending to turn in on herself, pretending to struggle with a shameful but irresistible love for her "inferior." She uses the triumph of love over station as a means of satisfying an affront to station. (Even with respect to that affront, Bélissaire is obviously doctrinally pure: it is the empress who sinned by loving out of place.) This diabolical creature is the enemy of grace itself: "Quelque part d'où l'injure ou la grâce procède" she begins her attack on Bélissaire for placing the scepter at her feet. Compared to this gesture, demeaning by the very lowliness of its source, "Mon exil m'affligeait bien moins que cette grâce" (IV.1). Grace may inhere in this world in Bélissaire, but through the dis-grace of Théodore that inherence is driven back to its source.

"Cette soumission, ce pardon généreux, / Est moins une pitié qu'un effet amoureux" (V.8), says the emperor of Bélissaire's earlier forgiveness of Théodore when he reads the "note to his wife." Claiming to be insulted by Bélissaire's base desire, Théodore splits the "selves" making up the "moi-même" of emperor and vassal. The emperor believes her. The evidence may not seem strong, but the belief nonetheless expresses the spiritual character of this play. Like many recent kings and lovers, the emperor prizes *amitié* over *amour*. There may even be signs of the homosexual motif of the early plays between the two men. The emperor calls the sleeping Bélissaire "la moitié de moi," a term applied elsewhere in Rotrou by heterosexual lovers or married characters to their beloved and mate.[32] Later, having read the fatal letter, the emperor tells Bélissaire: "Vous avez mal usé de mon *affection*" (IV.9; italics added). *Affection* is the term used in the early plays to express the emotion felt between heterosexual lovers. Finally, discovering the depths of his wife's perfidy in her very act of contrition at the end, the emperor punishes her by denying her forevermore "de part en mon lit" (V.8). Remaining latent, this homosexuality seems all the more "normal" in this play with its extremely spiritual emphasis. It adds to the many doubts cast on the "world as thing" in the last two acts. The "normal sexuality" of denouements in plays of the first half of the canon is condemned here. The pure lovers are never mated in body and, as reported by Philippe, Bélissaire died more the pure hero than the faithful lover, with no word for Antonie apparently. In the whole fifth act, Antonie is a pale figure whom her lover seems to have forgotten. Again, both in her old love and her present false charge of Bélissaire's base desire, Théodore presents physical union as "un bien source de mal." In the emperor's separation from his wife, we are far from the beautiful Alphrède's eloquent defense of sacramental marriage. Here, in annulling a license, the emperor seems to annul the order of the flesh itself. In his own way, like those heretics whom the historical Justinian brought under imperial ban, the emperor becomes Manichaean in his view of his wife and perhaps all women.

Heaven appears to be the only place of justice, and its light shines only for a short time on this dark earth. Like many other precepts of the theater of immanence, in this play the precept of rehabilitative time is rejected. Removing the emperor's ring and surrendering it to Léonse, Bélissaire declares:

> Le plus cher favori n'est rien qu'un peu de boue,
> Dont l'inconstant fait montre et puis après s'en joue;
> Et ses honneurs ne sont que des sables mouvants,
> Qui servent de jouet aux haleines des vents:
> Il n'est si haut crédit que le temps ne consomme,
> Puisque l'homme est mortel et qu'il provient de l'homme;
> Ce qui nous vient de Dieu, seul exempt de la mort,
> Est seul indépendant et du temps et du sort.
>
> (V.2)

Human time is not real. Only divine timelessness is real. The unreality of human time is beautifully rendered in the structure of these last scenes. They reverse the early moments of the play: each of the would-be assassins whom Bélissaire had forgiven earlier now comes in the same order (Léonse, Narsès, and Philippe) to take back from his savior some sign of Bélissaire's own worldly elevation. Léonse takes back the ring of office, Narsès, the papers of office, and Philippe actually arrests the saintly Bélissaire.

In the first three acts, with their independent "plot," we found Bélissaire casuistically falling away from his own ethical imperatives. Here, too, in his last moments he borders on a similar fall from virtue. In one of the longest speeches in Rotrou's theater, this champion of virtue for its own sake makes an impassioned plea for a recognition of his services to the emperor. He begins his speech of one hundred twenty four verses with an apostrophe to the emperor as "Prince l'espoir des bons et l'effroi des pervers/ Vive image de Dieu, Roi du bas univers." The separation of worlds has never been so stark in Rotrou: there is this *bas univers* and, by implication, there is the *haut univers*. Bélissaire gives us a splendid sacramental vision in the very feats of prowess for which he now seeks recompense. The emperor remaining silent, the long speech finally turns to condemnation of this *bas univers*:

> En me faisant du bien vous me fûtes barbare,
> En m'obligeant, cruel, en me donnant, avare;
> Le Crocodille, ainsi, tue en versant des pleurs,
> La sirène en chantant, et l'aspic sous les fleurs.

Earlier, Bélissaire had defended his fidelity as a rare "droit inviolable et pure,/ Dans le commun débris de tout la nature" (IV.8). Nature in the world of *Les Sosies* and of the early theater was sacramental in its beauty. That beauty was a visible sign of the providential order of both divine conventions and human institutions. Here, the hero describes his moral situation as an existing natural disorder of the kind unsuccessfully called for by Hermante at the end of *L'Innocente Infidélité*. In such a world, "les Rois ne sont plus Rois depuis que leur puissance/ Laisse à la calomnie opprimer l'innocence" (V.5).

Innocence is oppressed: Bélissaire does die. "C'est à vous, justes Cieux! à vous que je me plains;/ Voyez mon innocence et rendez témoignage/ De l'injuste riguer dont la terre m'outrage" (V.5). When he died, testifies Philippe, "son âme s'envolant par la brêche des yeux,/ D'un invisible effort a pris sa route aux Cieux" (V.8). The effort was invisible, but no less real, as the familiar repentance of both emperor and empress makes clear. All believe in Heaven as a Christian concept. In ascending to it, Bélissaire completes the final A portion of the drama that had its beginning in God's creation of the world. Through this ascension, the hero makes of this play, designated a *tragédie* on its title page, what it is called in the running heads of the printed version: *tragi-comédie*. We have already alluded to this expressive editorial discrepancy in *Iphigénie*, but *Bélissaire* is a tragicomedy of an even greater spiritual tendency. Key themes of Rotrou—*frères-amis* who become *frères-ennemis*, suspicion of the flesh per se, the instability of fortune—all come to spiritual focus in the hero's derisive view of "ce bas univers." The contrast with the apotheosis of "ce bas élément" in *Les Sosies*, the "high point" of Rotrou's theater of immanence, could not be greater. Here, God is no longer "consubstantially" available within the universe but only transcendentally accessible through it. Naturally, listening to the emperor pray to the intercessionary figure of the ascended Bélissaire in the closing lines of the play, we realize that God is not totally inaccessible (as he is in Racine, according to some critics). Though in its most somber mood thus far, Rotrou's Tridentine Christianity is still characteristically "beyond tragedy." God is obviously not *hidden* from the world. Nevertheless, more than in any of the plays thus far, He seems *beyond* it.

*Bélissaire* is followed by two comedies, *Célie, ou le Vice-roy de Naples* (1644 or 1645) and *La Sœur* (1645), and the famous tragicomedy with which we began, *Le Véritable Saint Genest*. In varying degrees, the comedies retreat from the extreme transcendental concepts of *Bélissaire*. Indeed, though *La Sœur* still shows marked influences of the spiritual stresses of the theater of transcendence, in mood, at least, it differs rather sharply from that theater. For this reason I shall discuss it in my next section.[33] As for *Le Véritable Saint Genest*, returning to it now in light of the analyses to this point, it is clearly a play marked more by transcendental than immanentist concepts. Nevertheless, the temptation to surrender to an extreme transcendence is obviously resisted both in the inner and outer plays of this remarkable work. This is a characteristic of Rotrou's theater, obviously. Again, the Christian specificity of the *Saint Genest* can now be seen to be as old as *La Pélerine amoureuse*, a play showing the effects of a strong pull toward immanence but seeking a balance. This is to remind us that the moments of Rotrou's theater up to this point are not to be divided into the "profane" and the "sacred" but into two different religious moments. Beyond this point, as we shall see, the influence of both moments, of immanence and transcendence, endures in an ambivalent fashion.[34]

CHAPTER FOUR

*Nostalgia for Immanence*

ONE of the most ribald of marriage jokes—wife-swapping—lies at the heart of *La Sœur*, Comédie (1645).¹ᴿ The play thus might seem a throwback to the extreme immanentism of certain early plays. Some support for this view can be found in Anselme's misgivings about the affection between his children:

> Ils en usent pour Nole avec trop de licence;
> Et quoique leur amour ait beaucoup d'innocence,
> Je ne puis approuver ces baisers assidus
> D'une ardeur mutuelle et donnés et rendus.
> Ces discours à l'oreille et ces tendres caresses,
> Plus dignes passe-temps d'Amants et de Maîtresses,
> Qu'ils ne sont, en effet, d'un Frère et d'une Sœur.
>
> (II.2)

However, the "trop de licence" does not prevail here. Rather, sensual license is set in a specifically Christian context in such a way as to suggest that Rotrou, at least momentarily, recaptures the sacramental equilibrium of plays like *La Pélerine amoureuse*.

This is apparent in the caresses to which the father improperly objects here. This affection is innocent because it is between a man and woman who love each other legitimately, with the "license" of chaste desire. "Volupté" is not very prominent in the relations between husband and wife. If anything, they behave throughout the play with the kind of affection they falsely claim for each other at the outset: "amitié" between brother and sister. The love of Lélie and Sophie for each other is a sublime love. Lélie could not have been first attracted by a more chaste part of her beautiful body: " . . . La table fut couverte/ Par des mains dont amour avait joué ma perte"; these hands belong to one whose unhappy fate is "infidèle à son sang" (I.3). The very name of this noble but poor creature is a sign of her divine purity: Sophie. Lest we think her wisdom is as secular as the ingenuity of Ergaste, another line of the play reassures us of its Christian character: "Mais dans Sainte Sophie où les Chrétiens s'assemblent" (III.2), says Géronte, by way of telling his brother that he knows Lélie has not been to Constantinople.

This line reminds us that, like *Bélissaire* before it and *Le Véritable Saint Genest* right after it, *La Sœur* is specifically Christian in setting as well as in theme. That the strain of Christian sacramental theology is sacramental is brought out repeatedly. Paradoxically enough, it is brought out even in connection with the hoary joke about wife-swapping. Eraste is shocked at the idea of marrying without possessing his beloved or of possessing her without marrying her. In Ergaste's plan, Eroxène's lover fears "d'un double adultère,/ De ce *lien sacré* profaner le mystère" (I.3; italics added). However, his orthodox view of the sacrament yields to Ergaste's more flexible doctrine. A friend can disguise himself (as a priest, presumably) and then, before the assembled parents, officiate at the wedding of Lélie and Eroxène, and of Eraste and Sophie, as a cover-up for the nightly wedding in the flesh of different partners. Naturally, the familiar doctrine of just intentions, of good ends over bad means, justifies the ruse: it is taken not to satisfy "sales désirs" but out of fidelity to one's first love. Ergaste's reasoning recalls the Jesuit concept of "intentionalism," soon to be condemned by Pascal in *Les Lettres provinciales*. Listening to Ergaste, one can understand why Jansenists and other *dévots* of the time opposed the idea of frequent Communion. True, sin may not have been a perdurable state of being for them, and the most conservative may have believed that the faithful could be prepared for frequent Communion by the sacrament of penance. Nevertheless, there was always the danger of sinning by relying on the very high probability of having that sin absolved later.[2] Ergaste's "casuistry" is amusing and ingenious, of course. This is a comedy. However, in the response of the young people, in their sincere wish to respect the sacramental character of marriage itself, we see the spiritualist emphases of Rotrou's more recent tragedies.

Ergaste's intentions nourish a legitimate hope for the happy life here on earth. The high point of the valet's scheming is his deception of Anselme in speaking a made-up Turkish. Coming from Rotrou's model, Della Porta's *La Sorella*, this scene has long been considered the source of the scene of Turkish tomfoolery in *Le Bourgeois gentilhomme*. The scheming translator is unable to speak the language he translates, but convinces his victim that "le langage Turc dit beaucoup en deux mots" (II.4). In the situation, Ergaste apparently needs no special grace to achieve his just ends of preserving Lélie's love. "Je ne sais quel génie, en ce besoin extrême,/ Me dictait un jargon que j'ignore moi-même" (IV.1), he tells Lélie. The mysterious force ("Je ne sais quel génie") directing such events in previous plays has acted like divine grace. And in spite of the "sacrilegious" implications of his false-marriage scheme, we might say that grace inheres in Ergaste's genius here. Even more than *Le Véritable Saint Genest*, *La Sœur* stresses both human ability and human responsibility in the co-operative act by which man achieves the good.

The stress on human *action* is closely tied to the idea of *acting* in the aesthetic as well as the ethical sense. Lélie presents his deception of his father to Eraste and Ergaste as a play. "J'ai fait mon personnage en cette Comédie," he says, but now he needs Ergaste to help him carry on. "Pour ce qui reste, il faut qu'- Ergaste y remédie" (I.3). In keeping with the theatrical motif of all this scheming, we may say that Ergaste is a sort of play doctor.

Not everybody is pleased with his ministrations. When Lydie overhears Eraste seek Aurélie in marriage, she cannot know he is playing a part in Ergaste's play. But she does think he's been making her mistress play a part in a very different play. "O noire perfidie!" she cries, "ô siècle, ô monde immonde!/ Source en crimes, en fraudes, en misères féconde!/ Vil théâtre des jeux et du sort et du temps" (II.7). When Lélie spoke earlier of his "comédie," he used the term as it was used in the period: generically for play. Envisaging a happy ending for himself, his term might also have been used specifically to designate a comedy. On the other hand, Lydie looks on the play as a tragedy because she does not realize that she is watching a pretense. We should thus be wary of assuming that we have a coalescence of planes here. Even Lydie's reference to "théâtre" shows that her aesthetic is exactly that of Eraste, who is only playing a part. She uses theater as a metaphor for illusion, for unreality, for pretense. Compared to true reality, the world is like a play. Reality for her is now spiritual and transcendental; like many of Rotrou's recent disappointed believers, she would reject this world, which is subject to fate and time. Like Bélissaire, she links fortune to the opposite sex (in this case, obviously, a man): "Un sexe . . . plus changeant que le sort, moins stable que la roue" (II.7).

When Ergaste's false datum breaks down in subsequent developments, it appears that we are restored to an initial A portion, whose real datum is that of a pretense; it is as if the structure of the play were B-A-B. When Constance identifies Sophie as Aurélie, she is not merely seeking to please her son: she is really welcoming the person she had raised as her daughter! Constance is less disturbed by this development than her son because, as she tells him, "Vous n'avez point péché, l'erreur n'est pas un crime/ Et n'a point fait outrage à ses chastes appas" (IV.6). Chastity is all a matter of intention. Even when confronted with civilization's primordially horrifying crime, incest, the doctrine of intention remains unshaken.

It does so, at least, in this mother whose own intentions have remained *constantly* good. The play on her name is even more persistent than that on Sophie's. The mother's constancy has been that of an unshakable faith in Heaven's goodness. Heaven shows that Ergaste's play had to stop so that Heaven could make manifest the real A portions of its play. In these, to the comfort of Lydie among others, Eraste does love Aurélie. Unwittingly, Ergaste has concocted a feint whose false terms turn out to be true: Lélie is to wed Eroxène, the girl he loves as Sophie but calls Aurélie; Eraste is to wed Aurélie, the girl he loves as Eroxène. The coalescence of Ergaste's and Heaven's plans suggests a meshing of the planes as in *Bélissaire*. Nothing could be further from the truth. The aesthetic resemblance is even more crucial in the second half of Rotrou's theater than in the first. Emphasizing the spiritual, this play, more than any other before *Le Véritable Saint Genest*, insists on the ethical aspects of pretense not by dissolving planes of real being and false being but by insisting on their distinction.

Now, that Sophie really is Eroxène is not brought out until the beginning of the last act. This revelation makes it seem that we have been viewing reality when we have been viewing falsity. Yet, Sophie has not *become* Eroxène—she *is* and always *has been* Eroxène. In the beginning was the word; true reality succeeds seeming reality. All play-acting comes to an end. Orgye penitently reflects on the meaning of the play in which he has been so long an actor. Its first act was written by his brother, Pamphile, but he collaborated in its composition by carrying it out for the sake of money at the expense of sacred love. "Maudite passion," he says, "dangereuse colère . . . Qui, dessus la raison, donnez l'empire aux sens/ Je crains bien de t'avoir trop crue à mes dépens" (V.3). His penance is obviously not perfect in its contrition; it is an act of attrition: the sinner fears either the loss of material good or the suffering of material punishment. But, as we know, sacramentally speaking, attrition is valid. More importantly in the context, this penance occurs "freely," not in a state of special grace but in a state of actual grace.

These doctrines of Christian theology are rendered specifically in this play. Reminding him that they are old and thus on the point of dying to this world, Anselme warns Orgye that when dead,

> . . . en ce compte exact que nous rendons à Dieu,
> La restitution tiendra le premier lieu;

Par elle seulement notre offence s'efface,
Et sans elle un pécheur ne trouve point de grâce.

(V.4)

Like his counterpart in Rotrou's Italian model, Orgye is impatient with such sermons; for him "grace" and "restitution" have distinctly material meanings. But in Rotrou's considerably expanded adaptation of this scene, material considerations are subordinated to Anselme's theology of sacramental penance:

Rendez grâces au Ciel, dont le soin provident,
De cet énorme Hymen divertit l'accident.
Car, quoique vous n'ayez qu'avec répugnance
Consenti cette injuste et funeste alliance,
Vous n'encouriez pas moins un supplice éternel:
*Qui pèche, y répugnant, en est plus criminel.*

(V.4; italics added)

Unlike the "incestuous" Lélie, Orgye cannot be held blameless for acting in error: the same doctrine of intention inculpates him, for his intention was both real and sinful. Sin is no longer a *folie*, a deprivation of full being for which Heaven itself is held responsible. The compulsion to do good is as strong as ever, as we see in the "rational" inclination to love each other both in young lovers (Lélie-Sophie, Eraste-"Eroxène") and old lovers (Anselme-Constance, Ergaste-Lydie). But, as Orgye shows, man is responsible for his "rational inclinations"; he can misuse his freedom by sinning.

Through grace, man is redeemed from sin. The last act of this play is a paean to divine grace. The scenes of Orgye's penitential grace yield to the still happier grace of Aurélie's "resurrection" in Sophie and the consequent prospect of the grace of the sacrament of "heureux mariage." Even Orgye is caught up in this communal grace. "Je demande une grâce," Constance says to him; "elle vous est acquise," he replies swiftly and succinctly. The "grâce" in question is the marriage of his true niece, brought back from captivity and thus bound to cost him 8,000 ducats. He does not flinch at the prospect; his contrition is now perfect; he has made full restitution and become one of this heaven-blessed family.

In *La Sœur* that character who has so often been left unwed and unwanted in Rotrou has become a cynosure of the utmost sacramental significance. Thanks to "un miracle inouï," a *sister* at last participates fully in the eschatological satisfactions of a universe whose sacramental purity is so well expressed by the very terms of her participation: " . . . femme et sœur légitime" (V.5).

Equally famous, if not in fact more so, than *Le Véritable Saint Genest*, is *Venceslas*, Tragi-comédie (1647), also considered by many critics as Rotrou's finest play.[3R] Calling attention to its superb portraits of the royal family, critics liken its author to Shakespeare, Corneille, Racine, and Sophocles, especially in his psychological penetration into the character of the aging king and his restive older son. On the basis of the confrontation between these two in the play's first scene, Voltaire came to his somewhat left-handed praise of Rotrou: that in just fourteen years Corneille had become the master of his own former master in dramatic art.[4] And though they are repelled by what they see as Rotrou's immorality in showing vice rewarded, other eighteenth-century critics are similarly drawn to this play. For most, Rotrou seems at last to break with the jejune psychology of swooning *généreux* and faultless females. Thus, in his paradoxical view of Ladislas as a detached, insipid spinner of proverbs and preciosities, Fréron stands apart from such admiring critics as La Harpe and Marmontel.[5]

In the very act of objecting to the contradictoriness of Ladislas' character, Marmontel unwittingly points to the inwardness of that character which has so fascinated later critics. Saint-Marc Girardin finds Rotrou as free of his Spanish model in characterization as Crane and especially Lancaster later find him in his dramaturgy.[6] Contrasting Rotrou's play with its model, Rojas' *No hay ser padre siendo rey*, the earlier critic finds in the expression of jealousy in the two plays the key to the difference between the Spanish and the French theaters. Based less fully on "le sentiment de l'honneur," the French theater "n'a pas surtout dans la jalousie cette inflexibilité vindicative qui est propre au théâtre espagnol. Les héros et les héroines de la jalousie française font volontiers le mal qui les venge, mais ils ressentent surtout le mal qui les tourmentent; ils appartiennent plus encore à la douleur qu'à la vengeance."[7] François Guizot comes to a similar formulation: "Corneille . . . avait peint l'amour combattu par le devoir; mais on n'avait pas encore vu au théâtre l'amour combattu par lui-même, tourmenté de sa propre violence, et tantôt suppliant, tantôt furieux, se manifestant par l'excès de la colère comme par l'excès de la tendresse."[8] The concepts obviously bring Rotrou closer to Racine in the very act of explicitly dissociating him from Corneille. Yet, as we know, Guizot is unjust to Rotrou in saying that we had not seen such "Racinian" complexities in his theater before *Venceslas*.[9]

If most critics are agreed on the psychological richness of Rotrou's portraits in this play, they are considerably less agreed on their dramatic and moral significance. Well before Mme de Pompadour asked Marmontel to "rectify" the vices of this fascinating dramatic heritage, the *Mercure de France* stated the view informing Marmontel's revision of the play: " . . . Dans quelle estime doit être un Prince à qui on impute tous les crimes que la nuit a dérobés aux regards du Public? De pareils caractères ont-ils jamais du être dans une Tragédie? Mais dans le reste de la Piece, les discours et les actions de ce monstre vont plus loin que le portrait."[10] Yet, from the eighteenth century well into our own, this view of the play has been argued. Curiously enough, it is Marmontel who makes us aware of the relative "goodness" of Ladislas. Because the prince is at the center of action, because he is to mount the scaffold only to be saved by his father at the last minute, says Marmontel, he ought to be of a character to win our sympathy.[11] The reviser thus relieves Rotrou's text of the "traits odieux" interfering with this interpretation. In and of itself, the procedure could be a naïve disfiguration of the play. Somewhat inconsistently, Marmontel then goes on to change the structure by having Cassandre punish Ladislas at the end. Later critics have found less discrepancy between original text and structure. Most recently, Mlle Van Baelen has shrewdly wondered if the text of the play before the attack on Alexandre really justifies the traditional maligning of Ladislas' character. Violent he certainly is, the critic says, but "de quels crimes est-il vraiment coupable"? Ambitious as he is, Mlle Van Baelen goes on, Ladislas nevertheless does not seize power. At most, the text shows him more accused than actually guilty of "les incartades d'un homme jeune et passionné, impatient de vivre et d'agir."[12] Mlle Van Baelen's insight is capital: after nearly three centuries of trying to understand Ladislas out of context, the best place to begin to understand this first angry young man of the French theater is within the context of the play itself and of Rotrou's theater.

In *Venceslas* Rotrou weaves many of his obsessive themes in a dramatic form seeming to restore the sacramental equilibrium of his earliest plays. The most recent editor of the play, W. Leiner, follows earlier commentators in pointing to Rotrou's long-standing prepossession with the very name of the aged king: Venceslas was also the name of the father of King Alfonce in Rotrou's second play of record, *La Bague de l'oubli*.[13] As I said of that royal hero, his sacrilegious surrender to "sales désirs" made him a worthy precursor of Rotrou's most famous lecher, Ladislas. Again, in his second play, Rotrou also showed an early preoccupation with the theme of generational conflict. On at least one of the grounds here dividing Venceslas and Ladislas, the duke of the early play reproached his daughter for a surrender to carnality. The confrontation of father and children has also been a key motif in numerous comedies and tragicomedies (although on somewhat different grounds—usually avarice). Again, on the basis of family relations in many previous plays, Lanson might have written of Rotrou that "Racine l'a beaucoup lu."[14] Ladislas and Alexandre are "frères ennemis": like the warring brothers of *Antigone*, one is a higher self of spirituality and the other a lower self of carnality or worldliness. Again, in the relations between Alexandre and Fédéric, Rotrou repeats the motif of plays as early as *La Céliane* or as recent as *Bélissaire*: the friends or even master and "slave" are in a bond of *amitié*; they are spiritual twins who vie with one another in *amitié*. Again, many have found echoes of Corneille in Cassandre's plea for Ladislas' head and her supposed eventual acceptance of him "in time." I would add that the "combat amical" of Fédéric and Ladislas resembles that between Antiochus and Séleucus in *Rodogune*. In that play Corneille also gives a defense of "les nœuds secrets," a concept of irrational love very like the concept of "secrets appas" that leads the Théodore of *Venceslas* to defend her "irrational" choice of Fédéric. In the very names of Théodore and Léonor, Leiner finds still further evidence of Corneille's imprint on Rotrou.[15] Yet, Rotrou's recent use of the name Théodore (*Bélissaire*) and Léonor (*Dom Bernard de Cabrère*) as well as the many motifs I have listed above show that Rotrou is drawing very largely on himself here.

His structural model is also found in his own practice. This observation is perhaps surprising in view of the apparent break with what Knutson calls the rule of "no surprise" in Rotrou. That rule seems suspended in the most famous and perhaps most widely admired scene of this or any other play of Rotrou: Ladislas' discovery that he has actually slain not Fédéric but his younger brother. In a striking departure from the play he imitated, Rotrou is said to have concealed from the audience and characters onstage the identity of the victim until it is announced by Cassandre. Yet, we may wonder if the break with previous practice is so apparent here. Details of language and aspects of the dramatic development indicate that when Ladislas first appears at this point, the audience knows that the real victim has, in fact, been Alexandre. However, the kind of knowledge in question does not provide information. That kind of knowledge is of the head, and in this play, Rotrou does not provide so much of it to his audience as he usually does. Nevertheless, he provides far more crucial knowledge here: of the heart. The heart tells the head that it is bound to be wrong, especially in heeding what is the overheard. Knowledge of the head creates a suspense based on curiosity and excitement, the emotional climate appropriate to tragicomedy. Knowledge of the heart creates a suspense—or, more accurately, an apprehension—based on anxiety and fear, the emotional climate appropriate to tragedy. Rotrou creates this climate masterfully in this scene. When the old king cries "O Dieu! L'Infant est mort!" (IV.6), his outburst tells us what we did not want to know but already felt in our "heart of hearts."

This dire news was as bound to be actualized in this moment as happy news was bound to be actualized in the resurrection scenes of earlier plays. Symbolically, in seeking to kill Fédéric, Ladislas is killing his brother: the lower self is killing the higher self—the carnal destroys the spiritual. This is a rueful inversion of the twin motif, for the king-to-be (builder of cities, in the myth) slays the spiritual part in which the civilizing resources of the "self" are said to lie. But the evidence for apprehension concerning the real identity of Ladislas' victim is both implicit in the mythical "structure" of the play and dramatically explicit as well. As early as the first scene, Ladislas threatens not only his spiritual *frère-ennemi*, Fédéric, but his biological *frère-ennemi* as well: "Pour mon frère, après son insolence,/ Je ne puis m'emporter à trop de violence" (I.1). Indeed, doubly enraged by his brother's support of Fédéric and open challenge to himself, Ladislas ominously portends the key event of the play by specifically setting himself against his brother in a mood of bloody vengeance:

> Mon frère contre moi veut prendre sa querelle,
> Et bien plus, sur l'épée ose porter la main!
> Ha! j'atteste du Ciel le pouvoir souverain,
> Qu'avant que le soleil, sorti du sein de l'onde,
> Ote et rende le jour aux deux moitiés du monde,
> Il m'ôtera le sang qu'il n'a pas respecté,
> Ou me fera raison de cette indignité.

(I.1)

This threat of fratricide broods over the entire play. The possibility of its realization is made only greater by the very scheme in which Frédéric and Alexandre have joined forces to frustrate the author of the threat. These spiritual *frères-amis* are worthy successors of such priggishly pure heroes as Dom Bernard and Bélissaire from Rotrou's recent plays and Ménechme-Sosicle from his early plays. In the political structure Frédéric, like Bernard, is of greater prowess but less station than Alexandre, the counterpart of Lope here. Again, when Frédéric reproaches his royal friend for thinking him capable of really wanting his friend's mistress, we see that he is loyal both as *généreux* and chaste lover. Like Lope, Alexandre is intimidated before the king, but the Bernard-like Frédéric speaks up—deferentially, to be sure, but articulately (except when he is interrupted by the angry Ladislas). He has concocted a "dessein" of traded identities because he must suffer the vice of his virtue: he is a perfect *généreux*, compelled to secret action only because the subterfuge "obeys" the desires of his royal friend. Like Genest, Frédéric feels compelled to drop the subterfuge in the name of truth, and he comes to this decision in a verse strikingly like Genest's: "Il faut lever le masque et t'ouvrir ma pensée." The duke urges Alexandre to speak up, to show himself for what he is: "De l'artifice enfin, il faut bannir l'usage,/ *Il faut lever le masque*, et montrer le visage" (III.2; italics added).

The advice not only recalls Genest's strictures against fiction, it also recalls that for Ladislas in theory, and for Venceslas in practice, kingship implies the opposite. He had learned from his father, Ladislas said to the latter earlier, that the art of governing meant: "Mettre bien la franchise et la feinte en usage,/ *Porter tantôt un masque et tantôt un visage*" (I.1; italics added). The parallel between the line of Frédéric and Genest reminds us that *pensée* and *visage* are in a virtually sacramental relationship: the face is the sign of thought, and what is signified is far more important than the sign. But for the king and his older son, the two are in a sacrilegious relationship: the face is at times but a mask of thought. Théodore, too, shows herself to be of a kind as well as kin in the matter: she conceals her love for Frédéric. In doing so she is more pathetic than blameworthy, somewhat like earlier queens in Rotrou. But she is not altogether blameless. In importuning Cassandre to accede to Ladislas, she is using the tenets of *générosité* to satisfy a private rather than a public motive.

In his adolescent hesitation, Alexandre, too, shows himself a part of this family. He and Cassandre reflect a suspicion of the carnal itself that predates even Rotrou's most overtly religious play. Cassandre rejects the reformed Ladislas because he first wanted her as an object of what the old king calls his "folles amours" (I.1) and what she calls his "sales plaisirs" (II.1). According to Alexandre, in his proposal of marriage, Ladislas only follows this unworthy desire: "On peut voir l'avenir dans les choses passées/ Et juger aisément qu'il tend à son honneur,/ Sous ces offres d'hymen un appas suborneur" (III.6). Obviously, for Alexandre and his beloved, marriage is of the utmost spiritual significance (as it was for the converted Adrien in Rotrou's famous play-within-a-play). Yet, the young prince cannot follow his fellow actor's advice here to "lift the mask," and declare his love for Cassandre under his own name. In this concealment lies still further dramatic foreordination of his death at his brother's hand. Names and other "conventions" point to essential realities for these *généreux*, and this leads logically to the ethic of fully open and fair relations with everybody. Therefore, concealment is wrong according to the codes by which the lovers claim to live: *générosité* and chaste desire. *Their* love does not violate a principle concerning rank and station. To Ladislas, Cassandre even proudly asserts of the man she loves: " . . . Son sang ne doit rien au sang dont vous sortez" (II.2). As the language reminds us, her lover's blood is of that very blood Ladislas threatened to shed before the day was out. And as that day comes to an end, we might well remember that still purer figures have suffered unjust death in Rotrou's theater (e.g., Bélissaire).

In the notion of the day's end, we have the most explicit evidence leading us to know the real identity of Ladislas' victim. Warned by the duke of Ladislas' impetuosity, Alexandre finally decides to put aside "les droits de la nature" in order to commit himself totally to "amour." Love is obviously the highest law for these lovers. Chaste desire tends to place Heaven in a transcendental relation to the natural law of family loyalty. The transcendence is not so absolute as in other cases in Rotrou, of course, for Alexandre does show that the world is of some value. Through its forms, one shows one's spirituality and so, "Je prends loi de Cassandre, *épousons dès ce soir* (III.2; italics added). He still hesitates, however, asking the duke to continue to deceive ("trompons") everybody else for a few more days "jusqu'à ses domestiques." This allusion to Cassandre's servants satisfies *vraisemblance* even as it offends the *bienséances*: it explains why the duke would be within Cassandre's palace in the dark of night, offending the strict proprieties by which we would expect so pure a princess to live. Yet, the allusion to a wedding in the flesh that very night must weigh equally for the attentive spectator. Its significance weighs even more heavily when it is reiterated in the next scene. Cassandre emerges from Théodore's room in great distress because of the princess' wish that she accept Ladislas. To comfort her, Alexandre says even more decisively:

> Coupons *dès cette nuit* tout *accès* à ses vœux,
> Et voyez *sans frayeur*, quoiqu'il ose entreprendre,
> Quand vous m'aurez commis une femme à défendre,
> Et quand *ouvertement* en qualité d'*époux*,
> Mon devoir m'enjoindra de *répondre* de vous.
>
> (III.3; italics added)

These words will echo in the heart of the spectator, who later listens as Ladislas describes how he gained *access* to Cassandre's apartment in order to slay him who *answers* as the *husband* he had heard she had taken *that very night*. The night conceals more from Ladislas than it does from the troubled spectator. The latter's apprehension must only increase at the end of the scene when the duke makes still one more allusion to this night in which one brother's marriage will only push the other to a homicidal ardor: "Prévenez *dès ce soir* l'ardeur qui le transporte" (III.3; italics added).

## NOSTALGIA FOR IMMANENCE

Further premonitions of fratricide are less explicit, but no less significant. Dreams have always had high predictive value in Rotrou. Like Valérie's dream in *Le Véritable Saint Genest*, Théodore's turns out to have a truth that even she did not suspect. It *is* a *brother's* head she sees "flying off" at a murderous blow. Ladislas tells us that he knocked on Cassandre's door "au nom du Duc," and we remember that when we last saw the duke and Alexandre, they had resolved to abandon their exchange of names. Théodore's shock at this news may momentarily still the heart's gnawing knowledge that the victim is really someone else. The gnawing starts again with the arrival of the king. Once again, Venceslas broods on his declining years and declining power. He seems considerably less sure of himself than he has in previous scenes. The atmosphere of uncertainty impends dire events. Thus, Fédéric's sudden appearance does not reassure us as similar "resurrections" have in early Rotrou plays; it increases our apprehension of the truth. This becomes still more acute when Fédéric is followed by the plaintive Cassandre. She does not announce immediately the name of the victim, as one might expect given the horror of the crime. Instead, she demands justice first, reviewing in a long speech the quality of one brother as compared with the lack of qualities in the other. These "delaying" tactics on the part of the dramatist only constitute the finishing touch of all the delaying tactics which satisfy our apprehension that "O Dieu! L'Infant est mort!" Indeed, had we not been warned in our hearts that it was Alexandre and not Fédéric who was to die? Had not the assassin himself threatened to shed before the day was out not the blood of his rival but of his brother? The consequences of the mask worn by Fédéric-Alexandre have come to term at a familiar point in a Rotrou play. The dramatist is true to his usual dramaturgy in this crucial scene of revelation.

He is also true to it in the larger structure of the play. The deception by Ladislas and Fédéric is the false datum giving rise to the "illusory" developments of the B portion of this play. As in *Le Véritable Saint Genest* and almost every other play by Rotrou, the second, third, and fourth acts of the total play constitute the middle portion of an A-B-A structure. Alexandre's death is undoubtedly gruesome, but the death of an innocent victim of deception or error is not new in Rotrou, as both *Crisante* and *Bélissaire* have shown.[16] This particular resemblance suggests that on either side of the B portion we might find A portions in which death and murder are justified in the light of a larger spiritual design. Looking at the end of the play, Morel has already perceptively demurred from the persistent condemnation of Ladislas and the view that the play is perforce tragic:

> Marmontel (et la plupart des commentateurs qui l'ont suivi) trouvait choquant que dans les derniers vers de la pièce Ladislas exprimât son espoir de conquérir le cœur de Cassandre. Il se méprenait sans doute sur la véritable nature du personnage, dont la générosité pleinement manifestée efface aux yeux de Rotrou tous les crimes antérieurs. Il se méprenait aussi sur la nature de cette pièce, qui, malgré les situations tragiques qu'elle comprend, est une tragi-comédie.[17]

Morel sees Ladislas' ascension to the throne as "symboliquement la résolution des conflits intérieur et extérieur auxquels le déroulement de la pièce a fait assister le spectateur."[18] The ending is perhaps not so clean-cut in its symbolism. Nevertheless, Morel's view of the symbolic value of the ending does correspond to what the dramatist probably thought he was conveying. In the process of relating the familiar B portions of the play to the specific rule of "no surprise" in the canon, I have already indicated many of the thematic constants giving weight to this view. A close reading of the A portions of the familiar dramatic structure lends even further weight to it. Let us look at the play in those parts.

In the earliest verses of the play, Rotrou has begun to move away from the transcendental theses of his most recent plays:

> J'attends toujours du temps qu'il mûrisse le fruit
> Que pour me succéder ma couche m'a produit;
> Et je croyais, mon fils, votre mère immortelle,
> Par le reste qu'en vous elle me laissa d'elle.

(I.1)

Recent transcendental heroes (Genest, Bélissaire) renounced time altogether. But here, Rotrou's aged king restates the view of time as rehabilitative, so central in his theater of immanence. Linked to this positive view of time is still another metaphorical notion from that theater: natural processes are evidences of the immanent divinity, actualizations of the fruit of full reason, of the potential lying in the seed of innate virtue. Still further, immortality is conceived not in terms of a transcendent realm to which the soul alone is transported but in the notion of generational continuity in the biological processes. In the king's disappointment with his son for his purported lechery, so at variance with his mother's goodness in beauty, we return to the premises of plays like *La Pèlerine amoureuse*. "Mais, hélas! ce portrait qu'elle s'était tracé,/ Perd beaucoup de son lustre et s'est effacé," the king goes on. As in the plays from the theater of immanence, Rotrou seems undisturbed by the transcendental doubts on the value of art and images of nature uttered by Genest just before his death. The beatific vision of a good woman is a sign of grace inherent in the world of things and men. The concept is considerably less simplistic than it was in early plays, of course. Here, for example, Venceslas sees his wisdom as directly connected with the process of aging. In this aging, the son and others see signs of another "natural" consequence of being—not the growth but the loss of efficiency in natural faculties. The debate between father and son on this score even has certain cynical overtones to which I shall want to return in my final assessment of the symbolic significance of the total structure. But for the moment it is important to note that there is nothing irredeemably wicked about the son's doubts about his father's effectiveness as king.

Nor is there anything irredeemably wicked about the crimes with which he is charged. Mlle Van Baelen's insight that, within the running time of the play itself, Ladislas is not guilty of any crimes is to the point. The critic overstates her case, perhaps, for the young prince *has been* guilty of lecherous desire in his initial desire for Cassandre. But like the "instinct" that drives many earlier *un*chaste lovers in Rotrou, his is not fatal. The queen of *L'Innocente Infidélité* saw her royal fiancé's instinct as the temporary and passing compulsions of youth. Here, too, the "instinct enragé qui meut ses passions" (III.7) is attributed to his youth. "Croyez-vous que le Prince en cet âge de feu," Léonor begins, in trying to soothe the princess awakened by her dream, "Où le corps à l'esprit s'assujettit si peu. . . . " She goes on to ask, "Cherchez-vous des clartés dans les nuits d'un jeune homme?" (IV.1). Well before this, the prince himself attributes his passion to his youth. "Ma jeunesse, d'abord, porta ma passion" (II.2), he pleads, having come before Cassandre in that spirit of repentance that has always redeemed faithless lovers in Rotrou. Telling Cassandre that he now seeks in her "une épouse et non une maîtresse," he pleads further that she give herself "au repentir profond,/ Qui détestant mon crime, à vos pieds me confond" (II.2). Like the hero of *La Belle Alphrède*, Ladislas begins the play with the reputation of a lecher; but very early in the action, on bended knee, he is redeemed of that charge. He repents and resolves henceforth to love Cassandre only as he should always have loved her—chastely and religiously:

> Car, enfin, si l'on pèche, adorant vos appas,
> Et si l'on ne vous plaît qu'en ne vous aimant pas,
> Cette offence est un mal que je veux toujours faire,
> Et je consens plutôt à mourir qu'à vous plaire.
>
> (II.2)

The sinner is not forbidden to worship, and none worship so spiritually as Rotrou's reformed "sacrilèges." His father's most frequent term for his lecherous penchant is *caprice*, and, in fact, that penchant is no more than a passing whim as it turns out.

For Ladislas, Cassandre is finally more than a whim: she is as much his beatific vision as Théodore is Fédéric's. This comes out especially in the spirit with which he seeks "punishment" for the death of his brother. Quite rightly, he argues that he could claim innocence of this crime. Like Constance in *La Sœur* when confronted with her son's presumed incest, the criminal claims, "Je pourrais . . . m'excuser sur l'*erreur*" (V.5; italics added). His sister adds that it was dark, besides. Again, as his infidelity through lust was rendered innocent by virtue of youth and repentance, so his fratricide is shown innocent by virtue of circumstances (the dark night) and his different intention. Intentionalism is a reasonable basis of justice in Rotrou's essentialistic ethic. I am aware of the dubiety of Ladislas' reasoning here on the evidence of the play itself. I might anticipate my conclusion to a certain extent by pointing out that his intentionalism and its implied notions of freedom are contradicted by Ladislas right after the crime itself: "De tout raisonnement je deviens incapable" (IV.2). But for the moment I wish to relate Ladislas' intentionalist argument to the theme of redemption to which Ladislas has been linked in so many other motifs before the murder. He is not guilty, he claims, yet he wants to be adjudged guilty because his mistress demands it. Such paradoxical devotion is perhaps horrifying, but it expresses the spiritual dedication to Cassandre that Ladislas has shown since the moment he appeared in the play. With Frédéric's appearance after the report of his death and Ladislas' spiritual regeneration we have two symbolic resurrections that, in a sense, make up for Alexandre's real death. In his devotion Ladislas loses his contradictoriness and thus joins the ranks of the rigidly pure "family" of characters found in Frédéric, Alexandre (with the reservations I've already noted), and especially Cassandre. A chaste *généreuse*, pure under each of the codes of Rotrou's sacramental ethos, Cassandre shows that in not loving her with such spirituality, Ladislas would offend the divinity itself.

If Ladislas is rehabilitated chiefly as a "private person," this is not to suggest that he is still somehow at fault as a *généreux*. We might expect that his devotion to Cassandre will also redeem his offenses to *amitié* against both his brother and his father's vassal. This is the gist of Morel's evaluation of the last act. Yet, given the hierarchies of *générosité*, we may wonder if Ladislas is basically wrong to feel insulted by the ascendancy of Frédéric. Ladislas behaves like the firstborn son of a royal family on most occasions in the running time of the play itself; his passionate self-assertion is in keeping with his position. Many critics have found the role of Frédéric and Rotrou's "invention" of Théodore insipid. Yet, as Sarcey recognized nearly a century ago, their relationship is crucial here: "Il était au seizième et au dix-septième siècle admis, comme vérité incontestable, qu'une princesse du sang royal ne pouvait, sans déchoir, épouser un homme dans les veines de qui un sang royal n'aurait pas coulé."[19] Saint-Marc Girardin notwithstanding, honor is as important here as in the Spanish play. Its key witness is Frédéric. Hence his silence, which enables him to play his pretense of love for the lesser Cassandre. And hence, more importantly, the basis for Ladislas' jealousy of him. Ladislas considers that the vassal usurps his prerogatives in loving the Princess of Cunisberg as much as he usurps them in taking his place in political affairs. It is a mistake to read Ladislas' enmity for Frédéric in the political realm as if it were a consequence of his unrequited love and jealousy. The relation between so-called public and private emotions here is one we have already found in Rotrou: "Quoi, Cassandre sera le prix d'une victoire,/ Qu'usurpant mes emplois, il dérobe à ma gloire." The loss of the beloved here is not an underlying cause but a "last straw." The insults Ladislas feels in one realm are causally independent of those felt in the other. Nevertheless, both derive from his exalted sense of self according to the twin codes of Rotrou's universe. In the state of *dis*grace in which he is slave to his passions, Ladislas is an ineffective ally of his father. The disordered reason deprives its sufferer of a sense of reality in all his pursuits. This is the brunt of Venceslas' reproaches to his son in the first act. However, restored to reason by repenting his *real* crime (the lust for Cassandre), he is eligible for kingship and, as king, "n'hérite point des différends du Prince" (V.9).

The potential kingliness of Ladislas was shown in the first two acts: in the attribution of his "sins" to a transitory stage of youth; in his repentance; in the very possession of what his father calls "le *secret pouvoir*, d'un *charme* que j'ignore" (I.1;

italics added) by which people cherish him even in criticizing him. This secret power is contrasted with the "instinct enragé" that leads Ladislas to his sacrilegious disrespect for the chaste Cassandre. The redeeming power in Ladislas resembles the redemptive grace of previous "sacrilèges" that was rendered by the formula "Je ne sais quel génie." Again, the designation of this power as *charme* reminds us of the compelling, benevolent power of sacramental beauty in earlier Rotrou figures (including men, as in *La Belle Alphrède*). This charm is Ladislas' actual grace in the initial A portion of the drama. Its potential is actualized through his freely chosen act of perfect contrition on two different occasions in the play, once before and again after the murder. Previous critics need not have looked to the denouement of *Le Cid* for the "influence" at work on Rotrou in order to determine how he arrived at his "happy ending." They had only to look to Rotrou himself.

And yet, the "happy ending" seems forced; the whole play seems forced—a nostalgic, flawed attempt to recapture the vision of the youthful plays. Drawn by the force of Ladislas' character and by the mere notion of "rehabilitative time" in the denouement, many critics have failed to pinpoint the really disturbing effect of this strange play. Undoubtedly, it is a tragicomedy if looked at as if the title were *Ladislas*. But the title is *Venceslas*, and it is basically a play about the old king's effort to reconcile fatherhood and kingship. He does not succeed. This is the real tragedy of the play. In the first scene, the father looks for the prince and future king in Ladislas:

> Toutes vos actions démentent votre rang,
> Je n'y vois rien d'auguste et digne de mon sang;
> J'y cherche Ladislas et ne le puis connaître,
> Vous n'avez rien de Roi que le désir de l'être.

(I.1)

But in the aftermath of the dark night of fratricide, the old king finds only his son. Significantly, coming upon his son in the midst of that terrible night, the first words the brooding old man addresses to Ladislas are: "Mon fils? . . . Hélas! . . . Est-ce vous Ladislas" (IV.4). Alas, for "je ne lui puis être et bon père et bon roi" (V.5). This dilemma comes back with such insistence that one is astonished that critics have become more indignant with the rewarded criminal than with the judge who gives him that reward! Ladislas is far less, and Venceslas far more, "criminal" than has been believed.

To be sure, the total action seems designed to absolve the father as well. "Lors," he had warned his son, calling attention to the danger of continuing his profligacy, "pour être tout Roi, je ne serai plus père/ Et vous abandonnant à la rigueur des loix,/ Au mépris de mon sang je maintiendrai mes droits" (I.1). Ladislas reminds us of Créon in saying that he preferred his hate to his quality as potential king (I.3). And the old king again reminds us of Créon in arguing that the stability of his power demands that he punish his son for what he clearly considers his crime: "Mais à l'état, enfin, je dois ce grand exemple,/ A ma propre vertu ce généreux effort" (V.4). There is something weak in this argument from *raison d'état* and self-interest. The argument is heard later, too: Venceslas asserts that in showing his horror of vice by punishing Ladislas, he will prove the legitimacy of the people's choice of him as king (V.5). In one sense this weak argument shows that the son was right in accusing his father of being an indecisive ruler (I.1). Furthermore, the argument is bound to crumble when Théodore, Fédéric, and Cassandre herself acknowledge that "reasons of state" dictate a quite contrary action. Of course, in seeing the play from Ladislas' point of view, the king's hesitancy happily leads him to that illumination in which he sees the justice of saving his son. In this light, he is a Créon who discovers his error in time and so saves his "defendant" from the injustice to which he has blindly condemned him in an abuse or misunderstanding of royal power. Even from Venceslas' point of view, this play would then fit nicely into what Aristotle considered the best of the four kinds of tragic action: " . . . When someone is about to do an irreparable deed through ignorance, and makes the discovery before it is done. . . . The last [fourth] is the best, as when in the *Cresphontes* Merope is about to slay her son, but, recognizing who he is, spares his life."[20] (The "rule" obviously applies as well to *Hercule mourant*, when the ascended god-man spares Arcas.)

But in the value system of *Venceslas*, Rotrou has added one argument too many to the reasons compelling the king to spare his son:

> Pour ne vous perdre pas, j'ai longtemps combattu,
> Mais ou l'art de régner n'est plus une vertu,
> Et c'est une chimère aux Rois que la Justice,
> Ou régnant à l'Etat je dois ce sacrifice.
>
> (V.4)

Kingship is apparently the virtue of rule, not the rule of virtue; kingship here demands that the king punish the murder of Alexandre. Yet, earlier for this king, virtue had nothing to do with the circumstances of Ladislas' homicide or the consequences of the prospective execution. To arguments from positive law, the king opposed the argument of absolute law. The latter is now seen to conflict with the natural law of paternal affection. We are reminded that, as in the case of Antigone and Iphigénie, for Rotrou natural law has always been defined in terms of Catholic theology. The king is God's power on earth. That the Polish king is elected here does not affect the validity of the concept of divine right that informs, or should inform, a king's behavior. Justice demands that Ladislas pay for his crime. That there is a crime according to the natural, innate (or *immanent*) conscience is somewhat obscured by Ladislas' appeal to intentionalism. But in this play there nonetheless has been a *real* effect of misintention (as there was not in the imputed incest of *La Sœur*): Alexandre has been killed. More importantly, Ladislas has committed a crime in the abuse of his reason. Ladislas cannot have it two ways: the moment after the act, he cannot claim that an uncontrollable consequence of a mad passion deprived him of his reason and then claim later that it was all due to a mistaken identity. To argue in this latter fashion is to say that, could he have seen that Alexandre had answered, he would have withheld his blow. This suggests premeditation and responsibility. These are the grounds explicitly informing Genest's assent to grace. Less explicitly but no less clearly, these are the grounds underlying the king's apposition of kingship and virtue in his first judgment of his older son's action. In his earlier advice that his son confess his sins to Heaven, the king is well aware that the excuses of positive law (the dark, the "murmure du peuple," etc), have no status before Heaven's absolute law:

> Allez vous préparer à cet illustre effort;
> Et pour les intérêts d'une mortelle flamme,
> Abandonnant le corps, n'abandonnez pas l'âme;
> Toute obscure qu'elle est, la nuit a beaucoup d'yeux,
> Et n'a pas pu cacher votre forfait aux Cieux.

(V.4)

In the end, Venceslas himself does not heed this stern, innate imperative of divine justice. He heeds another "natural" law: paternal feeling. As we have seen, the two have been increasingly at odds throughout Rotrou's canon. With its law of love, chaste desire in the theater of immanence seemed to lead to a logical connection between conjugal love and the "natural law." In the denouement of *Hercule mourant*, there was no necessary contradiction between natural love and its divine source. However, the emphasis most often fell quite naturally on the material expression rather than the spiritual reference. In Rotrou's theater of transcendence, the spiritual reference of chaste desire tended to be stressed. Virginity was increasingly prized and worldly marriage sublimated as the partners expressed themselves in fraternal and sisterly affection for one another. In *Venceslas* this sublimation has already been noted in the love of Alexandre and Cassandre. But in the feelings that finally move the father to protect his older son's life, we see a return to the linkage between "natural love" and the immanent deity. The old king ends where he had begun: by linking the latter code and its public imperatives to such notions as his wife's beauty being immortalized in her son. Venceslas breaks the sacramental equilibrium into its two components: kingship stresses the power of the spirit or of virtue; fatherhood stresses the power of natural feeling or love. There being no divinity appearing from on high to reconcile the antinomy, the French Venceslas is compelled to admit with his Spanish model that "no hay ser padre siendo rey". The "new law" of charity or mercy supersedes the old law of justice whenever they are at odds.

As the king yields to the father, one suspects that Rotrou might be seeking to return to the religious terms characterizing the resolution of *Hercule mourant*. The concept of "grace" is as persistent in the final scenes of this play as in *La Sœur*, for example. The last act begins with Théodore demanding that Fédéric ask her father "au lieu de notre Hymen, la Grâce de mon frère" (V.1). But one begins to doubt the spirituality of this "grace" as it is insistently linked to a number of purely material concerns. Fédéric is really moved by an ulterior motive, but he adds still more dubious colorations to the grace he asks: "L'état qu'il doit régir lui doit bien une grâce," he tells Venceslas, and then goes on to say that the blood of the infant alone had been shed by Ladislas, but the shedding of Ladislas' own blood will "wound" the entire state. Théodore speaks of "pitié" (like Hercule) but she seems to consider it on a par with reasons of state, self-interest, and so on. Finally, the king himself confirms the implicit argument here that virtue has little to do with the grace he is asked to grant. He poses a choice between a crown upon his son's head or the taking of that head. "Il vous en faut pourvoir, s'il vous faut pardonner," he tells his son. "Et punir votre crime ou bien le couronner."

Obviously, Venceslas is convinced that his son is still guilty. However, as he goes on, one sees the ambivalence in Rotrou's conception of this character and of the whole play. At first, Venceslas argues from reasons of state, including the people's "lesson" to him: "Voulant que vous viviez, [qu']il est las que je règne." As *Antigone* showed us, the people were not always considered so wise. Yet, Venceslas' reasons may be the signs of the immanent will of God and they may tie in still further with the Christian notion of the triumph of mercy over justice whenever these two seem to be at irreconcilable odds. But the king continues by separating his notion of absolute justice, a law that is really supernatural, from the people's notion of justice: "La Justice est aux rois la règne des vertus,/ Et me vouloir injuste est ne me vouloir plus." One might still believe that the king is saying: for me to slay you would be an injustice incompatible with the royal reign of virtues and so the people are right not to want me. But then the king goes on to illuminate his uncomprehending son of his real meaning: "Qui pardonne à son Roi punirait Ladislas,/ Et sans cet ornement ferait tomber sa tête" (V.9).

By definition, a king can do no wrong, nor can he suffer, as king, the imputation of any wrongdoing. The notion is sacramental. High station is the sign of pure spirit. We are reminded that in Corneille, kings are seldom found guilty of wrongdoing: this is attributed to their evil counselors. Few men can tolerate the thought that the highest exemplars of mankind can be guilty of evil. As Kantorovicz has shown, medieval political theory resolved this dilemma in the concept of the king's two bodies: the physical body, which was corruptible (and, at times, corrupting), as distinguished from (but not necessarily opposed to) the spiritual body. Yet, seldom has the concept been applied so cynically. It is evoked not only after the fact of a king's crime but *before the fact of his coronation* in order to preserve his physical body *after the fact of its corrupt act*. As king, the murderer will be beyond the reach of the law. The higher law is used in order to preserve the lower law. The relationship is far more tragic than the death of Ladislas. The play is properly called *Venceslas*, for it is the old king's tragedy.

At the height of the familiar eschatological euphoria of this scene, we seem to have had the abdication of sacrament and the coronation of sacrilege. Most critics of the play are convinced that the former king's invocation of rehabilitative time and the new king's "courteous" hope mean that, as in *Le Cid*, Cassandre will accept her husband's murderer in marriage. Undoubtedly, seen in connection with so many other motifs, this final one suggests that Rotrou was trying to write of a re-sacramentalized universe of the kind found in his earlier plays. Yet, one cannot escape the gnawing evidence of the play itself that the restoration is tragically imperfect. Time is not evoked here in the imperative of Corneille's adjudicatory king: "Laisse faire le temps, ta vaillance et ton roi" (*Le Cid*, V.7). Rather, this former king proposes the notion in an almost tentative fashion, as if aware of the feebleness of such an agency in the face of the loss Cassandre has suffered:

<blockquote>
Cassandre

Puis-je, sans un trop lâche et trop sensible effort,
Epouser le meurtrier, étant veuve du mort:
Puis-je.

Le Roi

Le temps, ma fille.

Cassandre

Ha! quel temps le peut faire?
</blockquote>

And this is all we hear from Cassandre. The play quickly comes to an end with Ladislas' hope that his "soumissions" will weaken her scorn, and with the former king's calls for the "dernières tendresses" toward the dead son and the praise of his own worthy successor to the throne. Over the gallant conditional of the young king and the hopeful imperatives of the old king, there hangs the pall of Cassandre's haunting interrogative. As she doubts time, one remembers her earlier lament in falling into tears when recounting Alexandre's murder: "En cet endroit, Seigneur, laissez couler mes larmes;/ Leurs cours vient d'une source *à ne tarir jamais*" (IV.6; italics added). This promise of eternal, if tearful, fidelity reminds us more of Andromaque than Chimène: In the resolute Cassandre as in the resolute Andromaque one feels that the "larmes" are also "armes." One thinks of Crisante, who was similarly determined to revenge the violator of her honor.

Ladislas has not actually raped Cassandre, of course. But he has done so in spirit, and this is just as bad for her. Moreover, he has murdered her husband. It is true that Cassandre does relent in her demand for Ladislas' head. As she heeds the reasons of state ("le bien public," she calls them), those critics who see a parallel with the denouement of *Le Cid* might find support for their thesis. Still further support might be found in the way in which the old king thereafter persistently includes Cassandre among those whose reasons he finally heeds: "Oui, ma fille; oui, Cassandre; oui, parole; oui, nature!/ Oui, peuple, il faut vouloir ce que vous souhaitez" (V.8). But Cassandre's motives here differ from those of the others mentioned by Venceslas in this moment of illumination. In her surrender to reasons of state, her concluding paradoxical combination of lassitude and resolve has not been sufficiently remarked:

> Je me tais donc, Seigneur, disposez de la vie,
> Que vous m'avez promise et que j'ai poursuivie,
> Au défaut de celui qu'on te refusera,
> *J'ai du sang, cher amant, qui te satisfera.*
>
> (V.6; italics added)

Crisante comes to mind once again: having been deprived of her honor, she slew herself. Occurring in those rare plays of Rotrou in which another threat of bloodshed has issued in real bloodshed, Cassandre's threat should not be taken lightly.

Understanding Cassandre's role better than he did Ladislas', Marmontel, in his revision more than a century later, had Cassandre slay herself. "Ma grâce est en vos mains," he has the repentant Ladislas tell Cassandre. "Voilà donc ton supplice," she tells him, thrusting a dagger into her breast. The irony on the word "grâce" is especially consistent with the *données* of

Rotrou's play. Nevertheless, one wonders if Marmontel has grasped the real grandeur and profundity of Cassandre's intention to commit suicide. One can conjecture that it would be on the very night of her wedding to Ladislas that she would deprive him of herself. However, any denouement other than that actually composed by Rotrou betrays the significance of the play and its place in Rotrou's canon. In its hesitancies, *Venceslas* shows the playwright longing for the immanent verities of his early plays, but clinging to the somber transcendence of his most recent ones.

In *Cosroès*, Tragédie (1648),[21R] one critic has said Rotrou looks back to Corneille's *Rodogune* and *Héraclius* as well as forward to that dramatist's *Nicomède*.[22] He also looks forward, another critic has said, to "the greatest creations of Racine."[23] The most recent editor of the play is reminded of *Hamlet*,[24] and Lancaster is reminded of Saint Germain's *Timoléon* (1639).[25] Certainly, such parallels do come to mind readily. As in *Nicomède*, an old king is beset by his wily second wife to name their child his successor, thus disinheriting the legitimate heir, the king's son by his first marriage. Again, Syra does resemble Corneille's Cléopâtre, the ambitious queen who is also obliged to drink the poison she has prepared for her stepson in *Rodogune*. To this resemblance we might add the parallels between the sets of brothers in both plays: Mardesane resembles Séleucus (at least until he usurps Syroès' power), and Syroès is a somewhat more complicated counterpart to Antiochus. In still another possible echo of Corneille, Narsée's dilemma is comparable to Chimène's in *Le Cid*: each finds that her lover has attacked her parent. On the other hand, noting such "pre-Racinian" motifs as the hesitancy of the young hero of this play, Orlando finds that Rotrou at last breaks with his usual "tempo della metamorfosi" in order to depict "quello dell' oscillazione".[26]

These parallels are helpful in understanding these other plays and, for my purpose here, *Cosroès* itself. However, within Rotrou's own theater, even more helpful parallels can be drawn for this purpose. As Schérer has noted, the theme of royal revolt is anticipated in *Antigone, Iphigénie,* and *Venceslas.*[27] In the latter, Schérer also notes, "Rotrou rencontre pour la première fois des conflits entre proches parents qui sont assez violents pour aller jusqu'au meurtre et qui mettent en jeu l'ambition, l'amour et des conceptions morales et politiques dérivées."[28] Schérer might have made the connection still more close: "J'aime mieux conserver un fils qu'un diadème" (V.9), the old king of the earlier play declared in abdicating; "Et ma tête à ce prix ne veut point de couronne" (V.4), says Syroès. The son has usurped Cosroès' throne only to learn that the final consequence of his act must be the command to execute his father. *Cosroès* offers a corollary to the lesson of *Venceslas*: one cannot be son and king. Here, too, numerous features suggest that the author might have posed the conflict only to resolve it through familiar religious concepts. But the resolution is perhaps even less successful here.

True, as Schérer and Orlando have remarked, by omitting Cellot's didactic Christian allusions in his reworking, Rotrou has, in one way, "de-Christianized" the story. Yet, with the possible exception of *Bélissaire, Cosroès* comes closer than any "secular" play in Rotrou to the special Christian way of looking at the tension between divine justice and divine mercy. Mardesane will reign, says the old king, "par le char éclatant du Dieu que je révère" (II.1). His image is the familiar one of God the Heavenly King in whose name the kings of the earth rule. Kings of the earth are regarded as the divinity immanent in the things of God's creation. This comes out more in the reign of Syroès than of his father, as I shall bring out below. For now, I wish to stress that Syroès' reign conveys a religious sense not only of justice but of charity. Recalling the officer sent to arrest his father, Syroès asks: "Condamné par mes *pleurs,* quel Dieu pourra m'*absoudre*?" (IV.2; italics added). A God of mercy is evoked in terms of a sacramental penance, even as a message of "pitié" by Hercule, another penitent son, recalled the same sacrament and its absolving grace. The overtones in both plays are Christian. Of course, the relation of justice to mercy is very different at the end of *Cosroès*. Rotrou's final tragedy does not present the clearly re-sacramentalized universe found at the end of his first tragedy. Here, one of these divine attributes prevails over the other in the realm of men. One feels that the only place justice and mercy can be reconciled is on high, in the heaven of saints rather than in the earth of sinners. However, before we explore this transcendental stress of the final moments of *Cosroès*, it will be interesting to see how the dramatist clings in almost every prior moment to the immanentism of his early plays.

Syroès' indecisiveness seems to make him "new" in Rotrou's canon for many critics. Yet, the theme is not new. Like many a previous hero, Syroès hesitates to act in a B portion of the play because he is confronted with a tension between values he had assumed to be reconciled in an initial A portion of the play. Characteristically, the tension rises because of a false datum. Indeed, there are two data whose falsity some critics tend to dismiss: first, Narsée's presumed identity as the daughter of Syra and, second, Syra's own report of Syroès' "threat" to her at the end of the first scene of the play. Since the latter is the least significant and the simpler to deal with, let us consider it first.

The debate between stepmother and stepson takes place according to the strictest interpretation of *générosité*. In the first two verses of the play, Syra charges Syroès with being "indigne" and "insolent," for he is born of lesser rank than she and her son. She contends that her son is the truer heir because *each* of his parents is of higher rank. Syroès is not unaware of Mardesane's dignity; he respects that son, he tells his adversary, because he sees in him "votre image" (I.1). We are on the grounds of immanent belief found at the beginning of *Venceslas*. However, on related grounds—primogeniture and patrilineal succession—Syroès opposes the queen's ambition. When Syra counters that his mother was of lesser rank than she, Syroès acknowledges that his mother may not have been "sœur, fille et veuve de Rois," but she had a *prior* dignity: the first love of his father. Chaste desire is invoked here as in Rotrou's theater of immanence: it is to be respected first whenever love and duty, nature and convention, charity and justice seem to be at odds. From the outset,

Syroès states the conflict that arises, in a different form, when he is asked to judge his father. But, for the moment, Syroès does not see any contradiction between the two codes. In an allusion to the divine, he reminds us that ambition like the queen's has always been sacrilegious in Rotrou:

> Il [Mardesane] prévoit le péril des trônes usurpés,
> A leurs superbes pieds il voit des précipices,
> Et sait que des Tyrans on fait des sacrifices,
> Il sait qu'il est au Ciel un Maître souverain,
> Qui leur ôte aisément le sceptre de la main,
> Et dont le foudre est fait pour ce genre de crimes,
> Pour tomber en faveur des Princes légitimes;
> Le crime lui plairait, mais la punition
> Lui fait fermer l'oreille à votre ambition.
>
> (I.1)

Standing apart from Heaven in this ambition, Syra stands aside from the "earth" as well. The co-operative relation between heaven and earth characterizes all of Rotrou's theater. Even in extreme moments of "transcendence," his heroes find it hard to view the things of this world as contradictory signs of divine intention. In varying degrees all of Rotrou's heroes have seen the world as a sacramental sign. At all points in the action, Syroès' so-called inaction is due to his scruples as a believer in the twin codes of the sacramental ethos. He is vindicated in this faith by all the signs intended to vindicate Ladislas and other heroes in Rotrou. Hired assassins can no more carry out the orders of Syra here than could the assassins, also hired by a vengeful queen in *Bélissaire*. Like Léonse or Narsès in that play, Sardarigue tells Syroès that he is so indebted to the prince for his bounty that he cannot arrest him; horrified by the murderous proposals of Syra, Hormidaste and Artanasde quit her service in order to join with Syroès. Again, the people are on Syroès' side as they were on Ladislas'. All this smacks of *raison d'état*, to be sure. When Syroès echoes Venceslas' litany of motives ("Oui, Princes, oui mes droits, oui Perse, oui mon Pays"

[I.4]), the syntactical parallel may add to the feeling that this prince's usurpation is as illegitimate as Venceslas' abdication. Yet, *raison d'état* is much purer here than in *Venceslas*, for it is guaranteed by the purity of Syroès.

(I am "reading" the play at this point to show its strong resemblance to Rotrou's early plays. I am aware that, in the end, the young usurper blames himself for the "maudite ambition" [IV.2] that his father attributes to himself earlier [II.1]. I shall return to this complexity in my final assessment.)

Syroès stands opposed to Syra. True, their names resemble each other, suggesting a oneness of self. But if so, we have the familiar divided self of Rotrou's theater of immanence: Syra is the lower self and Syroès the higher. This relation is repeated still more conventionally in the motif of the stepbrothers: the *frères amis* who become *frères ennemis*, as in *Venceslas*. Here, the richness of Rotrou's symbolic imagination is striking. Mardesane inherits the bad blood of both parents and thus succumbs to "maudite ambition," whereas in Syroès the good blood of the mother overcomes the bad blood of the father. The real mother is also opposed here to the stepmother: the *rang* and *sang*, in dramatic conflict in terms of *générosité* or justice, are reconciled in terms of chaste love or charity. Syroès' goodness through the mother also stands against the "evil" that some critics attribute to the king's counselors. Palmyras, in particular, has been especially suspect for his deviousness and ambition. There is no doubt that the minister is shrewd and opportunistic. He placed his own child in the crib of a dead princess in order to insure high fortune for that daughter. He suggests to the young prince that "le Ciel est inutile à qui ne s'aide pas" (I.3). We suspect that his advice comes from very different motives from those that inspired Genest's similar view on divine will and human responsibility. Still, Palmyras' "opportunism" cannot be viewed with the strictures leading Orlando to find "inaccettabile l'idea de considerare un Palmyras 'strumento' della Provvidennza."[29] A father's substitution of one infant for another to insure the prosperity of his child was the key to the providential ending of *La Sœur*. Even accepting

Palmyras' conduct as sacrilegious, the whole history of Rotrou's theater suggests that one can hardly doubt the possibility if not the probability that he is now using a "malheur" as the instrument of benevolent determinism.

The realistic advice of Palmyras (Heaven helps the self-helping) seems less casuistical on the lips of the pious captain of the guards, Sardarigue: "Le sort vous aidera, mais prêtez-lui les mains" (II.4). In the same speech Sardarigue also evokes the hallowed concept of rehabilitative time. Syntactically, the advice links Syroès (and all who support him) to such pure heroes as Genest and Fédéric (*Venceslas*):

> Issu du grand Cyrus et de tant de Monarques,
> Prince, de vos aieux conservez-vous les marques;
> *Il est temps de paraître* et temps de voir vos lois
> Dispenser les destins des peuples des Rois.
>
> (II.4; italics added)

"Il est temps de passer du théâtre aux autels" (IV.7), said the converted Genest; "il n'est plus temps d'aimer sous un nom empruneté," Fédéric told Alexandre. The essential dynamic of all of Rotrou's theater—the movement from potential to actual, from non-being (or incomplete being) to full being—characterizes *Cosroès* as well. And it must be emphasized that *being is appearance*: "Il est temps de *paraître*" is Sardarigue's advice here. In a sacramental universe appearance and reality coincide, for signs and names, words and deeds are not merely "nominal"; they are real. The opportunistic Palmyras himself follows this dynamic: after hearing his daughter, Narsée, attack him as an enemy, he cries, "O Nature, il est temps/ Que tu mettes au jour secret de vingt ans . . . (IV.4). In time, what had to be, is; the truth comes out.

Cosroès proves the thesis in its negative expression as surely as Syroès proves its positive. From the old king's first words we hear the ancient theme that vice is its own worst punishment. In those words we are also reminded that the sufferings of "hell" are real: "Ce corps n'a plus d'endroit, exempt de vos blessures," he tells the "noires divinités," who are "des vengences du Ciel ministres effroyables". He evokes the image of nature's monsters ("vos couleuvres") as still other agents of this heavenly vengeance. Now, Bélissaire, too, evoked nature's monsters as his enemies. Yet, the consonance of images could not dramatize more radically the difference between Rotrou's theater of immanence, recalled here, and the theater of transcendence in *Bélissaire*. In the latter play, monsters and other "commun debris de la nature" were to be found *everywhere*. In *Cosroès*, the sacrilegious old usurper alone suffers the "morsures" of such creatures in the "remords éternel" that Heaven sends him in punishment for his deed (II.1).

Usurpation is presented throughout the play in this light. Before he succumbs to ambition, Mardesane describes the same vice in his mother as "illusions . . . belles visions . . . un beau songe." In one of the most striking appositions of Rotrou's theater, Mardesane speaks disdainfully of "ce fantôme puissant,/ Ce pouvoir usurpé" (I.2). It was to this phantom power that Cosroès had given himself twenty years earlier and to which once again he succumbs with his "esprit *altéré* d'un père *furieux*" (I.3; italics added). Against this altered reason, Syroès rightly declares: "J'ai pour moi la raison, le droit et la nature" (I.3). He is speaking primarily according to the tenets of *générosité*, by which "nature" or natural law is really the law of Heaven. This law is implanted in the hearts and minds of men and "contingently" visible in such institutions as primogeniture and patrilineal heritage. Now, Cosroès had not exactly violated this law through his usurpation; he had only anticipated his inheritance in assuming the throne. He is nonetheless guilty of sacrilege, for he slew his father. Like many an earlier sacrilege in Rotrou, he broke the fused codes of chaste desire and *générosité*. The law of love was and is the higher one, as we see in Cosroès' remorse and in Syroès' reluctance to slay his father: " . . . De ma vie enfin je hasarde la course,/ Si mon impiété n'en épuise la source" (I.3). The explicitly religious concept of piety is linked in the play most often with the law of love. Syroès is unable to violate this religious injunction, but his hesitations on this score are signs of an inner strength. Among well-known critics of the play, Lancaster is unique in attributing to Syroès relative strength of character.[30]

Strength against sacrilege flows from a virtuous, rational understanding of reality and a fullness of being. Surrender to sacrilege shows a deprivation of reason and an incompleteness of being. The concept had already been implicit, of course, in the injunctions by both Palmyras and Sardarigue that Syroès help heaven in its work. The corollary of this notion is that freedom is not really a choice of ends but of means. To think it involves a choice of ends is to presuppose that ultimate reality is divisible or that one can sanely refuse to follow the "natural inclination" to do good. These are the concepts of freedom and rationality underlying the dramatic conflicts and resolutions of Rotrou's theater of immanence, we remember. (Certain conservative strains of modern psychiatric theory come close to the concepts of freedom and rationality in the sacramental ethos: criminal behavior is perforce insane, "adjustment" is the evidence of rationality, and so on).

The character of Syra, in particular, is best understood in light of these theological concepts. In spite of her fierce pride and generally open behavior, I think it a mistake to see her as a precursor of the modern, existentialist hero, on the one hand,[31] or of a *généreuse* from Corneille, on the other. Orlando finds that she may be excused for charging Syroès with an attempt on her life because he touched his hand to his sword at the end of their first confrontation. The critic is aware that the reader, at least, knows this charge is not true. Stage directions make it clear that Syroès merely touches his sword as a gesture of the power on which he can rely. The queen has even started off, is not near her stepson, and stops only when her own son appears. When the latter sees his brother's hand on his sword hilt, he asks the meaning of this "threat." The older brother then denies Syra's "calomnie" that he intended to attack her. However, Mardesane seems satisfied with Syroès' explanation: "Je lui montrais ce fer comme mon défenseur." The queen's son even criticizes her ambition, once she has gone. Now, Orlando sees the queen's later report of these events not as a calumny but "probabilimente sincera nella sua passionalità."[32] The accused Syroès calls it by another name: "imposture" (II.3). The context justifies Syroès more than Syra. In private with the old king, she had just charmed—indeed, given her manner, we might say seduced—him into breaking the laws of heaven and earth by giving the throne to Mardesane. Syra's public accusation of her stepson is only the final step in her scheme to have Cosroès abandon both the right use of his office and his reason.

In the relation between this husband and wife, we are far from the sisterly and brotherly affection of previous couples in Rotrou—Adrien and Natalie, for example. Instead, like Hermante in *L'Innocente Infidélité*, Syra uses the code of chaste desire in an impious ambition for worldly power as an end in itself. She urges the cause of Mardesane by reminding her husband of this son "dont vos chastes ardeurs ont honoré ce flanc" (II.1). (Theologically, this use of the sacred for the sake of the worldly is called a simony. In the religious climate of Rotrou's time, this view of her motivation would increase the audience's antipathy to her.) She has also spoken of Syroés' ambition, warning her husband that his first son could not tolerate his father's presence once he had assumed the throne. Knowing their characters at this point, the spectator is prepared to believe this insinuation more of Mardesane than Syroès! Preoccupied with the "tribunal céleste" to which he will soon go (II.2), Cosroès is only too ready to heed his wife's arguments, indebted as he is to her: "C'est un prix que je dois à l'amour de Syra" (II.2). Later, he will blame chiefly his ambition as the motive leading him to his marriage to Syra; but in this line as elsewhere in the play, we sense that he soiled his throne in soiling his couch. Whatever the first sin, carnal desire and ambition are obviously as intertwined in the disordered reason of Cosroès as they were in the disordered reason of Ladislas before his repentance.

When Syra is before us on stage, she maintains her sacrilegious outlook with a lucidity and rationality greater than anyone else's in the play. This intense spiritual self-possession is Lucifer-like. It has been the basis of the comparison of Syra with Corneille's Cléopâtre by traditional critics and for praise of her freedom by recent existentialist critics. Yet, it is hardly an image of fierce self-possession that Narsée evokes in speaking of the final moments of the woman whom she now knows is not her mother:

> J'ai jugé toutefois ne pouvoir sans faiblesse
> Ne point prendre de part au *malheur* qui la presse;
> L'éclat qui me jaillit de sa condition
> Me procure l'honneur de votre affection;
> Je suis sinon sa fille, au moins sa créature,
> Et du moins à ses soins je dois ma nourriture;
> Mais la voyant *en pleurs* sur le corps de son fils,
> *Appeler les destins et les Dieux ennemis,*
> A ce *triste spectacle*, interdite, éplorée,
> Sans pouvoir dire un mot je me suis retirée.
>
> (V.7; italics added)

Like Hermante, Syra acknowledges the gods in damning them: profanation is a religious act. One is hard put to find that the sacrilegiously defiant Syra has broken with "la morale traditionnelle" in any fundamental way. Like love of God, hatred of him is an ontological proof of his existence. One is hard put to find any of the dignity existentialist critics seek in the pathetic figure of the prostrate mother. In the end Syra is closer to the beaten Théodore of *Bélissaire* than she is to the chthonian Hermante of *L'Innocente Infidélité*. Syroès asserted his authority as king in an automatic generalization of the way things are: "Quittant le nom de Roy, c'est à moi qu'il le doit," he said of his father in arguing with the ambitious queen. She could invoke only opinion against this reality: "Il *croit* servir l'Etat par cette préférence" (III.3), she feebly retorted. In a world where the higher reason expresses itself in all things and especially institutions, opinion is not to be confused with insight. Guided by opinion to her doom, Syra occupies a fitting place among the heap of sacrilegious bodies at the foot of the scaffold to which Syroès and Narsèe run at the end of the play.

Among those bodies is that of Mardesane. Its presence there actualizes the threat, the potential of which his brother warned in the initial A portion of the play. Mardesane had even "warned" himself that he would end in such desecration, should he succumb to cursed ambition:

> Qui veut faire usurper un droit illégitime,
> Souvent, au lieu d'un Roi, couronne une victime;
> Et l'Etat est le Temple, et le Trône l'autel,
> Où cette malheureuse attend le coup mortel.
>
> (II.2)

This politico-religious insight concludes a long speech in which this strange character, ultimately sacrilegious by his own lights, gives a different perspective on the conception of freedom from the one found in what Vahanian describes as our modern, post-Christian era:[33]

> Un trône attire trop, on y monte sans peine,
> L'importance est de voir quel chemin nous y mène,
> De ne s'y presser pas, pour bientôt en sortir,
> Et pour n'y rencontrer qu'un fameux repentir.

For modern man, freedom may be a choice of ends. For a Rotrou hero once again, it is a choice of means rather than ends. Here, the choice is fundamentally between two negatives: either resistance to "unreason" or surrender to "unreason." Freedom consists in the commission of crime or, religiously speaking, sacrilege. In the final A portion of the play, each of the "sacrilèges" comes to his deserved death. Only Mardesane dies with some dignity: in a suicide answering to "un généreux conseil," as Narsée puts it. This dignity is perhaps a sign of Heaven's kindly regard for his relatively lesser sin: he had been the *purest* of the lot of sinners, no doubt. His death is no less just, for in his "trial" before the new king, he had proven the prideful ravages of the ambition that, he had been warned, would result from his usurpation of the throne.

Power corrupts and absolute power corrupts absolutely those who do not have just title to it: this is the lesson of the deaths of Mardesane, his mother, and Cosroès. The usurpation of power has proved to be the chief false datum of this play. In an eschatological justification with a familiar tripartite pattern, the consequences of this false datum are, happily, not realized.[34] Syra rather than Syroès has been the "indigne" and the "insolent." Lust and ambition, traditional imperfections of being in Rotrou's theater, have been only the illusions of a transitory middle part of the play. Syroès gives emphatic witness to the eternal "verities":

> Par quel aveuglement n'avez-vous pas jugé,
> Qu'ayant des Dieux au Ciel, j'en serais protégé?
> Doutez-vous que l'objet de leurs soins plus augustes,
> Est l'intérêt des Rois dont les causes sont justes?

(V.2)

Once again in Rotrou, the dramatic A-B-A supports an ethical Q.E.D.

The "orthodoxy" of *Cosroès* within the canon is still more clearly demonstrated if we give the role of Narsée its proper weight. Like Stiefel, Lancaster considers the role an afterthought, viewing the mention of her in the Elzévir edition as an addition to the original version.[35] Taking into account Schérer's inclusion of the role in his edition, Knight has been more perceptive about the role, seeing it as a "possible source of interesting dramatic tension." However, he finds that the role is "late and clumsily introduced," and he regrets that it is "withdrawn, after a long story of substituted babies which proves her to be someone else's daughter."[36] But in Schérer's edition, the first mention of Narsée occurs in I.3, starting at verse 289:

## NOSTALGIA FOR IMMANENCE

> Que peut contre Syra le courroux qui me presse,
> Si j'adore en sa fille une auguste Princesse,
> De qui l'autorité peut rompre mes desseins,
> Et faire à ma fureur choir les armes des mains.
>
> (I.3)

Coming fairly early in the first act, this news does not seem inordinately late either within the play as such or within the context of Rotrou's earlier dramatic practice. What is more important, the relative delay in introducing this news seems anything but clumsy: it gives signs of a superb psychological and dramatic understanding of the mechanism of repression. Finally forced to the surface at the end of the scene, this private motive casts a dubious light over the litany of public motives that Syroès has offered in his arguments with Syra and Mardesane. Even more seriously, within the "natural law of love," this motive casts a shadow over the "pious" love for his father that Syroès has just evoked (verses 273-86) to resist Palmyras' advice to seize power! The dramatic tension could not be greater.

In a footnote to this scene, Schérer perceptively describes the scene he has restored as "une indispensable préparation au rôle important que jouera Narsée à partir du III<sup>e</sup> acte".[37] Narsée is as important to the denouement of *Cosroès* as the traditionally minimized role of Aricie is to the denouement of *Phèdre*. In Racine's greatest play, Aricie is forbidden to Hippolyte on public grounds: she is the heir to a kingdom his father has dubiously acquired in one of his conquests. Yet, in fact, Hippolyte uses these public motives for private purposes. He says he comes to Aricie in order to restore what is rightly hers, but he knows that he has really come to see her as his beloved. He openly avows as much in one of the great lines of French drama: "Je vois que la raison cède à la violence" (II.2). Hippolyte, the chaste refuser of love, has been brought into love's tragic nexus. The nexus is tragic not because the mistress is "publicly" forbidden to her lover but because she is an object of love and he "privately" forbids himself love. To reverse a usual practice, we might apply the concepts of Rotrou's canon here to demonstrate the truly tragic character of Racine's vision. Like many Rotrou lovers, Hippolyte relies on *générosité* in order to realize a desire he knows to be forbidden by chaste desire. Nor is there a final peripety reconciling these two codes, an eschatological resolution showing that he had the right to love Aricie. On the other hand, in Rotrou's *Cosroès* the tension between the codes is relieved by the disclosure that its source is unreal, a mere illusion. The tragic potential is left unrealized because Narsée is *not* Syra's daughter.

The disclosure gives rise to what might be an inadvertently comic scene. As Palmyras teases his daughter with the knowledge that is his and ours, there is something grotesque in the playfulness of their exchange:

Narsée

J'ai malgré mon courroux du respect pour le Roi.

Palmyras

Quand vous me connaîtrez, vous en aurez pour moi.

Narsée

Quel objet de respect, l'ennemi de ma mère!

Palmyras

Votre mère plutôt m'a toujours été chère!

(IV.4)

Again, this familiar situation of substituted babies leads to a paradoxical expression of another favorite motif of Rotrou. When he learns Narsée's real identity, Syroés exclaims in joy:

Le reproche était juste, aux bouches de la Cour,
Que le sang de Syra, m'eût donné de l'amour;

Et son aversion, pour moi si naturelle,
Ne me pouvait souffrir d'aimer rien qui vint d'elle.

(IV.2)

The "cri *contre* le sang" is as expressive as the "cri *du* sang."[38] Furthermore, Palmyras' impulsion to reveal the truth is, in a non-satirical sense, a part of the comic spirit at work in this play as in all of Rotrou. The inevitability at work in Rotrou's universe is benign rather than tragic. Through the false datum of Narsée's identity as through the false datum of sacrilegious ambition (Syra, Mardesane, Cosroès), Rotrou remains faithful to his dramatic practice and moral vision. Usurpation and sacrilege are redeemed by divine foreordination.

And yet, there is the denouement:

Syroès (*furieux*)

Et bien, cruels, êtes-vous satisfaits?
Mon règne produit-il d'assez tristes effets?
La couronne, inhumains, à ce prix m'est trop chère,
Allons, Madame, allons suivre ou sauver mon Père.

Palmyras (*le suivant*)

Ne l'abandonnons point.

Sardarigue

Ses soins sont superflus,
Le poison est trop prompt, le Tyran ne vit plus.

FIN

Many critics have found a way of reconciling this tragic ending to "regular" dramatic practice in the period and, more importantly in this context, to Rotrou's usually hopeful outlook. Syroès' threat to commit suicide may be no more real than that of many another Rotrou hero and heroine. Calling attention to this previous practice, Schérer adds that Narsée and Palmyras will probably dissuade the prince from his intention.[39] In this light the "happy ending" of the final A portion of the drama lies beyond the running time of the play. By the same token, its initial A portion lay before the running time, in the play of Heaven with its inevitable condemnation of Syra and the substitution of Narsée for the dead daughter of Syra. Ironically, however, the role of Heaven suggests that the tragic premises of the play remain, whether the prince carries out his threat to self-slaughter or not.

The price of kingship, Syroès learns, is "tristes effets." He had had a glimmering of this truth in Mardesane's death: "Cruels," he had exclaimed at that news, "voilà l'effet de vos nobles maximes" (V.7). True, he himself had ordered that execution, and it would be surprising if he were not pleased that Mardesane had at least died with some nobility. Nevertheless, the news teaches Syroès that there is an irreconcilable conflict between human feeling and "nobles maximes." The news of his father's impending death brings the lesson home with even greater force. Like Mardesane's, Cosroès' death is self-inflicted. More importantly, neither the orders of Syroès nor of his minister lead directly to the old king's death. The son had resisted executing his father out of a mercy whose Christian overtones I have already stressed: "Condamné par mes pleurs, quel Dieu m'absoudra?" (IV.2). And in this final moment, in the "limit situation" of his father's "trial" he can no more get away from the view of patricide as an *impiéte* than he could before seizing power. When Palmyras warns him that he must retract his order to spare all three defendants, he replies:

> Je n'ai pu mieux défendre un cœur irrésolu,
> Où le sang a repris un Empire absolu;
> Vous deviez imposer silence à la nature
> Qui contre vos avis *secrètement murmure*,
> Et me fait préférer le péril d'une mort

A l'inhumanité d'un si barbare effort.
Il faut pour tant de force une vertu trop dure.

(V.6; italics added)

In an ideal, aristocratic world of royal *généreux*, the rhyming of *rang* and *sang* is moral as well as poetic. But now the two are no longer apposite; *sang* is a secret murmur opposed to *rang*: "Je ne sens plus mon rang/ Et [qu']en mon ennemi j'aime encore mon sang" (V.4). The concept and its formulation ("secrètement murmure") are familiar from Rotrou's earlier plays as the sufficient grace guiding offending heroes to repent their crimes and infidelities. Like so many of them, Syroès also repents an "infidelity" in the name of a natural law not of duty but of love.

In *Cosroès*, as in *Venceslas*, Rotrou seeks to reconcile justice and mercy and only leaves us with deep doubt about the possibility of such a reconciliation. At the outset, for the young Syroès as for the old Venceslas, there is a conflict between two values rather than between a value and a non-value. Understanding this, we not only appreciate the strength and poignancy of these characters but also see the unique moral status of *Cosroès* when we compare it with Rotrou's earlier "resolutions" of the same conflict. In *Hercule mourant*, for example, the *pitié* that God brings from on high corrects a potentially unjust act rather than a just one. Similarly, even in *Le Véritable Saint Genest*, Rotrou posits the possibility of reconciling the Roman and Christian concepts of piety. In that most obviously Christian of his plays, the conflict is not really between two different laws, justice and mercy, but between two different conceptions of justice. Here, paradoxically enough, in divesting Cellot's *Chosroës* of its overt Christian references, Rotrou has come closer than in any other play thus far to dramatizing the Christian tension between God's justice and God's mercy. In responding to the "natural law" of mercy, the son has not forgotten his father's usurpation of the throne. But love is a redeeming virtue here. "Mon *cœur* contre mon sang s'ose en vain révolter. . . . J'ai fait de ma *tendresse* une fausse vertu;/ A l'objet d'un Etat mon lâche sang s'est tu" (V.4; italics added). *Sang* and *tendresse* are opposed to *cœur*.

Once again, we must be wary of Pascalian overtones in studying both *cœur* and its etymologically-linked word *courage* in Rotrou. *Cœur* and *courage* evoke the public self in the dramatist's work. This is obviously the sense of *cœur* in *Cosroès*, where it seems to include not only the order of *esprit* as understood by Pascal but also his order of *chair*. Opposed to this order of *cœur* in Rotrou is an order of *sang* with its particular virtue of *tendresse*. Once we make these semantic adjustments, we see that the dramatist, like the philosopher, distinguishes between an order of love (Rotrou's *sang* or *tendresse*, Pascal's *cœur* or *charité*) and an order of justice (Rotrou's *cœur*, Pascal's *esprit-chair*). The orders are not necessarily at odds with one another in principle. Even in practice, some sense of Rotrou's touching desire to reconcile all antinomies can be found in Syroès' reproach to his blood as "lâche." The order of *sang* must not keep its reasons and values to itself; it must make them public. Nevertheless, Syroès shows us clearly that the order of charity conflicts with such public values as the defense of a throne. Here he accuses even himself of ambition. According to primogeniture and patrilineal inheritance, we know him to be wrong. However, according to the higher law of *sang* or love, he is right: concern with station is a false value. Redeemed by mercy in his own sacrilegious ambition, he has returned to a real value whose grace he wishes to extend to his sacrilegious family. *Returned* is a key concept here, for he now sees that rank and ambition are the false data that have led him to contemplate an even worse sacrilege: the execution of the members of his family. But in this A-B-A pattern, the thesis that is proven is an ominous one. The real datum of love is not vindicated; there are no miraculous repentances and resurrections in this denouement. Instead, the eschatological judgment vindicates the quality that Syroès has come to see as the very opposite of love. The loving son fails in his effort to incarnate divine mercy. Justice prevails instead.

*Divine* justice? That the justice could be viewed as divine is apparent from the many motifs I have reviewed. Heaven's surveillance of the world on behalf of just kings is proven in the final words of Cosroès himself. He died, says Sardarigue, with the awareness that

> Il faut du sort de Perse assouvir la furie,
> Accorder à mon Père un tribut qu'il attend,
> Laisser à Syroès le trône qu'il prétend,
> Et de tant de tyrans terminer la dispute.

(V.8)

As in *Venceslas*, Rotrou returns to the notion of the immanent deity whose presence gives both shape and meaning to the world. However, in *Cosroès*, the divinity gives undeniable evidence that He is a God not of love but of justice. He surveys the world on behalf of just kings, but not of loving sons. On the last occasion in which we see him in that world, Syroès has invited Narsée to join him in a choice between the suicide of the virtuous or the salvation of the sinful. The invitation is as disturbing as the haunting question of Cassandre: "Ha! quel temps le peut faire?" On the basis of Syroès' persistent "hesitancy," we might hope that he will not choose suicide. However, he had found the strength to withdraw the sentence of death he had imposed on his family. Should he find the strength to carry through his threat to suicide, should Narsée join him, they would deprive this world of its last signs of sanctifying grace.

CHAPTER FIVE

*Last Things . . . First Things . . .*

ROTROU'S prolific theater closes with *Dom Lope de Cardone*, Tragi-comédie (1649).[1] Here, a stern king and father forgives his son, Dom Pèdre, for his misdeeds as both lover and *généreux*. It is as if the playwright wished to correct the ambivalences of recent plays like *Dom Bernard de Cabrère* and *Venceslas*. Here, a deserving vassal, Lope, having himself incurred the king's displeasure, is rehabilitated by the king's son, the Bernard-like Pèdre. Again, both in his *sales désirs* and in his triumph over them, Pèdre reminds us of Ladislas. The grace he demands of his father on behalf of Lope manifests the power he has found in himself to overcome the flesh.

The grace would hardly seem sufficient, say, to many of the Jansenists whom Pascal defended in *Les Lettres provinciales*. For them the words Pèdre addresses to his mistress after his father's pardon of Lope will be more significant:

> Eh bien, inexorable, êtes-vous satisfaite
> De l'importunité dont je vous ai défaite?
> Et le barbare effort que j'ai fait sur mon cœur
> A-t-il quelque rapport avec votre rigueur?

(V.5)

Jansenists would probably find no greater sacrilege in all of Rotrou's theater: Pèdre has used the quality of mercy itself as a means of winning the woman after all. His eye has been cocked toward her, they could say, from the moment he demanded Lope's "grace" in a grotesque play on words. "Je demande sa tête et non pas son trépas," he tells his father, who has misunderstood his demand for Lope's head. This world is too full of such casuistical "misunderstandings," strictly Jansenistic critics might feel. They will understand that the world of this play is a market place of virtue. The prince uses his sister as a lever of love; the princess admits that her royal appearance conceals a demeaning love; a brother uses his sister as a lever of love in his relations with the murderer of the lover for whom she grieves; loyal vassals count on their past services to move the king to "discount" their violation of his law against dueling; and so on. Having condemned Lope as a matter of principle, the king himself at first refuses pleas of mercy from the women out of sheer expediency: "Qui, sujet seulement, m'a pu désobéir,/ Gendre un jour, se pourrait résoudre à me trahir" (V.2). Little wonder, the truly pious might say, that Heaven is mentioned only as an afterthought by this casuistical king of a world of spiritual money-changers.

And yet, this time that familiar formula of qualification must reject, rather than lead into, Jansenistic reservations. The quality of mercy is not strained in Dom Lope's resurrection through pardon. Nor is the quality of justice strained by the rejection of this world by Rotrou's transcendental heroes. For Lope and Pèdre, as for Adrien and Genest, the things of this world, including self-interest and reason, are the instruments through which divine mercy manifests itself. Even more than those Christian martyrs, Rotrou's men and women show in the last act of his theater that the order of charity *is* of this world. Caesar's realm has become permeated with the shaping truth of God's realm. The tendencies of Rotrou's theater of immanence rather than those of his theater of transcendence inform the epiphany of grace with which this play ends. In Rotrou we might well apply to this, and to every tragicomedy, Northrup Frye's insight into Shakespeare's comedy and romance: "His festive conclusions with their multiple marriages are not concessions: they are conventions built into the structure of the play from the beginning."[2] These conclusions are part of the "natural perspective" Frye finds in the great English dramatist to whom Rotrou has often been compared. It may seem that in his last play he has once again unduly emphasized the naturalness of his own perspective. Once again, it is a question of emphasis. True 'to his lifelong swing between the poles of sacramental figuralism, in a subsequent play the dramatist would perhaps have emphasized the spiritual rather than the material pole in this "natural perspective."[3] But, then, who is to say that the quality of mercy is not spiritual? Who is to say that it is not a forethought of the Heaven on which the king-father of this play calls in what prove to be the last words of Rotrou's theater?

> O Ciel! dont les décrets règlent nos destinées,
> Donne d'heureux succès à ces deux hyménées.
>
> (V.5)

Some may find that Rotrou satisfies his nostalgia for immanence no more successfully in *Dom Lope de Cardone* than in *Venceslas* and *Cosroès*. These plays give ethical as well as psychological premonitions of the dramatist of whom Lanson and others consider Rotrou a precursor in his last plays: Racine. In their dialectic of pride and sensualism, Rotrou's final plays anticipate those motifs of "rationalisme, naturalisme, monisme" that Butler finds more illuminating than Jansenism for explaining Racine's vision. That critic does not deny the validity of religious categories for understanding the dramatist whom Goldmann considers, with Pascal, the most extreme Jansenist of the seventeenth century. But where Jansenism is the very soul of Racine's theater for Goldmann, for Butler it is only a point of departure. He especially warns against seeing in the Racinian "concupiscence de la chair" Jansenistic theses about the "fall" of the natural order. For Jansenist theologians, acknowledgement of this "fall" may be the indispensable preparation for the return of grace (at the Almighty's exclusive will, of course). However, for Racine, says Butler,

> le naturalisme . . . , j'entends le fait de considérer la vie de la conscience comme un jeu de forces et de motifs purement naturels, se suffit à lui-même; il ne vise pas à humilier l'homme devant Dieu. Ce matérialisme, ou si l'on préfère, ce monisme racinien, n'est pas d'ailleurs . . .le pessimisme radical que l'on a cherché à voir chez lui.[4]

Unlike Goldmann, Butler finds grounds for optimism in such Racinian heroes and heroines as Hippolyte and Bérénice. The "désintéressement" of the one and the "délicatesse exquise"[5] of the other are clues for Butler that a natural *générosité* does exist in Racine. Butler links this complexly optimistic naturalism to Naudé, Gassendi, and other thinkers from the first part of the century, usually considered *libertins*. Contrasting this naturalism with the dominant baroque irrationalism of the first third of the century, the critic suggests that this early minority vision has become the majority vision of the classical writers of the last third of the century.

In this generational perspective, Rotrou seems neither a baroque irrationalist nor a classical naturalist, neither an adept of Corneille nor a precursor of Racine. The historical reference is helpful. In the still larger historical perspective—taking into account those from whom they take life, so to speak—all three dramatists stand as contemporary expressions of familiar stresses within the religious heritage to which they all explicitly turned at the height of their artistic powers. This heritage, which has informed my analysis of Rotrou's entire canon, seems especially relevant in an ultimate assessment of Rotrou's relation to his great classical contemporaries. Whether the naturalism of Racine be optimistic or pessimistic, libertine or Jansenist in its roots, those roots are themselves grounded in the long-standing tension within sacramental theology itself. As I have brought out in connection with Rotrou's theater of immanence, materialism under the sign of "les cieux" is a logical outgrowth of sacramental theology. Similarly, the otherworldly spirituality of his theater of transcendence is a logical outgrowth of that same theology. Whether in theologians from Augustine to Teilhard de Chardin or dramatists from Rotrou to Claudel, the sacramental vision has sought to reconcile matter and spirit, man's will and divine purpose, this world's justice and God's grace.

As Butler sees it, Racine describes this tension only to resolve it in favor of the former term in each polarity. "In favor of" only logically speaking, of course, since it is hardly a "favorable" view of this world and its "justice" that emerges from his plays! The great classical tragedian thus breaks with both Corneille and Corneille's "mentor," Rotrou.

Yet, if we accept Butler's view of at least some of Racine's "profane" heroes and heroines, his is not a universe totally without grace. Like Goldmann, some may want to find that grace in Racine's late theater: in the specifically religious plays, *Esther* and *Athalie*.[6] Appropriately enough, given the subject of these plays, the grace they proclaim is, in Vahanian's terms once again, "biblical" and "transcendent." But grace it is: Racine can no more look on the world as completely self-sufficient and irredeemable than Rotrou can look on it as completely self-sufficient and in no need of Heaven's tutelage. Rotrou stands between Corneille and Racine, then, not by moving from one to the other, but by including in his theater what Butler and others find univocal in each of the great classics. Corneille's is a theater of immanence in which the world seems blessed in its every sign and accident; Racine's, a theater of transcendence in which the world seems damned in its every sign and accident. Rotrou's is a theater of immanence and transcendence in which sacrament triumphs over sacrilege.[7]

Related to his contemporaries in this way, Rotrou is hardly a *modern* "tragicomedian." He is nonetheless essentially an author of tragicomedy. I generalize the term quite consciously, in spite of the fact that Herrick and others have preferred to see *Venceslas* and *Cosroès* as "tragedy with a happy ending."[8] Undoubtedly, these and some other tragedies of Rotrou do not fit the definition of tragicomedy given by Herrick, Lancaster, and other literary historians: presence of both lowly and noble characters; the concomitant mixture (often, merely juxtaposition) of comic and serious scenes; a grave situation (usually peril of life) issuing nonetheless in a "happy ending"; and so on.[9] Rotrou's other plays may answer to this definition, especially the plays of his theater of immanence. But *Venceslas, Cosroès, Crisante, Bélissaire,* and perhaps others escape these characterics of external form. More importantly, they show an inner form that links them to modern tragicomedy as we know it first in Ibsen and Strindberg, then in Chekhov and Pirandello, and presently in "absurdist" drama. In whatever genre we place their fascinating plays, these dramatists show the fusion of comic and tragic. They are concerned with such themes as: the bleak "everydayness" of the human condition at every social level; the lies by which we seek to make the pity of our existence more bearable to ourselves and, perhaps, to others; the prison of subjectivity that makes pity for any but ourselves a dubious hope; the assertion of every man's heroism by the assault on every man's cowardice; the elucidation of our misery by the baring of our spiritual ambiguities; and so on. Some may find these themes at least in the Rotrou of the late plays. As for the earlier plays, some will perhaps be prepared, with a modern student of tragicomedy, to dismiss them as a "hybrid" form, a jumble of "faraway outlandish settings . . . unlikely happenings and situations . . . farfetched juxtapositions of the ludicrous and the serious."[10]

To dismiss Rotrou and his contemporaries on these grounds is to pay less attention to the philosophic and cultural setting of Rotrou's time than to the setting of modern tragicomedy. Inured to alienation, many moderns will find the B portions of Rotrou's tragicomedy more attractive than the A portions. For such moderns, the world gives less than it takes away. The neat pairings and constrained passions of the A portions must strike some moderns as the real illusions of Rotrou's vision. These critics will look on that total vision as, at worst, an abominable deception and, at best, a prologue to paranoia. To sanctify the world in its beauty and then to deny the enjoyment of that beauty on purportedly the same religious grounds—this is an invitation to madness and, in religious terms, to the sacrilegious rather than the sacramental celebration of the world.

Seen in this light, the Rotrou of the B portions of his plays looks forward more to Baudelaire than he does to Racine. To the "converted" Baudelaire of *Mon Cœur mis à nu*, the "incarnational" postulates of Rotrou's theater of immanence would seem a euhemerist surrender to the lesser of the "deux postulations simultanées, l'une vers Dieu, l'autre vers Satan."[11] Baudelaire finally surrenders to "l'horreur de la vie," which he admits had always existed in his heart with a contradictory "extase de la vie."[12] In these notions he shows himself a quintessential Christian in the terms of Harnack, which I cited in my Introduction and which bear repeating here within the context of a fuller statement:

> At bottom, only a single point was dealt with, abstinence from sexual relationships; everything else was secondary: for he who had renounced these found nothing hard. Renunciation of the servile yoke of sin (*servile* peccati iugum discutere) was the watchword of Christians, and an extraordinary unanimity prevailed as to the meaning of this watchword, whether we turn to the coptic porter, or the learned Greek teacher, to the Bishop of Hippo, or Jerome the Roman presbyter, or the biographer of Saint Martin. Virginity was the specifically Christian virture, and the essence of all virtues; in this conviction the meaning of the evangelical law was summed up.[13]

Citing this passage, Philip Rieff has said: "Historically, the rejection of sexual individualism (which divorces pleasure and procreation) was the consensual matrix of Christian culture."[14] Yet, at key points in the history of that culture, the consensus was challenged from within the culture itself. Various Christian thinkers sought to wed pleasure and procreation. The effort is undoubtedly doomed to failure for those who stress that current in Christian culture which culminated in Protestantism. For them, the Christian consensus is based on what Rieff calls a "predicate of renunciatory control."[15] However, from within the largest Christian group, the Church of Rome, have come the strongest efforts to modulate this predicate of renunciation through a predicate of indulgence. On the specific sexual renunciation emphasized by Harnack and Rieff, it is significant that the Roman church considers marriage a sacrament, whereas Protestant sects can measure their distance from Rome on this very point. Nevertheless, the Protestant consensus can be measured within Rome itself by the hierarchy of the sacraments in Rome's sacramental theology: Orders are higher than Marriage and, within Orders, celibacy and chastity are as much watchwords today as they were for the early Christians cited by Harnack. In heroines like Crisante, Antigone, and Iphigénie, in heroes like Adrien and Genest, Rotrou depicts the power of the predicate of renunciatory control. Yet, even in the worlds of these heroes and heroines, Rotrou is reluctant to relinquish the Catholic predicate of indulgence. Whether subordinated in those plays or stressed in the theater of immanence, this predicate is permissive as well as remissive. Having remitted the sacrilegious abuse of natural faculties, man is permitted the sacramental use of those faculties.

Reconciliation is the goal of action in Rotrou's theater of ambivalent religious forces. As a poet, the seventeenth-century dramatist never succumbs to that "horreur de la vie" which leads Baudelaire to assert that "il se fait un divorce de plus en plus sensible entre l'esprit et la brute."[16] In his darkest moments, Rotrou never looks on the world as the comitragedy Baudelaire came to see in it.

Rotrou always writes tragicomedy. In arriving at a minimal definition of seventeenth-century French tragedy, Knight does not include those very plays in which he, like Lanson before him, finds that Rotrou "prefigures Racine." One assumes that Knight excludes all of Rotrou from his definition on the grounds that all of the plays violate *vraisemblance* and *les bienséances*. The late plays do meet the other *minimal* conditions, it is true: "a dramatic action in which personnages above the common have to react to a situation above the common, in that it involves a danger usually of death."[17] Yet, beyond these minimal conditions, in both his theater of immanence and his theater of transcendence, Rotrou's plays are tragicomedies. They express in their plots the movement of the parts in that compound word: they move through the tragic to the comic, from the conjectured loss of value to the actual retrieval of value. However things work out in "modern tragicomedy" in the Age of Anxiety, they always work out as planned in the tragicomedy of an Age of Reason that is still an Age of Faith. Rotrou manipulates his plots toward their "happy ending," just as God manipulates the world toward its "happy ending." To apply certain concepts of modern linguistics, Rotrou's plays are "transforms" of a "deep grammar" of eternal meaning. To apply the chief concept of the more optimistic school of thought in modern theology, his is a "theology of hope."[18] Even in moments of greatest stress on either of its major tendencies, Rotrou's tragicomedy remains within the bounds of a religious vision in which the transcendent God is said to have resanctified the fallen world through the sacramental gift of His Merciful Son Become Man. In its specific Christian as well as in its secular expression, Rotrou's vision restates an ancient, enduring faith in the holiness of the human condition.

In life and in death, Rotrou reflected on the meaning of this world's signs. "Au moment que je vous écris," he informed his brother in his last hours, "les cloches sonnent pour la vingt-deuxième personne qui est morte aujourd'hui. Elles sonneront pour moi quand il plaira à Dieu."[19] The sights and sounds of this world are at one with those of another world. In a long canon of dramatic witness, Jean Rotrou unfailingly testified that, in the last things as in the first things, Heaven's decrees "règlent nos destinées."

APPENDIX A

*Rotrou in Legend and Criticism:*

*A Brief Summary of Positions*

ROTROU'S serene pronouncement of faith and citizenship during the plague has been integrated into Charles Maillier's one-act verse drama *La Mort de Rotrou,* composed for the tricentenary celebration of the dramatist's death (Dreux, 1950). This twentieth-century celebrant of the playwright's legend continues a poetic tradition of long practice. For example, in 1811, poems of the same name, one by Latouche and the other by Millevoye, were selected by the Academy in its desire to honor the poet-patriot of Dreux. Again, Ferdinand Simon de Laboullaye and Pierre Etienne Piestre Cormon collaborated on a one-act comedy, *Corneille et Rotrou,* obviously commemorating the legendary championship of Corneille by Rotrou. Until the early twentieth century and especially until the studies by Morel, Orlando, Knutson, and Van Baelen, most critics have prized the legendary "mayor-martyr" rather than the prolific dramatist. This view informs the largely biographical studies of Peysonnié and Saint-René Taillandier, for example.

Rotrou, then, has been celebrated for deeds that have but a casual or, for some critics, contradictory, connection with his literary achievements. The most celebrated of these deeds are his "defense" of Corneille and his exemplary death during the plague at Dreux in the early summer of 1650. The latter "legend" does have a solid core of fact. And, as Mme Deierkauf-Holsboer has shown, there is also some basis in fact to the "legend" of Rotrou as a *poète à gages* exploited by the actors of the Hôtel de Bourgogne.[1] But legend with less solid core has also made Rotrou the unacknowledged founder of the Académie Française, mysteriously and unjustly kept out of that institution; a *poète maudit* whose amatory and bibulous exploits were surpassed only by his gambling excesses; a profligate who repentantly assumed the magistracy at Dreux when thirty years old and thereafter heeded his saintly compatriot, the poet-prelate Antoine de

APPENDIX A

Godeau, to dedicate himself to works of civic duty and Christian piety. In more strictly literary legend, Rotrou has also been hallowed as the founder of the French theater, the mentor of the father of French tragedy, and the precursor in tragedy of Racine and in comedy of Molière. For a skeptical review of these and other legends concerning Rotrou's life, see especially Henri Chardon, *La Vie de Rotrou mieux connue*, and the studies by Léonce Person cited in the Bibliography.

Common sense suggests that, on certain legends, the skepticism of these critics is largely justified. For example, Rotrou produced some ten plays after he was thirty. Obviously, his rate of productivity had diminished, but the figure and the variety of subject are still impressive enough to cast doubt on the legend of his pious renunciation of the theater. On the other hand, a too literal-minded skepticism in approaching certain of the legends might obscure the likelihood that the legends have arisen as a kind of indirect literary criticism, an application to the life of impressions derived from the work. In this connection we might recall an observation made by Ramon Fernandez concerning the legends attached to the career of Molière: "Les biographes qui prennent ces récits pour de l'histoire commettent une faute; mais ceux qui les rejettent dédaigneusement n'en commettent pas une moindre. Ils devaient les donner pour des illustrations symboliques de l'âme de leur héros."[2] The caution is well taken, at least as long as we begin with the work as the primary source of such symbolic illustrations. Thomas Frederick Crane's introduction in *Jean Rotrou's "Saint Genest" and "Venceslas"* is also useful in its study of Rotrou's literary relations with his contemporaries.[3] The most thorough examination of specific points of contact between Rotrou's plays and plays of his contemporaries (including those outside of France) as well as those of his predecessors is to be found in Lancaster's *History*. At appropriate chronological points in his multivolume survey, the learned historian considers each of Rotrou's plays in several relations. He is especially perceptive with respect to the dramatist's Spanish sources. Lancaster's demonstration of Rotrou's frequent independence of his source corrects the extreme Spanish bias of Federico del Valle Abad's *Influencia Española sobre La Literatura Francesa: Juan Rotrou (1609-1650)*. I trust the reader closes my pages on the dramatist with the same feeling with which one closes Lancaster's pages on him: Jean Rotrou is very much his own man.

APPENDIX B

## "Sacrement" and "Sacrilège":

## A Brief Etymological and Historical Review

LET us begin with a seventeenth-century scholar's definition:

Sacrament. s.m. Les Théologiens le définissent en général, Signe d'une chose sacrée. En ce sens ils y comprennent les *Sacrements* de la Loi naturelle, qui est la saine Morale conforme à la droite raison, avec la manière d'offrir le pain et le vin comme fit Melchisedech; ceux de la Loi Mosaïque, comme la Circoncision, l'Agneau Pascal, la consécration des Prêtres, les Purifications. Mais à l'égard de l'Eglise Chrétienne, ils disent que c'est un signe visible ou sensible d'une chose ou Cérémonie sacrée instituée de Dieu, dont l'usage confère la sainteté et la grâce. Il y a deux objets dans les *Sacrements*; l'un est le signe matériel, et voilà l'objet des sens: l'autre la chose signifiée, et voilà l'objet de la foi. Ainsi Dieu a voulu donner comme un corps à ces mystères spirituels, afin que notre foi fût aidée, et fortifiée par ces signes visibles et matériels. CL. L'Eglise Romaine reconnaît sept *Sacrements*: le Baptême, la Confirmation, l'Eucharistie, la Pénitence, l'Extrême-onction, les Ordres, et le Mariage. La Protestante n'en reçoit que deux: le Baptême et l'Eucharistie. Tout *Sacrement* consiste en matière, et en forme. Les gens de bien fréquentent les *Sacrements*; les hypocrites en abusent. Ce mot chez les Anciens signifiait un *serment*, et particulièrement celui que les soldats prêtaient entre les mains de leurs capitaines.

The scholar is Furetière, and the definition is from his *Dictionnaire universel*. The work dates from 1690, somewhat beyond the period of Rotrou's theater. Nevertheless, the applicability of his definition from well before Rotrou's time can be judged from Godefroy's *Dictionnaire de l'ancienne langue française et de tous les dialectes du*

APPENDIX B

*IX<sup>e</sup> au XV<sup>e</sup> siècles.* In Volume VII of that work, under the initial entry for *Sacrement, sacrament, sagrament, saigrement,* we read: "Commémoration solennelle, Partie de la Messe qu'on appelle la Consécration, l'élévation, Moment de la consécration, Mystère, Serment—Norm., *sacrement,* moment de la Messe appelé la consécration ou l'élévation." In the complementary Volume X, under the entry for *sacrement,* Godefroy reports: "acte religieux institué de Dieu pour la sanctification des âmes; cérémonie destinée à la consécration religieuse de chacune des sept phases de la vie privée des fidèles. *Partic., en parlant du mariage*" (italics added). In the latter sense the philologist cites one literal use of the term from the *Poésies* of Robert de Blois: "Que Deus ne fist nul saicrement/ Fors mariage soulement"; and one figurative extension of the term in Clément Marot's *Temple de Cupido*: "Qui sont beaux lictz, encourtinez de soye,/ La ou se font d'amour des sacrements."

The tendency to limit the term *le sacrement* to marriage alone is undoubtedly related to many philological and sociological phenomena. By the seventeenth century, on a statistical basis, for example, the connection between the terms is bound to be greater than between *sacrament* and any other of the seven sacraments, with the exception of baptism and possibly extreme unction. Nevertheless, the connection *sacrament-marriage* also points to a philosophical tension within the concept of sacrament itself, a tension heightened in the specifically Christian development of the concept.

The world as sign of divine immanence, particularly the world's beauty, precedes the specific religious notion of "signs instituted by Christ." Thus, the Narcissus myth as a "genesis" is sacramental: a god looks into a "mirror" and sees himself, the world is his reflection. Etymologically, too, the linkage between divine and human shows that the concept is not specifically Christian and Roman Catholic. *Sacramentum* was the word for the sum of money that, deposited in the treasury of the temple of Saturn at Rome, was surrendered by him who lost a lawsuit, the money being consecrated to the divinity. The word also had a military usage, signifying the oath sworn by recruits upon entering military service. Thus, in its very origin, the word shows the attempt to link sign and signified. Its origin also provides the grounds for that special tension between sign and what it signified when the word was adapted for theological use by Christian thinkers. In *sacramentum* understood as a sum of money, we have the grounds for an emphasis on the material sign. In *sacramentum* understood as the oath sworn (whence, etymologically: Modern French, *serment*), we have the grounds for emphasis on the signified, the spiritual entity to which the words of the oath refer.

APPENDIX B

This tension between the material and the spiritual is accentuated in Christian adaptations of the concept. In the comprehensive article on "Sacrement" in the *Dictionnaire de théologie catholique*, A. Michel finds that "l'existence du *sacramentum militiae*, parfois attestée par un signe (*fidei signaculum*) a exercé par son symbolisme une certaine influence sur la notion de mystère qui s'est attaché au concept du sacrement chrétien."[1] As Michel and other historians of the word note, *sacramentum* is the word usually used by the early fathers of the church to render the Greek μυστέριον, "désignant philosophiquement la nature intime et secrète d'une chose pour l'appliquer au rite symbolique produisant la grâce qu'il figure, puis, aux vérités incompréhensibles qui dépassent les lumières de la raison."[2] Yet, Michel notes that some of the most original theologians in the early church emphasized as much, if not more, the material, visible, and hence apprehensible aspect of what was considered sacramental: thus Tertullian, Ambrose, and the greatest of the early church fathers, Augustine. According to Michel, this materialistic strain persisted until the ninth century, when, through a mistaken etymological connection with Latin *secretum*, Saint Isidore gave the concept an excesively spiritual emphasis. This was corrected only by the Angelic Doctor himself three centuries later.

Other historians of the subject are less disturbed by the emphasis on the material in Augustine. For Joseph Mazzeo, Augustine's notion of the sacramental is derived from his rhetorical theories and "extends beyond the traditional sacraments of Church tradition to include the transcendental meaning of the events and realities of Scripture, all of which, like the sacraments, are to be understood as pointing beyond themselves."[3] Though he stresses importance of the material sign as "an adaptation to human sensibility of eternal truths,"[4] Mazzeo finds Augustine to be constantly referential: the sign is allegorically subordinated to the divine reality that is its referent. This interpretation tends to place Augustine in line with Origen and Cyprian. For them, as Michel notes, *sacramentum* in its Greek equivalent was also synonymous with "symbole, figure, allégorie, mystère ou chose secrète et cachée, disposition, plan, ordre divin, prophétie."[5]

Yet, the synonymy *sacrement-figure* reminds us that Erich Auerbach, even more than Mazzeo, stresses the notion of an equilibrium between the material and the spiritual, between the historical and the eternal in the Augustinian and medieval concept of *figura*. By tendency, as Mazzeo stresses the spiritual, so Auerbach stresses the material. He sees Augustine playing a leading part in the compromise between the historical and realistic interpretation of Scriptures by Tertullian and his adepts, on the one hand, and the ethical, alle-

## APPENDIX B

gorical approach by Origen and his adepts on the other hand. Auerbach concludes that "on the whole, [Augustine] favored a living, figural interpretation, for his thinking was far too concrete and historical to content itself with pure abstract allegory."[6] Augustine is a capital moment in that development of medieval figuralism which culminated in Dante and for which "*figura* is something real and historical which announces something else that is also real and historical."[7] Auerbach also notes that "the whole classical tradition was very much alive in St. Augustine, and of this his use of the word *figura* is one more indication. In his writings we find it expressing the general notion of form in all its traditional variants, static and dynamic, outline and body; it is applied to the world, to nature as a whole, and to the particular object; along with *forma*, color, and so on, it stands for outward appearance (Epist., 120, 10 or 146, 3); or it may signify the variable aspect over against the imperishable essence."[8] In the history of sacramental theology as well as in the more literary history of "figuralism," it is clear that, within the Christian tradition, the logic of sacramentalism tends to defeat attempts at limitation of the concept. A rampant sacramentalism of a strongly materialist cast characterizes the development of the concept in Augustine, as Auerbach shows; and a rampant sacramentalism of a strongly spiritualist cast characterizes the development in Isidore, as Michel shows.

It is to this rampant sacramentalism, particularly in its materialist tendency, that the Protestant of the Reform reacts so violently, seeing in it a decidedly un-Christian commitment to the things of this world. Protestantism is by tendency non-sacramental and in some forms, profoundly anti-sacramental. As a modern Catholic theologian, Louis Bouyer, has put it, " . . . Dans tout sacrementalisme, le protestantisme flaire de la magie." Bouyer relates this suspicion to Saint Augustine, not the Augustine of Auerbach's history of *figura* but rather the Augustine

> d'une tendance . . . plus ou moins platonisante, qui était déjà sensible à travers tout le moyen âge, mais qui a prédominé sans plus de contre-partie dans les Eglises de la Réforme. C'est la tendance à réduire le spirituel à l'intérieur,—à regarder tout ce qui est corporel, sensible, dans la religion, comme au mieux superflu, et facilement douteux.[9]

Such a tendency reaches its most pessimistic expression in Rotrou's time in those "Catholic Protestants," the extreme Jansenists, who see worldly things and most human events as signs not of incarnation but of "dis-incarnation," signs of the world's loss in the sight of the Divine.

APPENDIX B

This particular antagonism gives the so-called Protestant Baroque poets of the late sixteenth century their special quality, a quality not wholly absent from Rotrou. For such poets the world cannot be an occasion of grace. They remind us that the theological debate between the partisans of grace *ex opere operato* and those of grace *ex opere operantis*, between partisans of the sacraments and partisans of pure faith, is not a mere quarrel of preachers or pedants; it is a quarrel of poets as well.

This observation seems to me capital when related to French classical writers, among them Rotrou, for whom also the "whole classical tradition was very much alive." The return to pagan antiquity in the late sixteenth and seventeenth centuries has too long been regarded as one with a Renaissance humanism presumably at odds with a supposed anti-humanistic, medieval, Christian tradition. Auerbach notes that the baffling "mixture of spirituality and sense of reality which characterizes the European Middle Ages" and which he studies in the concept of *figura* persisted as a mode of interpretation up to the eighteenth century.[10] Still more recently, O. B. Hardison has suggested that the central dramatic form of the Middle Ages has had a much more direct bearing on Renaissance drama than the familiar way of looking at both medieval and Renaissance drama has allowed. Abandoning the secularist aesthetic he sees forged in the Renaissance, Hardison argues that rite and drama are not so separate as Chambers, Young, and Craig had argued in famous theses. For him, the Christian rite is indeed a play, so that

> recognition of the persistence of ritual form inherited from the Mass and the liturgy may provide a way of coming to terms with the variety of views now current [concerning the transition between medieval and Renaissance drama.] This form is, after all, the dominant form for medieval drama. As such, it both fulfilled the expectations of audiences conditioned by their experience of Christian worship and educated them in what to expect from representational drama.[11]

What they were to expect according to this model was a structure which, as Hardison put it, ". . . is comic, not tragic. The mythic event celebrated is rebirth, not death, although it is a rebirth that requires death as its prelude. The experience of the participants is transition from guilt to innocence, from separation to communion."[12] Hardison sees this particular structure in Shakespeare.[13] In less specifically Christian terms, Northrop Frye has also argued along archetypal grounds that this is the typical pattern at least of Shakespearean comedy and romance.[14]

APPENDIX B

This conception of certain plays is obviously "sacramental," but it differs, of course, from the true idea of sacramental drama given by Bruce W. Wardropper:

> Dramatists approached the true idea of the *auto sacramental* to the extent that they conceived it as an intrinsically sacramental drama, and not merely as a drama "in honor of" the Eucharist. The composition of a sacramental drama entails the acceptance for dramatic purposes of a sacramental "world:" a scale of values, a concept of reality and time, an attitude to history—all of which are different from, and may be opposed to, the "real" world of the secular theatre. The sacramental world lends itself to the altar, rather than to the stage. Any attempt to reproduce the sacramental world on the stage must be a compromise: a compromise between the Mass and the *comedia*. The most successful sacramental play was that which succeeded in blending theatre and sacrament while still preserving an artistic interest.[15]

In answer to the question "What was the nature of the sacramental world?" Wardropper quotes the "allegorical language" of Pope Urban IV, instituting the Corpus observances in 1264: "Canta le Fe, la Esperanza salte de placer y la Caridad se regocije! Alégrese le Devoción, . . . la Pureza se huelge!" As the critic sees it, these words forecast the "language used three or four centuries later by those Spanish dramatists who succeeded in finding the dramatic formula of the sacramental world."[16] Considering the tensions of sacramental theology itself, one must say that these Spanish dramatists find *one* of the dramatic formulas of the sacramental world. This formula is linked to the specifically Christian notion of divinely instituted sacraments, of course. The critic regards timelessness and especially allegory as the "two principles of sacramental art". The signified is more important than the sign in the sacramental art dissected by Wardropper. He calls attention to the innovative "enlargement of the scope of allegory" in the form at the end of the sixteenth century when:

> It was recognized that, since it is the function of the *auto sacramental* to compare the world of the less known with that of the known, the effectiveness of the comparison often *depends on the hostility between the two worlds*. Completely secular themes were exploited as illustrations of the Christian mysteries: the *Celestina* material is blended with the tender story of the pardonned adulteress in *Los amores del alma*; the Don Gayferos of the ballads, forced to rescue his captive wife as a

penalty of losing a game of backgammon, is identified with Christ the Redeemer in *El rescate del alma*. This readiness to make use of *the clash between two worlds* opened the way for the audacities of the seventeenth-century *autos sacramentales*: the use of the *serrana de la Vera* theme by Valdivielso, of *La Araucana* by Lope, of the Minotaur by Tirso.[17]

Historically, this view of sacramental theology values the spiritual. The "hostility" and the "clash" between "the two worlds" is inevitable: between the world of the spirit and the material world, between heaven and earth. Significantly, in this same vein, Wardropper stresses Valdivielso's realization of the "sacramental world's independence of the earthly world."[18] Obviously, in terms of the history of sacramental theology in the early church, the *auto sacramental* continues that current of spiritual emphasis represented by Origen and Cyprian.

There is another current, one that, to use Wardropper's terms, leads to a different "dramatic formula." This is the current in which the sign is given more weight, if not so much weight as what it signifies. In such a relation there is no necessary clash or hostility between the two components of a sacramental object or sacramental event. By definition the natural is the reflection of the divine, and only human nature, with its peculiar attribute of freedom, creates an antagonistic relation between this world and the next. Human misconduct is thus the basis of one of the formulas of sacramental art as much as timelessness and allegory are principles of the formula dissected by Wardropper.

In religious terms this misconduct is defined under the categories of sin and sacrilege. "Au sense stricte," writes Nicholas Jung in the *Dictionnaire de théologie catholique*, *sacrilège* is "la profanation d'une personne, d'une chose ou d'un lieu sacrés, ou, pour mieux dire, publiquement dédiés par l'autorité de Dieu ou de l'Eglise au culte divin."[19] But the same authority reminds us that the ancients, too, had a concept of sacrilege, calling by that name "le vol d'une chose, publiquement protégée par la sainteté du temple, où elle se trouvait."[20] Here, as in the history of *sacrement*, we are reminded that the sacramental view of the human condition is not specifically Christian but, rather, universally religious. In certain interpretations of the Narcissus myth, the self-admiration leading to creation also leads to suicide: Narcissus plunges into the waters to embrace his own lovely image and drowns. Otto Rank reports the adaptation of this myth by certain Gnostic and Neoplatonists of the early Christian era: "Adam a perdu sa nature céleste parce qu'il était devenu amoureux de sa propre image."[21] The sign of the spiritual can also become the

## APPENDIX B

occasion for its violation; like capitalism, in early Marxist thinking, sacramentalism carries the seeds of its own destruction.

# Notes

In order to keep annotation to a minimum in this highly allusive study of a writer who has drawn on several literatures, I have not provided footnotes for references to works already identified in my text. Full information for such references may be found in the Bibliography.

Except where otherwise indicated, quotations from Rotrou's works are from original editions. Except where otherwise indicated, as well, I have modernized both spelling and punctuation, but have respected act and scene divisions in the originals.

*Preface*

1. *Commentaires sur Corneille, Œuvres*, XXXI, 180-81.
2. Those interested in Rotrou's relation to the Baroque should consult especially Imbrie Buffum, *Studies in the Baroque from Montaigne to Rotrou*; Jean Rousset, *La Littérature de l'âge baroque en France*; Wilhelm Fries, *Der Stil der theaterstücke Rotrous: Eine Untersuchung über Formprobleme des barocken Vorstadiums der französischen Literatur des Klassizismus*; Raymond Lebègue, "Rotrou: dramaturge baroque," *Revue d'histoire littéraire de la France*, L (1950), 379-84. Orlando (op. cit.) turns to Rousset in making strong links between Rotrou and the Baroque, and Philip Butler (*Classicisme et baroque dans l'œuvre de Racine*) frequently uses Rotrou as what might be called a "Baroque counter" to Racine's *eventually* classic integrity.
3. *The Liberal Imagination*, p. 191.

*Introduction*

1. In one context Morel sees Rotrou's thematic relationship with Corneille as parallel to the famous Corneille-Racine contrast: " . . . Le drame cornélien est celui de l'immanence, le drame de Rotrou est celui de la transcendance" (*La Tragédie*, p. 51). However, the critic's context is the history of tragedy. He thus excludes the comedies and tragicomedies that, in the context of Rotrou's entire theater, provide the basis of my study of Rotrou as the dramatist of both immanence and transcendence. For a technical discussion of the "immanentist current" in sacramental theology from the early church to the church of Rotrou's day (Augustine to Francis de Sales), see Appendix B.
2. *Corneille: His Heroes and Their Worlds*, p. 19.
3. Loc. cit.
4. "Au temps de Bérulle, la crise est encore latente. L'Eglise catholique se relève après des années d'épreuves; les Turcs ont été défaits à Lépante, les progrès de l'hérésie paraissent arrêtés. Les grandes œuvres de Belarmin et de Baronius semblent assurer, dans le domaine de la science religieuse, le triomphe de la vérité catholique. La Rome des Papes a retrouvé la splendeur de la Rome an-

tique. Il y a chez les catholiques du temps une sorte d'optimisme triomphal qui s'exprimera magnifiquement dans l'œuvre éclatante de Rubens et naïvement dans *L'Imago primi saeculi.* La décoration de la Bibliothèque Vaticane, achevée en 1591, exprime d'une façon plus didactique le même état d'esprit. . . . Dans [cette] série de fresques, le progrès de l'esprit est toujours associé au triomphe de l'Eglise. L'œuvre des législateurs et des philosophes apparait comme préparation évangélique. Nulle rupture dans cette harmonieuse histoire: Dieu est le Père des lumières, lumière naturelle qui révèle le monde de l'invisible à travers la création visible, lumière de la foi, lumière de l'Evangile: tout vient de Dieu. L'humanisme est alors ivresse d'harmonie, ivresse d'unité" (Jean Dagens, op. cit., pp. 67-68).

5. Quoted in René Bady, *L'Homme et son institution de Montaigne à Bérulle (1580-1625),* p. 81 (italics added). In the context Bady notes that this "très orthodoxe successeur de Montaigne au Parlement de Bordeaux" offers his analogies in response to attacks on pagan antiquity by Protestants.

6. Quoted in Loukovitch, *L'Evolution de la tragédie religieuse classique en France,* p. 2.

7. P. 285. As for the rest of the public, according to Loukovitch, Corneille counted on their favor to overcome the opposition of the "lettrés" (p. 27).

8. Loukovitch quotes this report from *Les Mémoires pour servir à l'histoire de Port Royal* in his *L'Evolution,* p. 22.

9. *L'Art poétique,* III, 881-85.

10. Robert Barroux would even correct the view of Gassendi as an outright *libertin*: "Les libertins, qui tentent de compter parmi eux ce séduisant esprit, si ingénieux et si cultivé, ne lisent qu'une partie de son œuvre et ne peuvent être tenus ni pour ses maîtres ni pour ses disciples" (*Dictionnaire des lettres françaises: XVII*e *siècle,* p. 451).

11. *L'Homme et son institution de Montaigne à Bérulle (1580–1625),* p. 249 (italics added).

12. Quoted by Bady, op. cit. In his *Histoire littéraire du sentiment religieux en France,* Henri Bremond defends Richeome against the charge of semi-Pelagianism: "Semipélagien, soupirerait Sainte-Beuve. Laissons-le faire et n'allons pas perdre le temps à venger l'orthodoxie plus que manifeste du jésuite" (I, 52).

13. "La Compagnie du Saint-Sacrement et la Contre-Réforme catholique," *Revue des deux mondes,* 5e période (1903), 542. Under the over-all title *Un Episode de l'histoire religieuse du 17*e *siècle,* Rébelliau's masterful survey of this fascinating movement appeared in separate articles over several years in this journal. See Bibliography. Acknowledgment is made to the estate of the author.

14. *Dictionnaire universel,* 3e édition. See Appendix B above for a further discussion of this connection between marriage and "le sacrement." Here, I would recall the linkage as established by a modern lay theologian who is also a dramatist, Charles Williams: "The Way of Affirmation was to develop great art and romantic love and marriage and philosophy and social justice; the Way of Rejection was to break out continually in the profound mystical documents of the soul, the records of the great psychological masters of Christendom" (*The Descent of the Dove: A Short History of the Holy Spirit in the Church,* pp. 57-58).

15. Queried by La Compagnie d'Anger, La Compagnie de Paris offered the following justification of secrecy: " . . . le désir d'imiter la vie cachée du Sauveur dans cette Eucharistie dont elle [La Compagnie] portait le nom." Rébelliau is inclined to credit still more the justification in a "mémoire . . . sur l'esprit de

la Compagnie" circulated in the provinces in 1660: "La fin de ce secret . . . est de donner moyen d'entendre les œuvres fortes avec plus de *prudence*, de *désappropriation* (entendez: de désintérressement), avec plus de succès et moins de contradiction. Car l'expérience a fait connaître que l'éclat est la ruine des œuvres . . . et que le *propriété* (entendez: l'amour-propre, l'intérêt de vanité) est la destruction du mérite et du progrès en vertu" ("La Compagnie du Saint-Sacrement," p. 60).

16. "En 1637-1638, elle [La Compagnie] fait adopter l'usage de voiler le Saint-Sacrement avant et pendant le sermon" (a report quoted by Rébelliau, "La Compagnie du Saint-Sacrement," p. 76.) With even the visible sign of the sacrament of the Eucharist thus hidden, little wonder that the Compagnie would be especially concerned to conceal the " 'nudités de gorge' que les femmes étalaient aux offices" (ibid., p. 65). One can imagine the reaction of the "compagnons du Saint-Sacrement" to those many scenes in Rotrou in which a lover looks on his mistress' breast as a sign that she is "l'abrégé mortel des merveilles des cieux."

17. *L'Art poétique*, Chant III, vv. 235-36. Similar strictures can be found in Chant II, vv. 187 ff. On the other hand, Boileau calls for a full-fledged mythologism in non-Christian subjects, should the theme allow for it "dans une profane et riante peinture" (Chant III, vv. 217 ff.).

18. See *Laure persécutée, tragi-comédie*, édition critique publiée par Jacques Morel, p. 11 (a transcript of which M. Morel has been most gracious to lend me in copy), where the editor notes the substitution of plural for singular references to the Divinity as if the *bienséances* had already grown to great force.

19. *Wait without Idols*, p. 32. In this book Vahanian studies the signs of our "Post-Christian" era in a number of major literary figures: Hawthorne, Eliot, Faulkner, et al. The theologian's most famous expression of his thesis is to be found, of course, in *The Death of God: The Culture of Our Post-Christian Era*. I should add that in both books, for Vahanian, Christian is synonymous only with "biblical" and "transcendental."

20. *Wait without Idols*, p. 44.

21. *La Civilisation de l'Europe classique*, p. 457.

22. Writing of the first few centuries of the Christian era, Harnack maintains that "at bottom, only a single point was dealt with, abstinence from sexual relationship. . . . Renunciation of the servile yoke of sin . . . was the watchword" (cited by Philip Rieff, *The Triumph of the Therapeutic: Uses of Faith after Freud*, p. 16).

23. Henry Carrington Lancaster, *A History of French Dramatic Literature in the Seventeenth Century* (9 vols.; Baltimore, The Johns Hopkins Press, 1929-42).

24. Summarizing the scholarship on Rotrou's collaboration in the commissioned plays and adding his own measure of internal and external evidence, Lancaster concludes that Rotrou composed Act I of *La Comédie des Tuileries* (*History*, Part Two, I, 97-101) and Act II of *L'Aveugle de Smyrne* (*History*, Part Two, I, 205-8). As for *L'Illustre Amazone*, first attributed to Rotrou by Beauchamps in his *Recherches* of 1735 (II, 115), Viollet-le-Duc is inclined to believe it is by Rotrou (V, 508) and thus includes it in his edition. Lancaster finds that its French subject, treatment of place, and use of the uncounted mute *e* cast internal doubt on the attribution. In addition, the dedication to Fouquet gives strong external evidence that the play is not Rotrou's: the dramatist died in 1650, and Fouquet did not rise to power until after that date. See *History*, Part Three, I, 182-83.

25. Schérer discusses all but *Les Captifs, Clarice, Dom Bernard de Cabrère,* and *La Pélerine amoureuse* in *La Dramaturgie classique en France*. He also sets Rotrou's "originality" in a favorable Racinian perspective: "Rotrou, dont l'œuvre abondante et brillante a connu un grand succès, n'est pas un novateur en dramaturgie; il fait son profit, avec beaucoup de talent et de souplesse, des acquisitions de sa génération. On en dirait autant de Racine, qui a utilisé, avec l'art le plus raffiné, des procédés dont en général il n'est pas l'auteur,—n'était que sa première pièce, la *Thébaïde*, témoigne d'indécisions et d'archaïsmes qui indiquent un accord moins profond avec le public chez Racine débutant que chez Rotrou ou Corneille débutants" (p. 428). On the other hand, Knutson finds that Rotrou is genuinely innovative in technique: the dramatist builds his comedies according to a principle of polarized types, as functions of "ironic contrast." He sees Rotrou as interested "in using stock figures to accentuate polarity of tone and to provide contrasting perspectives" so that "the simultaneous vision of two extremes creates a balanced picture of human conduct." (See *The Ironic Game*, pp. 18 and 20.) Knutson also makes a technical observation that I find of greater thematic consequence than he does: "that the playwright was reluctant to mystify his audience for any length of time" and that his "limited use of surprise proves that he chose not to disrupt too often the audience's godlike vision of the total spectacle" (pp. 39-40).

*I. Immanence and Transcendence in "Le Véritable Saint Genest"*

1[R]. In this tragedy of 1645, Valérie, daughter of the Roman emperor Dioclétien, dreams that she is to wed a lowborn suitor whose court her own father will support. Putting more faith in this dream than her maid, Camille, Valérie is vindicated when she learns the origins of her fiance, Maximin. Just returned from far-off campaigns to marry her with her own and her father's approval, he is a lowborn shepherd raised to co-emperor by her father, himself a lowborn, self-made man. To celebrate the wedding, Dioclétien asks the actor Genest to present a play. After some discussion of possible plays by ancient and modern authors, the emperor decides on a play showing the folly of the Christian martyrs whom the empire persecutes. Genest suggests the subject of the martyrdom of Adrien, one of Maximin's officers who was converted. Rehearsing the play before going onstage, Genest is interrupted by Marcelle, who plays Natalie, Adrien's wife. The conceited, beautiful actress finds it difficult to play a Christian, for she finds renunciation of the world foolish. Genest convinces her she can play the part. Returning to his own rehearsing, the actor is so moved by his lines that he finds himself beginning to believe them in fact. He is assured by a voice from above that his playing will not be in vain. Thinking his fellow actors may be fooling him, Genest returns to his concerns as actor and director, but he goes onstage inviting both pagan gods and Christ to vie for his faith. In the play Adrien is shown converted by the very courage of those he persecutes. He resists threats, enticements, and appeals to return to the faith of the Romans, and is unmoved by the anger of Maximin himself. Urging his wife, Natalie, to share his faith, he discovers that she has been a Christian since birth but has kept it a secret both at her mother's orders and out of her own fear. She wants to proclaim her faith openly now, but her husband persuades her that it is God's will that she keep it secret. At this point, as earlier during Genest's presentation, the spectators become unruly, and the actor appeals to the emperor to calm the audience. When the play resumes, Adrien appears to Natalie in apparent freedom. She berates him for his apostasy and her own cowardice. But he assures her that he is still firm in his faith. Adrien is, in fact, about to suffer execution, his baptism of blood, when Genest stops playing to announce his own conversion. The audience thinks he is still acting, but he finally convinces all that the play is over. Dioclétien orders his execution. Genest willingly goes to his death, refusing Marcelle's entreaties on behalf of the troupe that he renounce his sacrilegious conversion to Christianity. The troupe loses the favor of the emperor as Genest gains the favor of God.

I have used the critical edition of the play prepared by Thomas Frederick Crane (Boston: Ginn and Co., 1907). The following analysis of this play differs in a number of respects from my earlier essay on Rotrou's play about the actor-martyr: "Rotrou. The Play as Miracle" in my *Play within a Play*, pp. 36-46.

2. In *Rotrou: Dalla Tragicommedia Alla Tragedia*, Francesco Orlando has written most incisively of the technical aspects of this same pattern, calling particular attention to the motif of the false datum in the central portion.

3. See, for example, Judd Hubert, "Le Réel et l'illusoire dans le théâtre de Corneille et dans celui de Rotrou," *Revue des sciences humaines*, XCV (July-September, 1958), 336.

4. Op. cit., p. 262.

5. Thus, in Rotrou's very first play, *L'Hypocondriaque, ou le mort amoureux* (1628), the heroine, Perside, and her cousin, Aliaste, plan to go off, with the girl disguised as a man, in search of her lover, Cloridan. Before leaving, they test their plan by exchanging garments and appearing before her parents. The mother, Clarinde, sees through her daughter's disguise from the outset. Only the father, Oronte, is fooled, but he is shocked by the consequences of the transvestism. However, lest we dismiss such art as mere "entertainment," let us also note that this aesthetic playing-around has served another purpose. If art is a cause of pleasure, it is also an occasion for reflection and reassurance. "Aliaste!" exclaims Oronte:

> . . . Est-ce vous? Dieux! cette ressemblance
> Me charme et tient encor mon esprit en balance,
> Ma fille a même poil, mêmes yeux, même teint.
> L'agréable transport dont je me sens atteint:
> Qu'en ce déguisement mon esprit se récrée!
> Et que le souvenir de mon erreur agrée.
>
> (IV.4)

Oronte at last becomes an on-stage spectator with his wife. The play's resemblance to life is disturbing, but the truth of life is not found in the play; the truth of the play is found in life. Life guarantees the meaning of art. Because life's truths are sure, art's "transport," even when apparently disagreeable, is "agréable." Art is neither a romantic extension of life's glorious potential nor a Pirandellian solace for life's pains. Art returns one to life and its happy meanings.

6. Thus, Lancaster, *History*, Part Two, II, 541.

7. The famous critic complains of Rotrou that "on entrevoit ici un beau dénouement qui est manqué: on conçoit possible, vraisemblable, selon les lois de la Grâce et l'intérêt de la tragédie, la conversion de toute la troupe; on se la figure aisément assistant au supplice de Genest, et, à un certain moment, se précipitant tout entière, se baptisant soudainement de son sang, et s'écriant qu'elle veut mourir avec lui. Mais rien de tel" (*Port Royal*, I, 219).

8. Lancaster suggests that the play was probably first called *Le Feint vérit-*

*able*, an exact translation of the title of Lope's play which, in part, served as Rotrou's model. The author would then have presumably called it simply *Saint Genest*, but his publisher retained the adjective from the original "in order to help sell the work in competition with that of Desfontaines" (*History*, Part Two, II, 539).

9. "Une scène inédite de 'Saint Genest'," *Revue d'histoire littéraire de la France*, L (1950), 395-403.

10. Challenged by certain critics that his conception of rationality denied the exercise of "le libre arbitre," a positive power of will to choose one of two contraries, Descartes explained his position in a letter to Le Père Mesland as follows: "Cette faculté positive, je n'ai pas nié qu'elle fût dans la volonté. Bien plus, j'estime qu'elle y est, non seulement dans ces actes où elle n'est pas poussée par des raisons évidentes d'un côté plutôt que l'autre, mais aussi dans tous les autres; à ce point que, lorsqu'une raison très évidente nous porte d'un côté, bien qu'en, *moralement parlant*, nous ne puissions guère aller à l'opposé, absolument parlant, néanmoins, nous le pourrions. En effet, il nous est toujours possible de nous retenir de poursuivre un bien clairement connu ou d'admettre une vérité évidente, pourvu que nous pensions que c'est un bien d'affirmer par là notre libre arbitre" (*Œuvres et lettres* [Pléiade edition], p. 1177; italics added). Obviously, for Descartes as for Rotrou's rational heroes, freedom consists only in going against one's conscience.

11. *Le Romantisme des classiques*, p. 96.

12. The theological justification for this possible working of grace is provided by Henry VIII in his famous *Defence*. Citing I Cor. 7:12 ("If any Brother have a wife, an Infidel, etc."), Henry comments: "Do not these words of the Apostle shew, that, in Marriage (which is an entire thing of itself, after one of the Parties is converted to the Faith) the Sanctity of the Sacrament sanctifies the whole Marriage, which before was altogether unclean?" (p. 386). Leeming provides an explicit theological justification of the sacramental character of this marriage formally contracted under pagan auspices by a Christian and a pagan who becomes Christian: "The marriage of pagans becomes a sacrament *ipso facto* upon reception of Baptism, without any renewal of consent, and the reason for this is that the bond contracted in paganism remains and becomes a sacramental bond by the mere fact of existing between Christians" (*Principles of Sacramental Theology*, p. 279).

13. Pensée Number 274 in the widely known Brunschvicg enumeration, but Number 530 in the edition by Louis Lafuma, which I have used here. See Bibliography.

14. In his edition of the play, R. S. Ladborough observes in a note to these lines that they "imply the orthodox Catholic doctrine that grace is sufficient for salvation, but is only made efficacious by human cooperation" (p. 58). Some theologians may find that the critic makes man the author of the much disputed efficacious grace that, to the dismay of Pascal and other Jansenists, had to be added to sufficient grace! Strictly speaking, God alone can make any grace efficacious, but man can benefit from that efficacy by co-operating with the Divine intention through a proper disposition of spirit. When he does so, as Leeming reports, there is restored to him the gift of *integrity*: "Adam and Eve were free from concupiscence, which means that their faculties were perfectly harmonious, reason being subject to God, and appetite to reason" (*Principles*, p. 104). Rotrou does not indicate the special power by which Genest finds himself better disposed than his colleagues and rulers to heed the call presumably delivered to them as well as himself.

15. For a review of this question, see Leeming, op.cit., pp. 295-313.
16. Op.cit., p. 163.
17. Op.cit., p. 279.
18. The hero of Rotrou's first play, *L'Hypocondriaque, ou le mort amoureaux*, suffers from the hallucination that he has died after what he believes to be the death of his mistress. He is restored to his senses by a pistol shot and declares:

>Mais Dieux! Ce coup me laisse un libre mouvement,
>Et je n'en puis trouver la marque seulement.
>*Ma raison voit enfin la fourbe découverte:*
>On me rend *la santé* sous le front de ma perte.
>Refuser du secours c'était me secourir,
>Et vous me *guérissez* par la peur de mourir,
>Je ne puis reconnaître un si *pieux office*,
>Qu'offrant un cœur tout nu pour ce doux artifice:
>Que j'ai gardé longtemps des charmes si puissants;
>Et qu'une longue erreur a gouverné mes sens!
>Maintenant *ma raison, qui règne et la surmonte*,
>M'en laisse seulement la mémoire et la honte.
>
>(V.6; italics added)

The terms are virtually those of the Christian concepts informing *Le Véritable Saint Genest* explicitly.
19. Brunschvicg, number 284; Lafuma, number 380.
20. "Burke and Marx," *New American Review*, No. 1, 252.

## II. The Temptation to Total Immanence

1[R]. Léonor, the sister of the young king of Sicily, Alfonce, is in love with Léandre but cannot hope to wed him because of his lesser station. The lovers, wishing that Léandre could somehow be elevated to kingship short of regicide, call on Alcandre, a benevolent magician. He gives them a magic ring that changes the outlook of the king when Léandre manages to trick him into wearing it. The king is carnally in love with Liliane, daughter of Duke Alexandre, who has, in fact, promised her hand to a suitor of truly pure intention, Count Tancrède. Tricked into wearing the ring, the king reverses a number of political and other "tactical" decisions. These had been to further his illicit desire. Under the spell of the ring, he is pure in his behavior toward Liliane, respectful of the political allies he had so shamefully used, and forgetful of the debt he owes Fabrice. Moving in and out of the spell on various occasions, he comes to recognize the effect of the ring on him. At last spiritually in love with Liliane, he rescues her parent and the count, whom he had ordered executed on the advice of Léonor and Léandre while still under the spell. He also proposes legitimate union with Liliane. In a final gesture he pretends to be under the influence of the ring, "surrenders" his throne to Léonor and her consort, who is "now" king. As a "subject," Alfonce asks the "king" to judge a case that in effect describes the trick of Léandre and Léonor. Léandre proposes another case for judgment: a king has tried to seduce a virtuous woman and unjustly condemned her father and pure suitor. The true king recognizes the equal injustice of both cases and forgives Léonor and Léandre, accepting the argument that love was to be blamed. Count Tancrède receives a cousin of the king in marriage, and so the play ends with the prospect of three weddings.

    2.           Le Roi, lavant, dit, ayant mis l'anneau sur le bassin:
> Amants, qu'on ne verse plus d'eau
> Qu'on ne se plaigne ni soupire,
> Par la prison d'un œil si beau,
> L'Amour a perdu son empire.

                Léandre, prenant l'anneau, dit tout bas:
> Léandre, ne verse plus d'eau,
> Ne craint désormais, ni soupire:
> Car, pouvant changer cet anneau,
> Le Roi va perdre son Empire.

                Le Roi:
> Je tiens cet objet précieux,
> Je ne répandrai plus de larmes,
> Et malgré tous mes envieux,
> Je serai maître de ses charmes.

                Léandre, lui ayant rendu l'anneau enchanté:
> Il tient cet anneau précieux,
> Je ne répandrai plus de larmes:
> Et malgré tous mes envieux,
> Je serai maître par ses charmes.

                (II.6)

    3.    "*Magic, Science and Religion*" *and Other Essays*, p. 40.

    4.    Loc. cit.

    5.    The model is Lope's *Sortija del Olvido*. Its difference from Rotrou's play is discussed at length by Lancaster, *History*, Part One, I, 361-65. Georg Steffens, *Rotrou Studien—I: Jean de Rotrou als nachamer Lope de Vegas*, pp. 33-49, and Stiefel, "Uber Jean Rotrous Spanische Quellen," *Zeitschrift für französischen Sprache und Literatur*,XXIX (1901), 195-234, give extremely detailed comparisons (and contrasts) between Lope's play and Rotrou's "imitation" of it.

    6.    After *La Bague*, Rotrou composed three comedies ( *Les Ménechmes, La Céliane*, and *La Diane*) in which the emphasis on the material world is especially strong. The licentiousness of certain situations in *La Céliane* is so excessive that, religiously speaking, the play might be considered a Feast of Fools, whose sacrilegious spirit is taken back in the sacramentally balanced *La Pélerine amoureuse*.

    7[R].    Lucidor smugly speaks of the favor he enjoys with Célie over another suitor, Céliante. The latter warns Lucidor that heaven has more to do with such matters than might appear. Confident that he will marry Célie, whose father, Erasme, is on his side, Lucidor nonetheless looks back on his "dead" mistress, Angélique, with love. Célie herself is only following her father's wishes, but she really loves another Lucidor—a nobleman who pretends to be her painting instructor, Léandre, and by whom she is pregnant. Célie pretends to be mad as a way of putting off the marriage with Lucidor until "Léandre" can prove his nobility. Ersame calls on a pilgrim with mysterious powers to help his daughter in her madness. This pilgrim is really Angélique, coming to find out what her lover is up to. She learns the reason for Célie's condition and urges her to continue to pretend madness. However, a servant, Filène, overhears the Nurse and Célie talking about the girl's pregnancy by "Lucidor," and Filidan spies the girl and the painter making love. Confronted by her father, Célie declares her love for "Léandre." The latter is corroborated in his claim to nobility by Céliante, who turns out to be his brother. Meanwhile, Lucidor urges his valet, Filidan, also a poet, to prepare a poem commemorated to his dead mistress, Angélique. Erasme asks him to meet with the pilgrim, who will put an end to their misery—which she does, easily enough, being revealed to her former lover as his mistress. Accepting his explanation of infidelity as due to her reported death, Angélique accepts him as well. They, too, will marry.

8. C. S. Lewis summarizes the premises of courtly love in Andreas Capellanus' *De Arte Honeste Amandi* as follows: "The definition of love on the first page of this work rules out at once the kind of love that is called Platonic. The aim of love, for Andreas, is actual fruition, and its source is visible beauty: so much so, that the blind are declared incapable of love, or, at least of entering upon love after they have become blind. *On the other hand, love is not sensuality.* [Italics added.] The sensual man—the man who suffers from *abundantia voluptatis*—is disqualified from participating in it. It may even be claimed that love is a "kind of chastity," in virtue of its severe standard of fidelity to a single object. The lover must not hope to succeed, except with a foolish lady, by his *formae venustas*, but by his eloquence, and above all, by his *morum probitas*. The latter implies no mean or one-sided conception of character. The lover must be truthful and modest, a good Catholic, clean in his speech, hospitable and ready to return good for evil" (*The Allegory of Love*, pp. 33-34).

9. Ibid., p. 36.

10. ". . . Le mariage est indispensable parce qu'une fois consommé, il indique parfaitement l'union du Christ avec l'Eglise." A. Michel, *Dictionnaire de théologie catholique*, XIV, I, Column 634.

11. See "Question LXII: The Theological Virtues" in *Basic Writings of St. Thomas Aquinas*, II, 475-80, especially "Third Article," which examines the relations between the theological virtues (faith, hope, and charity) and the intellectual virtues. "First, as regards the intellect, man receives certain supernatural principles, which are held by means of a divine light; and these are the things which are to be believed, about which is *faith*. Secondly, the will is directed to this end, both as to the movement of intention, which tends to that end as something attainable,—this pertains to *hope*—and as to a certain spiritual union whereby the will is, in a way, transformed into that end—and this belongs to charity. For the appetite of a thing is naturally moved and tends towards its connatural end and this movement is due to a certain conformity of the thing with its end" (II, 478).

12. Lancaster, *History*, Part One, II, 558-60.

13. Ibid., p. 559.

14. *La Pélerine amoureuse* occurs under the title *La Pérlerine* as entry no. 55 in *Le Mémoire de Mahelot*. Lancaster thus feels justified in dating it as early as 1632-33. It may even have preceded *La Diane* (no. 58 in Mahelot's list). As for its model, Stiefel has shown that Rotrou used Girolamo Bargagli's *La Pellegrina* (published 1589), but made substantial changes (*Unbekannte Italianische Quellen Jean Rotrou's, Zeitschrift für französische Sprache und Literatur*, Supplementheft V, 3-39).

15. Lancaster also notes that *Amélie* is a reworking of many elements in his entire theater to date. The historian does draw attention to other possible models, however; e.g., Mairet's *Duc d'Ossone* for the girl's confession of her love in a

dream at the beginning of this play (*History*, Part One, II, 561-62). Again, Robert Garapon notes that in *Amélie* "l'intérêt demeure concentré autour du groupe des personnages qui, à deux ou trois années de distance, annoncent et préfigurent les héroes de *L'Illusion comique*." Garapon rejects the hypothesis that Rotrou may have influenced Corneille. He prefers to believe in "une source commune où nos deux poètes ont puisé leur inspiration." See "Rotrou et Corneille," *Revue d'histoire littéraire de la France*, L (1950), 388-89. As for the specific sources of *La Célimène*, I shall comment on them in the next few pages.

16. *History*, Part One, II, 639.

17. *La Pastorale dramatique en France à la fin du XVI$^e$ et au commencement du XVII$^e$ siècle*, pp. 361-64. Tristan's adaptation is entitled *Amarillis, pastorale*. See Bibliography.

18. *Un Paradis désespéré: L'Amour et l'illusion dans l'Astrée*, pp. 15-16.

19. Ibid., p. 27.

20. For the man, writes Ehrmann, "la prière est la manifestation de sa fidélité, de sa soumission, de son obéissance. Instrument de libération de sa nature animale, elle est aussi asservissement aux mots qui, dans leur ambiguïté, ne peuvent jamais être débarrassés de leur noyau d'illusion" (ibid.).

21$^R$. Théane admits to her sister, Céphise, that she has at last surrendered to love in the person of Thimante. Céphise is in love with Thimante herself, she tells Filandre, another suitor of his sister, but says she can bear her sorrow. He accuses her of not really being in love, else she would suffer as he does from the unrequited love he bears Nérée. Nérée loves, and is loved by, Filandre's own brother, Célidor. Filandre proposes that they separate Thimante and Théane, then Célidor and Nérée, and make it seem that Nérée loves Filandre and Thimante loves Céphise. Knowing Théane overhears, Filandre pretends to bring a letter from Thimante to Céphise who presumably repels his courtship. Céphise is then "forced" by her sister to reveal Thimante's treachery. When Thimante despairs of Théane's new coolness, Céphise stops him from killing himself. Meanwhile, Filandre plants distrust in his brother concerning Nérée and then tells Nérée that Célidor really loves Céphise. When Célidor appears, Nérée angrily flees; the despairing lover succumbs in a sleep he wishes were eternal. Céphise appears and, drawn by such beauty, clips a lock of hair from the sleeper. Then for the approaching Célidor, Céphise and Filandre allow themselves to be overheard as Filandre reports that Nérée has confessed her love for Filandre. Céphise offers her love to Célidor. When he refuses, she threatens to drive his sword into her body. He laughs when she does not carry through on the gesture. Meanwhile, Théane and Thimante quarrel and separate, so Filandre offers his love to Théane, who ignores it just as Célidor had ignored Céphise. She is too preoccupied with Nérée, who reproaches her for turning her brother away. Céphise comes upon the quarreling mistresses to claim that she has won the favor of both of their lovers. Théane becomes suspicious. She reassures Nérée that all will turn out well, and sends her after Thimante. However, Thimante will not heed Nérée; he throws himself in the river. Unaware of this, Filandre reappears and is accused of treachery by Nérée, Célidor, and Théane. He denies the charges, but is prepared to meet his brother in combat were the duel not prevented by the horrified women. Célidor and Nérée are reconciled. Filandre and Céphise see heaven's hand against them and pledge their love to one another. Then a shepherd arrives announcing the drowning of Thimante. Théane rushes upon Filandre promising vengeance. He and Céphise confess, but Théane postpones their punishment of death until she has conducted a further search for her lover. Nérée then appears. Filandre informs her of her brother's death. The two join in the search for the body. Thimante appears to Théane, who accepts his apology for having presumed to love her. Meanwhile, Thimante's rescuers, an old boatman, Menalche and the peasant, Damète, appear, followed by Filandre, who is ready to die at Célidor's hands to expiate Thimante's death. But Thimante forgives Filandre and Céphise, so that all couples can look forward to happy marriage.

22. Morel notes the use of these *stances-méditations* in several tragedies of Rotrou: *Antigone, Le Véritable Saint Genest*, etc. "Les Stances dans la tragédie française au XVIIe siècle," *XVII[e] Siecle*, Nos. 66-67 (Numéro spécial, 1965), 43-56, especially 53.

23. The historian believes that, "had it been written a little earlier," *Le Filandre* probably would have been classified as a pastoral (*History*, Part One, II, 642).

24. "Les Criminels de Rotrou en face de leurs actes," *Le Théâtre tragique*, ed. Jean Jacquot, p. 237.

25. *Dogmatic Canons and Decrees*, pp. 90-92.

26. *History*, Part One, II, 643.

27[R]. Hercule, half-god, half-man, son of Jupiter and Alcmène, asks his heavenly father to take him to heaven for his great feats. As the action begins he has just triumphed over the king of Oetolie and taken the latter's daughter, Iole, as a prize for his own bed. When his wife, Déjanire, accuses him of such plans, the husband denies it. The disbelieving wife, jealous of the captive, has her suspicions confirmed by seeing Hercule on his knees beseeching Iole's favor. Iole denies Hercule out of family and national pride, but he accuses her of shielding love for her countryman, Arcas. Hercule threatens bloody vengeance on the lover. Meanwhile, the furious wife invokes a charm she had received from a would-be abductor, the centaur Nesse. The centaur was carrying Déjanire across a river when he was struck by Hercule's arrows: as he died he gave the wife a garment that would oblige her husband to "rendre son âme" should he be unfaithful. She sends the garment to Hercule. Iole pleads with Déjanire to intercede with her husband for the innocent lovers. The wife thinks the plea is a trick and refuses. Arcas arrives and offers to slay himself so that his mistress will not have to compromise her honor. She says she will die first. Meanwhile, Hercule prepares an offering at the altar to consecrate his recent victory. As he prays, the garment begins to consume him with its fiery poison. Philoctète, his loyal follower, blames the goddess, Junon, jealous at the infidelity of Jupiter that caused the hero's birth. However, Hercule sees a human hand in his fate. Back at the palace, Déjanire begins to have misgivings. As the garment was being carried to her husband, she noticed that drippings of Nesse's blood had eaten through wood and stone. The wife's fears are confirmed by the report of Hercule's distress; she repents, deciding to punish herself by suicide. Imploring heaven's mercy in murderous thunderbolt, Hercule now meets his mother, Alcmène. She fears the ignoble end of her son's life will cast doubts on her union with Jupiter. While her son cools his pain in the waters of the Penée, an attendant, Agis, announces that Nesse's gift has driven Déjanire to suicide. When Alcmène explains the cause of his torment to her son, he rejoices. He sees in it the fulfilment of an ancient prophecy that he would die victim of one of his own victims. For his death he orders a huge fire atop Mount Oethé and commands Philoctète to complete his vengeance by the execution of Arcas afterwards. Hercule's death is glorious as reported by Philoctète: the dying hero even reproached his mother for berating the gods. He also insisted that his fatal desires concerning Arcas be carried out. The mother returns with her son's ashes and scornfully orders Philoctète not to heed the pitiful entreaties of Arcas and Iole. Philoctète is about to proceed, when Iole seizes his sword to kill herself. At this moment the heavens open thunderously: Hercule descends to order that Arcas be spared and joined with his mistress. He then reascends. The lovers rejoice in his command.

28. Lancaster attributes both simply to "early in 1634" (*History*, Part One, I, 310, n. 2). Whatever the order of these two plays, Lancaster is convinced that *Hercule mourant* precedes Mairet's *Sophonisbe* and that, in spite of its lesser "regularity," thus deserves an equally important place in the development of French classical tragedy, since it "marks . . . the first application of the new rules to tragedy" (*History*, Part One, II, 689). After *Le Filandre*, Rotrou wrote *Les Occasions perdues* (1633), *L'Heureuse Constance* (1633, or possibly earlier according to Lancaster, *History*, Part One, II, 492), and *La Doristée* (1634, also known as *Cléagenor et Doristée*). All three are tragicomedies very much on the model of *Le Filandre*.

29. In *La Doristée*, Théandre gives a trenchant expression of a motif that becomes especially important in plays like *Iphigénie* and *Bélisaire*: beauty itself as a lure to sacrilege.

> O Nature, peux-tu sous un si bel aspect
> Cacher tant d'infamie et si peu de respect,
> Courir d'un front si doux une flamme brutale
> Et dans un si beau corps mettre une âme si sale?
>
> (IV.4)

The words, of course, seem especially ironic on the lips of an unfaithful husband.

30. *History*, Part One, II, 685.

31. Defining suicide as "le meurtre de soi-même volontairement accompli," the theologian A. Michel stresses that " 'volontairement' indique ici que le crime de suicide n'existe plus lorsqu'on se donne la mort dans un accès de folie ou dans une crise maladive" (*Dictionnaire de théologie catholique*, XIV, 2, Col. 2739).

32. See note 5, p. 200. Morel's commentary on *Hercule mourant* is also to the point here: "C'est donc bien comme chez Sénèque une éthique de la grandeur qui nous est proposée dans l' *Hercule mourant* de Rotrou. Mais la leçon prend dans le poème français une coloration et des dimensions nouvelles, Hercule n'est plus le héros solitaire qui triomphe par la volonté des atteintes cruelles du destin. Il est le pécheur par amour appelé paradoxalement à la sainteté, auprès duquel deux héroïnes de l'amour parviennent, au nom même de leur passion, à un dépassement et à un sacrifice qui paraissent figurer les siens" (Jacques Morel, "L'*Hercule sur l'Œta* de Sénèque et les dramaturges français de l'époque de Louis XIII," in *Les Tragédies de Sénèque et le théâtre de la Renaissance*, ed. Jean Jacquot, p. 110).

33. "Discours du poème dramatique," *Œuvres*, I, 26-27.

34. For a radically opposed, "existentialist" interpretation of this play, see Jacqueline Van Baelen, *Rotrou: Le Héros tragique et la révolte*, pp. 19-44.

35[R]. The lowly Hermante regrets the surrender of her honor to Félismond, Roi d'Epire; she blames the aged seer, Clariane, for leading her to hope that the surrender would induce the king to marry her and make her queen. The young king now disdains his mistress, for he intends to marry the chaste Princess Parthénie. Calling on the powers of darkness, Hermante obtains a magic ring from Clariane. Wearing it at the king's wedding to Parthénie, she is able to win back his lascivious love. Hermante urges the king to rid himself of his wife. It is planned that she shall "accidentally" drown while being escorted to another castle by the king's servitor, Evandre, who has all along tried in vain to dissuade the king from his lust for Hermante. Evandre decides to deliver the queen safely to the other castle and falsely report her death. Meanwhile, Clarimond, a former suitor of Parthénie has engaged Clariane to help him win Parthénie to himself in spite of her wedding. Knowing of Evandre's plans to save the queen, Clariane bribes Léonie, one of the queen's attendants, to have the queen delivered without Evandre's knowledge into a place where Clarimond, his cohort Thersandre, and Clariane can approach her, confident that she will submit to her former suitor. But Léonie reveals the plan to her mistress and Evandre. Thus prepared, they frustrate it, killing the intruders. Clariane surrenders and reveals the cause of the king's infidelity. When Evandre returns to announce the "drowning" of the queen, he wrests the magic ring from Hermante's finger while the king is momentarily absent. Félismond is now disenchanted. Cursing the vicious object of his former lechery, he has her arrested and imprisoned in the royal tower. Allowing the king to think Parthénie dead, Evandre fetches her while the king repents the effects of his "crimes." During the funeral ceremony for the drowned Parthénie, the "corpse" reappears. Instead of a funeral, the play ends with a prospective consummation of marriage.

In seeking to date the play, Lancaster writes: "It was hailed by La Pinelière (cf. above, Part I, p. 691) at the end of 1634 or the beginning of 1635 as a new play and the most beautiful that its author had composed" (*History*, part Two, I, 73). Actually, commenting on the opinions of "les idiots, ou des gens nouvellement venus de la Campagne," La Pinelière said that such people will claim that "*L'Innocente Infidelité* est la plus belle pièce de Rotrou, quoiqu'on ne s'imaginât pas qu'il put s'élever au-dessus de celles qu'il avait déjà faites" (quoted by Lancaster, *History*, Part One, II, 691).

36. *History*, Part One, I, 74. Lancaster adds: "The dramatic value of the play lies especially in the scenes between Hermante, a jealous and violent woman, stopping at nothing to gain her ends, and the king, divided between his physical desire for his mistress and his idealized love for his wife. These scenes are rendered passionate to a degree that is not found in other tragicomedies of the time." The historian is also pleased that "the unities of time and action are carefully preserved."

37. Sainte-Beuve has added this theological disagreement to the many bases for Richelieu's imprisonment of Saint-Cyran in 1638: " . . . qu'on y joigne même la doctrine sur l'insuffisance de l'attrition et sur la nécessité de l'amour dans la pénitence, qui blessait directement l'opinion posée par Richelieu théologien dans son Catéchisme de Luçon: et Richelieu, entiché sur ce point comme en matière de bel esprit, ne voulait pas plus la contrition que le *Cid*" (*Port Royal*, I [Pléiade edition], 356-57).

38. *The Mind's Ascent to God*, p. 224.

39[R]. In a prologue Junon, the wife of Jupiter, complains that she once again has been displaced in heaven by a mortal whom her husband prefers: Alcmène, wife of Amphitryon. But she promises revenge on the fruit of this union. In the play Mercure, son of Jupiter, aids his father in his escapade by assuming the appearance of Sosie, Amphitryon's servant. The latter is on his way to Alcmène from battle with a message of his master's victory and a cup of gold, booty that is offered to Alcmène as a token of love. Frightened by his double, Sosie returns to his master. Meanwhile, Jupiter, in the husband's form, departs from Alcmène, leaving a cup of gold. Refusing to believe his servant's tale, Amphitryon returns to his wife, who expresses surprise at his return. When she explains her surprise, Amphitryon doubts her fidelity. His suspicion is justified when Sosie opens his sack to find the gift missing. Amphitryon is sure his unknown rival has received it and then presented it to his unfaithful wife. Amphitryon gone, Jupiter appears in order to reassure Alcmène that in his recent anger he was just testing her. The disguised god then sends Sosie off to invite Amphitryon's captains to a dinner. When Amphitryon himself returns, he is greeted insolently from an upstairs window by Sosie, really Mercure. When the real Sosie returns with the captains, Amphitryon doubts the valet's word as to this mission. Jupiter appears and confounds matters only further. Resembling Amphitryon, he answers difficult questions as convincingly as Amphitryon. The witnesses believe Jupiter and follow him as their "captain," leaving Amphitryon alone and dejected. Mercure is then seen beating Sosie, and Jupiter is seen leaving Alcmène, promising her that the fruit of their union will be a creature hailed as the son of Jupiter. Amphitryon returns with his captains, having convinced them he is the victim of an imposter. But he and they are struck down by a noise from the heavens. When they recover, Alcmène's servant, Céphalie, informs Amphitryon that, during the burst of thunder, his wife gave birth to twins, one of whom strangled two serpents appearing in the crib. This creature was identified from on high as Hercule, son of Jupiter. Accepting this report as beautiful rather than shameful, Amphitryon is reassured by the descent of Jupiter in all his glory. When the god returns to the heavens, Sosie closes the play with a rueful comment on the value of the honors his master and he have received.

40. With the exception of *Crisante*, the series of plays culminating in *Les Sosies* seems an almost motif-for-motif corrective of the somber themes we find in the B portion of plays like *Le Filandre* and *L'Innocente Infidélité*. In *Clorinde*, Comédie (1635), *La Florimonde*, Comédie (1635), *La Belle Alphrède*, (1635 or 1636), and *Les Deux Pucelles*, Tragi-comédie (1636), the problematic B portions of the familiar tripartite structure are quickly resolved—so quickly that it is difficult in some cases to speak of a resacramentalized universe at the end. The sanctified character of the universe has been established almost from the outset. The immanentist character of the divinity is so stressed that some might consider the plays hardly religious, or at least not Christian. On the other hand, liberal observers might think that in a play like *La Belle Alphrède*, Rotrou's belief in divine immanence has never been more fully elaborated. The orthodox confidence in human nature and in the "state of nature" is orchestrated in almost every relation with unusual insistence. *La Belle Alphrède* is also interesting for its use of a ballet that is integral to the development of the action. In her study of this form, Margaret McGowan discusses this ballet briefly. However, she is more concerned with linking the ballet to other spectacular effects in Rotrou's theater: for example, the "machines célestes" in *Hercule mourant*, *Les Sosies*, and *Iphigénie*. See *Le Ballet de cour en France: 1581-1643*, pp. 235-36.

41. Pp. 81-82.

42. *Don Juan*, p. 163.

43. *Beyond Psychology*, p. 91.

44. Ibid., p. 92.

45. In reviewing the young man's plea, Sartre concludes: " . . . Le sentiment se construit par les actes qu'on fait; je ne puis donc pas le consulter pour me guider sur lui. Ce qui veut dire que je ne puis ni chercher en moi l'état authentique qui me poussera à agir, ni demander à une morale les concepts qui me permettront d'agir. Au moins, direz-vous, est-il allé voir un professeur pour lui

demander conseil. Mais, si vous cherchez un conseil auprès d'un prêtre, par exemple, vous saviez déjà au fond, plus ou moins, ce qu'il allait vous conseiller. Autrement dit, choisir le conseiller, c'est encore s'engager soi-même" (*L'Existentialisme est un humanisme*, p. 45-46).

46. For Bérulle, through the Incarnation, the flesh became Word: "Et comme la Personne du Verbe est divine & infinie, elle a aussi une toute extraordinaire & indicible application à la nature humaine, qui étant dépourvue de sa subsistence, a besoin de celle du Verbe éternel; laquelle, pour le dire ainsi, est actuante & pénétrante cette Humanité & en son Essence & en ses puissances, & en toutes ses parties; & ce encore selon l'étendue de son pouvoir & de son infinité, autant que la Créature en est capable au plus haut & dernier point de son élèvement. Et comme la divine Essence est toujours subsistente au Verbe éternel; aussi l'humanité n'a jamais été, & ne sera jamais un seul moment sans être toujours actuée & pénétrée, & toujours comme informée & comme animée de cette même subsistence" (*Discours de l'estat et des grandeurs de Jésus* in *Œuvres complètes*, I, 215 and 218).

47. For a discussion of this link, see Appendix B.

48. The quotation from the abbé's book and that from the Compagnie are given in Rébelliau, "La Compagnie du Saint Sacrement d'après des documents nouveaux," *Revue des Deux Mondes*, 78ᵉ année 5ᵉ période [1908], 859 and 861 respectively.

49. In its extreme immanentism, *Les Sosies* expresses that "modern . . . Promethean iconoclasm" of the post-Christian era which Vahanian contrasts with the "biblical" iconoclasm of the Christian era: " . . . Modern iconoclasm is an antidivine manifestation, whereas the biblical form is a deflation of man's natural inclination to deify himself, or his society, or the State, or his culture. In this light, any reader of the Bible will discern the relentless exposing of this manifold, constant proclivity to elevate the finite to the level of the infinite, to give to the transitory the status of permanent, and to attribute to man qualities that will deceive him into denying his finitude" (*Wait Without Idols*, p. 24). Such a "biblical" perspective on Rotrou's theater of immanence was not missing in his own day. Commenting on *La Belle Alphrède*, a play with many of the same themes (see note 40, above), one scandalized contemporary found it "l'extravagant poème de l'amour, fléau de vices et perte des cœurs" (quoted in Gaquère, *Le Théâtre devant la conscience chrétienne*, p. 14). In that play as in *Les Sosies*, analogues with symbols of Christian hagiography are close. The motif of the half-man, half-god born of the ruler of heaven and the chaste earthly spouse of a mortal might seem especially scandalous in its parallel to the most sacrosanct of Christian motifs. However, as I have indicated, the motif does express the "religious substratum" (Vahanian's phrase; see n.20, p. 201) of Rotrou's time. Moreover, Rotrou, in particular, develops it in a respectful manner as Molière does not. The latter's play is dominated by the satirical servant-figure; Rotrou's, by the serious spouses and the romantic Jupiter.

*III. The Temptation to Total Transcendence*

1ᴿ. Manilie, general of the Roman army that has just conquered the army of Corinth, assigns his lieutenant, Cassie, to hold in honorable captivity Crisante, the queen of Corinth. She has been separated from her husband, Antioche, who has fled from the conquerors. Cassie agrees, but he has no intention to respect his oath, blinded as he is by his desire for Crisante. Aware of Cassie's intentions, the queen is hardly assured by her attendants, Marcie and Orante, who insist on Heaven's tutelage and Cassie's honor. When Cassie makes it clear to Orante that he will not be checked in his desire, the attendant urges her mistress to yield in secret and preserve her life. Outraged, Crisante slays Orante. Then, when she is about to slay herself, Cassie prevents her. Claiming to be horrified at the consequences of his desire, he convinces her of his change of heart. But he has only been pretending, and violates the queen. Crisante recovers from the violation remorseful at her inability to avenge her stained honor because of her fear of death. Meanwhile, Cassie also shows remorse but forsakes suicide at the advice of his friend, Cléodore. The latter suggests they report the death of Crisante's guards (slain by Cassie) as due to the queen herself in her flight. When Crisante reports the offense to her honor to Antioche, he condemns her for not having slain herself rather than suffer dishonor. He tells her to give herself completely to Cassie, to whom she obviously surrendered willingly. Determined to revenge herself and to prove her integrity, Crisante appears before Manilie and demands justice. The Roman general puts Cassie's fate in her hands, and she, in turn, puts his fate in his own hands. The remorseful lieutenant is only too willing to slay himself. Crisante asks for his head. Meanwhile, Antioche despairs of Heaven's help and sees himself as a victim of fate. Crisante appears before him, throws the head of Cassie at his feet and then kills herself. Convinced but remorseful, Antioche slays himself and dies with a warning that a similar fate awaits Rome.

2. On the basis of Lancaster's detailed discussion at successive points in his *History*, *Crisante* might be thought of as preceding *Florimonde* and *Clorinde*. For the thematic reasons indicated, I have placed it as close as possible to the plays of the late thirties and early forties.

3. Op. cit., p. 81.
4. *History*, Part Two, I, 65, n. 20.
5. Op. cit., p. 87.
6. W. G. Moore, *French Classical Literature: An Essay*, p. 69.
7. Crisante's suicide might also be theologically absolved on rational grounds as one of those "actes de force" that the theologian A. Michel acknowledges as morally justified, especially in the case of a chaste woman's imperiled virtue: "Faut-il ajouter que cette conception du suicide, acte de force, ne semble pas étrangère à certains actes ou légendes de martyrs? On cite le cas de martyrs qui ont recherché le suprême sacrifice. Plusieurs vierges n'hésitèrent pas à se donner la mort pour éviter le déshonneur" (*Dictionnaire de théologie catholique*, Vol. 14, Pt. 2, col. 2740). To be sure, Crisante's suicide is undertaken not to avoid dishonor but because she has presumably already been dishonored. She thus seems reprehensible even under the large dispensation Michel here gives. However, Michel gives grounds for an even larger dispensation when he notes that under the pressures of such circumstances as imperiled virginity or chastity, a woman's "domaine" over her actions "lui échappe tout au moins partiellement" (ibid., col. 2745).

8. A concept I apply from the review of scholastic philosophy in Leslie Dewart's *The Future of Belief: Theism in a World Come of Age*, pp. 29-35, and especially p. 32, where the lay theologian writes: "The doctrine of St. Thomas, in the last analysis, rests on the hellenic principle that man's perfection *is* happiness."

9[R]. Jocaste, mother-wife of the dead Œdipe, king of Thebes, commiserates with her daughters, Ismène and Antigone, on the imminent clash of armies led by their brothers, Etéocle and Polynice, rivals for the throne of their father. The women learn from Etéocle, present occupant of the throne, that Ménécée, youngest son of Créon, has killed himself in order to fulfill a prophecy promising peace when the last blood of the race of Python will have been shed. Confident that this has been the meaning of this act, Etéocle tries to still the anger of his uncle, who reproaches the gods for working out their justice on his innocent children. Meanwhile, Polynice resents his brother's breach of contract whereby he, Polynice, was to have the throne at a certain time. He determines on mortal combat with Etéocle, thus horrifying even his chief ally, Adraste, father of his equally horrified but sympathetic wife, Argie. Before the walls of Thebes, Polynice refuses to heed the pleas of Antigone and their mother to forego battle with his brother. Both brothers die. Unlike her fearful sister, Antigone is determined to bury Polynice with the same honor to be accorded Etéocle, thus violating Créon's order, as new king, against such honors for Polynice. Meanwhile, the counselor Ephyte vainly beseeches the new king to respect the laws of heaven and earth by allowing honorable burial to Polynice. Learning of Antigone's breach of his law, Créon condemns her to death as she proudly refuses claims to complicity in her deed by Argie and Ismène. When his son, Hémon, Antigone's lover, pleads for the retraction of his father's sentence, the father attributes his gesture to a lover's interest. Hémon is determined to save his mistress even at the risk of rebellion. The king hears the warning of the blind priest, Tirésie, that his condemnation of Antigone is heinous to the gods. At first resentful of the priest's counsel, Créon finally decides to retract his orders concerning both Polynice and Antigone. But it is too late: Antigone has taken her own life. When the king arrives in her prison, he is met by his son, who takes his own life before his father, fulfilling the prophecy of such a loss made earlier by Tirésie to the resentful king. The king faints while Ismène closes the play berating herself for not following her sister's example.

10. "Préface" to *La Thébaïde* in *Œuvres*, I, 393. The two plays in question are Euripides' *The Phoenissae* and, of course, Sophocles' *Antigone*.

11. *History*, Part Two, I, 155.

12. *Classicisme et baroque dans l'œuvre de Racine*, p. 210.

13. "Le Mythe d'Antigone, de Garnier à Racine," *Revista de Letras*, V (1964), 200.

14. *Greek Tragedy: A Literary Study*, pp. 120-92, passim, but especially Chapter VI, "The Philosophy of Sophocles," pp. 151-55, from which I give this emblematic sentence: "The Aeschylean universe is one of august moral laws, infringement of which brings certain doom; the Sophoclean is one in which wrongdoing does indeed work out its own punishment, but disaster comes too without justification; at the most with 'contributary negligence'" (p. 154).

15. Op. cit., pp. 210-11. Citing the verses I have just quoted, Butler observes: " . . . Lorsqu'il s'agit de justifier le défi d'Antigone à Créon, les dieux païens se transforment en une Providence chrétienne."

16. Ibid.

17. Ibid., p. 212.

18. The phrase is the title of a book by Niebuhr, which is subtitled: *Essays on the Christian Interpretation of History*.

19. Before *Iphigénie*, Rotrou composed *Laure persécutée*, Tragi-comédie (1637), and *Les Captifs, ou les esclaves*, Comédie (1638). In both there is a reprise of many of the motifs of the resacramentalized universes of earlier plays. However, as Morel has noted in his critical edition, *Laure persécutée* is important in the aesthetic development of Rotrou. The playwright seems to be

forsaking the "structure romanesque" of his earlier work: "En revanche, les tragi-comédies qui suivront (*Iphigénie, Bélissaire, Célie, Don Bernard de Cabrère, Venceslas, Don Lope de Cardone*) seront construites au fil d'une intrigue serrée, et toujours précisément 'signifiante.' *Laure persécutée* constitue donc un précédent important. Parallèlement, on constate qu'à partir de cette tragi-comédie, et même lorsque Rotrou s'inspirera des Espagnols, unités et bienséances seront toujours assez étroitement observées" ("Introduction," *Laure persécutée, tragi-comédie*, publiée par Jacques Morel, p. 4).

20[R]. With the vessels of his Troy-bound forces trapped in a port by a becalmed sea, the Greek leader Agamemnon regrets having heeded the oracle that promised him release of his forces if he would sacrifice his daughter, Iphigénie, to the goddess Diane. He sends a second note to his wife, Clytemnestre, presumably at home. This note revises earlier terms in which he had induced his wife to bring Iphigénie to him on the pretext that she was to marry Achille. This second message has no sooner gone than the general begins to have second thoughts, and he almost recalls the messenger, Amintas. Finally, he resolves to heed his love as father rather than his duty as king. However, his brother, Ménélas, intercepts the message and berates Agamemnon for his flaccidity of purpose, reminding him he had sought his high post. But Agamemnon rejects this lack of family feeling, especially Ménélas' desire to sacrifice his niece for his wife's sin. Agamemnon determines to spare his daughter. At this, bent on victory and sustaining Diane's will, Ulysse appears, announcing the imminent arrival of Clytemnestre and Iphigénie. Defeated by fate, Agamemnon consents to the sacrifice, but urges that all try to conceal their real purpose from Clytemnestre. Discovering the reasons for her husband's distracted greeting and strange request that she return home alone, Clytemnestre curses her husband for his preoccupation with glory. She berates herself for ever having wed this assassin of her first husband and her infant son. When Achille appears, she trusts that this prospective husband will rescue his bride-to-be. Although Achille knows nothing of this marriage, he regards the use of his name as an insult and agrees to defend Iphigénie. His decision is reinforced as he falls in love with her on sight. Though she is herself astonished at her father's unnatural intentions, Iphigénie reproaches all those who oppose her sacrifice. At the altar itself, only she and Ulysse consistently sustain the will of Diane. However, Iphigénie finally brings her father around to accepting that will, as well. Her mother and her lover see only cruelty and pride in her self-sacrifice, but their opposition is ended when Iphigénie is assumed into the heavens by Diane. The goddess appears to announce her satisfaction with the sacrifice even though it has not actually drawn blood. The army can now proceed on its mission.

21. Op. cit., p. 120. I cannot, however, agree with this critic that Agamemnon himself is of a kind with the members of this unseemly band.

22. " . . . Il n'est pas rare que l'homme qui va sacrifier se trouve déjà marqué d'un caractère sacré, d'où résultent des interdictions rituelles qui peuvent être contraires à ses desseins. La Souillure qu'il contracte en n'observant pas les lois religieuses ou par le contact des chose impures, est une sorte de consécration. Le pécheur, comme le criminel, est un être sacré" ("Essai sur la nature et la fonction du sacrifice," *L'Année sociologique*, II [1897-98], 91). This author, Henri Hubert, a distinguished anthropologist, is not to be mistaken for the eminent literary scholar Judd Hubert, whom I cite in another context here.

23. Op. cit., pp. 45-46.

24. Whitney J. Oates and Eugene O'Neill, Jr., "Introduction," *Iphigenia in Aulis* in *The Complete Greek Drama*, II, 287.

25. In Rotrou's theater, *Bélissaire* follows *Clarice, ou l'amour constant*, Comédie (1641). This comedy shows some attempt at that balance of immanentism and transcendantalism which I study in *La Sœur*.

26[R]. Léonse, confidant of the emperor of Constantinople, plans to murder Bélissaire, the emperor's chief vassal, on the latter's triumphant return after a series of successful campaigns. Disguised as a pilgrim claiming to have served Léonse, the assassin follows the orders of the emperor's wife, Théodore. She is angry with Bélissaire for rejecting her love before her marriage and for his growing political esteem. However, Bélissaire gives a gold chain to the pilgrim because of Léonse, whose face he has forgotten but whose deeds he recalls. Repentant, Léonse throws off his disguise and warns Bélissaire that he is pursued by a woman whose name Léonse dare not give. Welcomed in the court by the emperor, Bélissaire is repulsed by Antonie, whom he loves. Though she loves him, Antonie has been warned by Théodore not to show it. Bélissaire is convinced that Antonie is the enemy whose name Léonse dared not give. Pursuing her vengeance, Théodore engages Narsès to murder Bélissaire. But when he is about to stab the sleeping Bélissaire, Narsès discovers a letter of appointment in which, at the emperor's behest, Bélissaire has named him sovereign of Italy. Narsès also repents, penning a message to Bélissaire and pointing to an unnamed woman as his employer. As the emperor begins to suspect his wife, she hires a third assassin: her cousin, Philippe, to whom she promises Antonie, who has already rejected him for Bélissaire. Earlier, Bélissaire had come upon Philippe in a park, at the mercy of several attackers. Rescuing Philippe, Bélissaire refused to identify himself (his face was covered) and to accept a reward, but he did accept a token of Philippe's gratitude: a ring. Thanks to this, the third assassin later recognizes his would-be victim as his one-time rescuer, Philippe, too, repents but refuses to name his employer. Before Philippe's attempt, Bélissaire had discovered from Antonie that she does love him and that his true enemy is Théodore. Bélissaire fears offending the emperor by a direct accusation, but, pretending to be asleep and dreaming aloud in the emperor's presence, he names Théodore as his enemy. The emperor warns his wife that he would give Bélissaire half his realm. But Bélissaire refuses, laying the scepter at the empress' feet. Her hatred intensified, Théodore resolves to seduce Bélissaire into destruction: she would have him caught with a scarf, evidence of his courtship of her. But he has Antonie pick up the garment and slips a love note to her. The empress gets hold of the note. In the vassal's hand but without an address, she tells the emperor that it is addressed to her, one of Bélissaire's many salacious letters over the years. Enraged, the emperor orders Bélissaire's death, refusing even to reply to his denials and his plea for justice in view of his service. However, beginning to regret his orders, the emperor learns that his wife has also repented. The emperor orders the salvation of the prisoner, but too late. Repudiating his wife forever, the emperor remorsefully waits for his own death.

27. The Manicheans' attitude toward woman is seen in their particular view of the first woman, Eve, and her role in the cosmic struggle between "light" and "darkness." As one student of the movement has summarized this attitude: "In the production of the human species the demoniacal forces played not an involuntary part but an active role of their own wicked designing, the creation of the two sexes being especially the work of the Evil One. His fiendish aim was by this means to incarcerate the light perpetually in the bonds of the carnal body. . . . In Adam, however, the luminous particles predominated, while Eve was composed wholly of dark elements" (A. V. Williams Jackson, *Researches in Manichaeism, With Special Reference to the Turfan Fragments*, p. 11).

28. *Modern Language Notes*, XXVII (1912), 226-27.

29. *History*, Part Two, II, 533.

30. In *Bélissaire*, as in *Les Captifs* before it, Rotrou is obviously returning to the theme of the twins, which he first treated in *Les Ménechmes*.

31. This editor puts stage directions just before the verse beginning "Achevez, mes soupirs . . . " (op. cit., IV. 523).

32. For example, most recently in Anselme's "Cet écrit . . . lui laisse . . . rechercher Clarice, au nom de sa *moitié*" (*Clarice*, V. 4; italics added).

33. Between *Bélissaire* and *La Sœur*, Rotrou wrote *Célie, ou le Viceroy de Naples*, Tragi-comédie (1644 or 1645). It anticipates some of the motifs of both *La Sœur* and *Le Véritable Saint Genest*, but is distinctly inferior to both.

34. As I have indicated, I shall illustrate Rotrou's final ambivalence by analyses of *La Sœur*, *Venceslas*, and *Cosroès*. To a certain extent, this ambivalence is anticipated by the play composed after *Saint Genest*, *Dom Bernard de Cabrére*, Tragi-comédie (1646). The play is really about Dom Lope, Bernard's friend, who is repeatedly frustrated in receiving the reward obviously due him for his outstanding services. In the last sixteen verses of the play, the king of the play does send after the disconsolate Lope in order to reward him. Lope finds himself, at least by royal promise, where the *données* of birth and performance put him in the initial A portion of the play. *Dom Bernard de Cabrère* thus seems a familiar immanentist tragicomedy. However, the dramaturgy establishes Lope as a comic figure: like Molière's Dom Garcie, his role is to be always on the verge of triumph over the fate that plagues him (an inner fate in Molière's hero, an outer one in Rotrou's). Lope's "comi-tragic" story thus sets the happy story of his friend, Dom Bernard, in a parodistic light; it makes the immanentist truths of Bernard's story seem mere illusions.

*IV. Nostalgia for Immanence*

1[R]. Lélie despairs when his valet, Ergaste, says that his father, Anselme, wishes him to marry Eroxène, niece of the wealthy Orgye. Lélie is secretly married to Sophie, a servant he passes off as his sister, Aurélie. The sister had many years before gone with her mother, Constance, to rejoin Anselme when the latter was serving in Poland. However, en route the mother and daughter had been captured by Turks. Sent to recover them when he had grown to manhood, Lélie had gotten only as far as Venice. Falling in love with a servant in an inn there, he married her and returned to his home in Nole. Thus, the news that he must marry Eroxène seems fatal not only to him but also to his friend Eraste, who loves Eroxène. Ergaste comes to the aid of the lovers by proposing that Lélie marry Eroxène and Eraste marry Lélie's "sister," Sophie, known as Aurélie. By night the men can swap wives and once the fathers are dead, legitimize their unions in proper marriage. This will also frustrate the plan by which Anselme had promised his "daughter" to the aged Polidor. Meanwhile, Anselme's brother, Géronte, returns from Constantinople with his son, Horace. He convinces Anselme that Constance is alive and that the girl in his house is not Aurélie but Sophie. These convictions are shaken by Ergaste, who claims to have learned in Turkish, Horace's only language, that Géronte was joking. Anselme's convictions are somewhat restored, however, by Géronte's demonstration that Ergaste does not know Turkish. Meanwhile, dressed as a pilgrim, Constance returns from Turkey. Lélie is overjoyed to regain his mother but fears to lose Sophie. The mother agrees to pretend that this girl, whom she has not seen, is Aurélie so that the plan for switching wives can be carried out. However, when she sees Sophie, Constance recognizes her daughter in the girl. Thinking he has wed his own sister, Lélie despairs. Meanwhile, Eroxène's servant, Lydie, is seen by Orgye with Eraste. Lydie has actually been chiding Eraste, because, not knowing Ergaste's plan, she had heard Eraste "wickedly" agree to marry Aurélie (Sophie). But Orgye thinks she is arranging something to his own financial detriment and so he mistreats Lydie. Vengeful, Lydie tells Anselme that years before, Pamphile, Orgye's brother and the father of Eroxène, had actually switched infants to insure a better life for his daughter. Exroène is really Aurélie, and Aurélie (Sophie) is Eroxéne. Orgye has kept this secret because his brother's will provided that, if rescued from the Turks, Eroxène was to receive 10,000 ducats. Were she not rescued, the false Eroxène (Aurélie) was to receive only 2,000. Repentant, Orgye confirms Lydie's tale. Three marriages are in view as the play ends: Lélie and the real Eroxène (Sophie), Eraste and the real Aurélie (the false Eroxène), Ergaste and Lydie.

2. Ergaste's doctrine might be designated "proleptic absolution." It is probably sacrilegious, since it involves the use of what St. Thomas considers a *strictly* necessary sacrament in order to obtain what he considers the less necessary one of matrimony: "Trois sacrements sont nécessaires de la première nécessité, c'est-à-dire, strictement, dont deux, par rapport aux individus particuliers, le baptême et la pénitence; le baptême simplement et absolument, la pénitence dans la seule hypothèse de péchés mortels commis après le baptême. Le sacrement de l'ordre est nécessaire à l'Eglise: *là où il n'y a pas de gouvernement, le peuple croulera* (Prov., xi, 14). Mais les autres sacrements ne sont nécessaires que d'une nécessité moins stricte: car la confirmation n'est en quelque sorte que le perfectionnement du baptême, l'extrême-onction, le perfectionnement de la pénitence; quant au mariage, il assura la perpétuité de l'Eglise par la propagation de la race chrétienne" (quoted by A. Michel in his article on the sacraments, *Dictionnaire de théologie catholique*, XIV, 1, col. 633). In commenting on this passage, Michel restates the widely held theological view that "le mariage est indispensable parce qu'une fois consommé, il indique parfaitement l'union du Christ avec l'Eglise" (col. 634).

3[R]. The aged king Venceslas orders his younger son, Alexandre, from his presence in order to reprimand his older son, Ladislas. The father reminds the latter of the crimes and indecencies attributed to the passionate prince. Impatiently waiting for his father to finish, Ladislas finally defends himself by admitting that he is eager to assume his father's throne. He feels supported because of the dissatisfaction of others with the king's failures due to age. Ladislas also claims that the charges of indecency are due to his father's favorite, the vassal Fédéric. The latter usurps his own rightful place, says Ladislas, both in affairs of state and affairs of the heart through pursuit of Cassandre, princess of Cunisberg. When the father attempts to reconcile his older son with both Alexandre and Fédéric, Ladislas angrily prevents his rival from mentioning the name of the woman whom he is about to request as a reward for his services to the king. Ladislas will not forsake his passion for Cassandre. The latter refuses his love, even though he says it is purified of its early lascivious motives. Insisting on her noble station, she can never forgive him the initial insult of such a desire. She admits, moreover, her love for another easily his equal. Convinced that his rival is Fédéric, Ladislas tells his sister, Théodore, of his anguish. She herself cannot gain the rational control she urges on her brother, for she is in love with Fédéric. Meanwhile, Fédéric assures Alexandre that he is only pretending to love Cassandre and she him. Nevertheless, Frédéric counsels his royal friend to give up the pretense now. Alexandre wants to prolong the ruse a few days longer, but when Cassandre tells him that Théodore wants her to wed Ladislas, Alexandre assures her that they will be wed that night. Meanwhile, Ladislas claims to have overcome his passion and is prepared to ask his father to grant Frédéric the woman he wants. Still seeking to protect Alexandre, Frédéric hedges, but finally obeys the king when the latter orders him to name the woman he wishes as a reward. Once again, Ladislas angrily interrupts his rival. Not yet having named his beloved, Frédéric pleads with the king not to be too severe with his own son. Later, Théodore recounts to her maid a dream in which she saw her brother, Ladislas, slain. The maid tries to reassure her: being a young, passionate man, one should expect Ladislas to be out in the middle of the night. When the wounded Ladislas appears, Théodore's fears are confirmed in a way she did not expect. She is overcome to hear from her brother that he has slain Frédéric when the latter answered his knock at Cassandre's very door. The king, brooding and unable to sleep, is the next to be shocked by his son's news. But all are shocked then to see Frédéric himself appear, soon followed by Cassandre demanding vengeance for the real crime Ladislas has committed—the murder of his own brother. Ladislas could claim absolution on the grounds that he struck Alexandre thinking him another, but he is glad to suffer because it pleases his beloved. The king promises justice to Cassandre, but he is troubled. Also, first his daughter, then Cassandre, then Frédéric propound reasons for him not to take his surviving son's life in punishment: Ladislas acted in error and in the dark; people think the king acts out of fear; the king owes Frédéric whatever he asks, etc. (Frédéric has been obliged by Théodore to make his plea.) The king yields, solving the dilemma between justice and natural love by abdicating in favor of his son. The old king, the new king, Théodore, and Frédéric, all hope that Cassandre's sorrow will yield in time and that she will accept King Ladislas in marriage.

I have used the critical edition prepared by W. Leiner (see Bibliography).

4. *Commentaires sur Corneille, Œuvres,* XXXI, 180-81.

5. Fréron finds Ladislas, Venceslas, and Frédéric admirable, but the other characters "médiocrement dessinés." He reproaches the play as departing from tragic grandeur in being "purement domestique" since "les ressorts qui font mouvoir cette machine sont frêles et voisins du comique." Fréron also objects that the action is built on the fragile premise of Ladislas' mistaken belief that the duke loves Cassandre: "Otez cette équivoque, toute la pièce tombe. . . . La vraie tragédie dédaigne ces petits moyens; elle ne se resserre non plus dans l'enceinte d'une maison . . . " (*L'Année littéraire: 1759,* 105-6). The sense of Marmontel's admiration will emerge in my commentary on his revisions. As for La Harpe, characteristically, he apes Voltaire in his judgments on Rotrou as on so many others: "De tous ceux qui ont écrit avant Corneille, c'est celui qui avait le plus de talent; mais comme son *Venceslas,* la seule pièce de lui qui soit restée, est postérieure aux plus belles du père du théâtre, on peut le compter parmi les écrivains qui ont pu se former à l'école de ce grand homme." And like Marmontel, he finds the denouement of this finest of Rotrou's plays "défectueux." Cited in Crane, "Introduction," *Jean Rotrou's "Saint Genest" and "Venceslas,"* p. 120.

6. Crane notes that the changes from this play's Spanish model are fewer than those in *Saint Genest* with respect to its Spanish model (op. cit., p. 113), but still finds that "the general result of Rotrou's changes is a play more compact and dramatic than the original, while the repulsive character of the hero has been softened and rendered more attractive" (p. 115). Lancaster is more aware of Rotrou's independence of his model: "Rotrou's play is by no means a translation

of Rojas and can hardly be called even an adaptation of it, for, while he drew from it the four main characters and suggestions for many of the situations, he added and altered so extensively that over half of the play, including all of the second and third acts, four scenes of the first, and nearly four of the last, are new" (*History*, Part Two, II, 546).

7. *Cours de littérature dramatique*, II, 341.

8. *Vies des poètes de Louis XIV*, p. 427.

9. On the other hand, Henri de La Pommeraye later found Rotrou a precursor of the realists and the naturalists: "Corneille mettait sur la scène des caractères; Rotrou y a mis un tempérament, comme on dit aujourd'hui; par là, il est plus romantique que classique; par là il se rapproche de Shakespeare, qui est un physiologiste admirable, et le type de Ladislas devrait être admiré sous ce rapport par les réalistes, les naturalistes, qui pourraient revendiquer Rotrou comme ancêtre." From a review on the occasion of a reprise of *Venceslas* at the Odéon, on August 30, 1885. I have consulted the review in *Recueil de pièces sur reprises du "Venceslas" de J. Rotrou* at the Bibliothèque de l'Arsenal (Rf. 7061).

10. "Lettre de M$^r$ de . . . à M de . . . sur la tragédie de Venceslas," *Mercure de France* (December, 1730), 2693.

11. Marmontel's commentary is contained in a June, 1759, reply to the May, 1759, criticism by Fréron in *L'Année littéraire* as well as in his "Avis au lecteur" to his corrected edition of the play: *Venceslas*, tragédie de Rotrou, retouchée par M. Marmontel (Paris: Sébastian Jarry, 1759) and in an *Examen du "Venceslas"* accompanying an edition of the original in 1773. Generous quotation from the *Examen* is to be found in Crane, op. cit., pp. 116-18.

12. Op. cit., pp. 172-73.

13. Op. cit., p. xiii.

14. *Esquisse*, p. 93.

15. Op. cit., p. xx.

16. Rotrou's consistency here leads one to question Orlando's contention that "attendosi . . . malgrado tutto al *dénouement* originario Rotrou ha sovrapposto, se cosi puo dire, un ultimo atto da tragicommedia ad un penultimo de tragedia" (op. cit., p. 340).

17. "Les Criminels de Rotrou en face de leurs actes," p. 236.

18. Ibid.

19. In *Le Temps*, September 14, 1885, in a review of the reprise of *Venceslas*, August 30, 1885. Contained in the same *Recueil* in which I read La Pommeraye's commentary (see note 9 above).

20. S. H. Butcher's translation in his *Aristotle's Theory of Poetry and Fine Art*, 4th ed., pp. 51-53. Obviously, this type of action is to be found in all of Rotrou's plays denominated *tragédie*.

21[B]. Syra, wife of King Cosroès of Persia, quarrels with her stepson, Syroès, the king's son by a previous marriage. She wishes to have her son by Cosroès, Mardesane, succeed his father on the throne. Mardesane, also leery of his mother's ambition, tells his brother that his warnings about the power of ambition are pointless, since he recognizes Syroès' legitimate claim. However, Palmyras, a minister, fallen from esteem because of Syra, warns Syroès that he must preclude any further inroads by seizing the throne from Cosroès. (Cosroès himself had seized it years before by murdering his own father, Hormisdas.) Syroès hesitates, constrained by the natural law and fearing that his opposition to Syra will alienate Narsée, Syra's daughter by her previous marriage. Tormented by remorse for his own usurpation, Cosroès heeds Syra's warnings about Syroès' ambition. He commands that Mardesane succeed him and that Syroès be arrested for a purported threat to the queen. However, the arresting officer, Sardarigue, urges the prince to seize power himself. Meanwhile, thinking Syroès in prison, Syra plans to have him either take poison or be stabbed if he refuses. Instead, Sardarigue arrives to arrest her, announcing that Syroès has seized power. Having ordered Syra to prison, the new king finds it hard to carry through with the next steps—the arrest of his father, in particular. His doubts are increased when Narsée arrives and accuses him of betraying their love. He submits to his mistress' request that her mother be turned over to her. Meanwhile, Hormidaste, the hired poisoner, has informed her brother, Artanasde, of the queen's plans. Repelled by such horror, they reveal the plan to the new king. Artanasde also reveals that at the time of the marriage of Syra and Cosroès, his sister had accepted the daughter of Palmyras in substitution for the child of Syra, who had died in her care. Palmyras, too, begins to tell his daughter her true identity, but he is called off by Artanasde in order to strengthen the new king in his wavering rule. That rule is firm enough when it comes to ordering first Syra and then Mardesane to death, but it weakens when Cosroès stands before his son in judgment. The son relents in the name of nature and turns the fate of his other prisoners over to the old king. When the latter has gone off, the new king learns that Mardesane has killed himself. Sardarigue then returns with the news that Syra has poisoned herself and that her husband is about to take his own life. Castigating Palmyras for having urged him to such justice, Syroès asks Narsée to help him either to save his father's life or to follow his example. Palmyras rushes after the couple, but Sardarigue declares that the pursuit is vain: the old king has died.

I have used the critical edition established by J. Schérer (see Bibliography).

22. Lancaster, *History*, Part Two, II, 550-53.

23. R. C. Knight, "*Cosroès* and *Nicomède*" in *The French Mind: Studies in Honor of Gustave Rudler*, p. 53 and passim.

24. Schérer, "Introduction," op. cit., p. xxiii.

25. Op. cit., p. 551.

26. Op. cit., p. 385.

27. Op. cit., pp. xxxiv-xxxv.

28. Ibid.

29. Op. cit., p. 405.

30. "The action primarily depends upon the character of Syroès, a highly interesting personality, neither altogether good nor altogether bad" (*History*, Part Two, II, 551).

31. See for example, Van Baelen, op. cit., p. 200.

32. Op. cit., p. 373.

33. See note 19, above p. 000.

34. Schérer speaks aptly of the three "trials" of the last act (op. cit., p. xv).

35. *History*, Part Two, II, 553.

36. Op. cit., p. 55.

37. Op. cit., note to verse 296, p. 22. Schérer also discounts the influence of Corneille's *Héraclius* (p. xxxiv) and reproaches d'Ussé de Valentine for cutting out the role of Narsée in his 1705 adaptation of the play (p. xxix).

38. Commenting on the "cri du sang" in this play, Cherpack has rightly

observed that *sang* cannot here "be conceived of as instinct" (*The Call of Blood in French Classical Tragedy*, p. 33). Taking "instinct" in the sense of a blind, irrational force to which a sentient being automatically surrenders, Cherpack is right, of course. However, it must be stressed that the "cri du sang" to which Syroès and other Rotrou characters respond in such dilemmas is implanted within them in all its "rationality," just as biological "instinct" is implanted in them in all its "irrationality."

39. Op. cit., note to verse 1736, p. 118.

V. Last Things . . . First Things . . .

1. See my remarks above, p. 16, concerning *L'Illustre amazone*, considered by some to be Rotrou's truly last play.

2. *A Natural Perspective: The Development of Shakespearean Comedy and Romance*, p. 119.

3. In 1649, the same year in which *Dom Lope* was produced, *Les Sosies* was presented in a spectacular production for which a densely printed, twelve-page brochure was published: *Dessin du poème de la grande pièce des machines de "La Naissance d'Hercule," dernier ouvrage de Monsieur de Rotrou.* The brochure suggests that the producer gave an even more "materialist" stress to Rotrou's play than the text itself.

4. *Classicisme et baroque dans l'œuvre de Racine*, p. 293.

5. Ibid.

6. "Avec *Athalie*," writes Goldmann, "le théâtre racinien se-termine sur une note optimiste de confiance et d'espoir, mais d'espoir en Dieu et l'éternité qui n'implique aucune concession sur le plan du réalisme terrestre, et nous ne sommes pas très sûr que la note dont M. Henri Maugis a accompagné dans l'édition scolaire des classiques Larousse, les derniers vers d'*Athalie*: 'La pièce se termine sur une impression d'apaisement et de sérénité', ne soit pas un contresens assez grave. C'est au contraire l'ange exterminateur, la menace contre le roi et la cour, l'espoir d'une promesse pour les persécutés que nous croyons entendre dans ces derniers vers que Racine fait encore dire sur la scène de son théâtre" (*Le Dieu caché*, p. 446).

7. I remind the reader that Morel sees the Rotrou *of the tragedies only* as the dramatist of transcendence, in contrast with Corneille, dramatist of immanence (see note 1, Introduction). However, in his more recent and comprehensive book on the dramatist, *Jean Rotrou: dramaturge de l'ambiguité*, the critic testifies to the dramatist's equal preoccupation with the immanentist motifs of his religious heritage. (See my Preface, p. x.).

8. Herrick, *Tragicomedy: Its Origin and Development in Italy, France and England*, p. 207.

9. See Lancaster, *The French Tragicomedy: Its Origin and Development from 1552 to 1628*, p. xxiv and passim.

10. Karl Guthke, *Modern Tragicomedy: An Investigation into the Nature of the Genre*, p. 17.

11. *Mon Cœur mis à nu* in *Œuvres* (Pléiade edition), p. 1203.

12. Ibid., p. 1220.

13. Cited by Philip Rieff, *The Triumph of the Therapeutic: Uses of Faith after Freud*, pp. 16-17.

14. Ibid., p. 17.

15. Ibid.

16. Op. cit., p. 1220. This is not to say that such an expression is not to be found within that theater. The dark moments of its B portions prove otherwise. Again, the non-dramatic poetry of Rotrou contains some of the most striking formulations of just the kind of "divorce" between "l'esprit et la brute" of which Baudelaire speaks here. Thus, from the very early "Les Pensées du religieux à Tyrsis":

> Les Charmes les plus ravissants
> Dont les objets touchent les sens
> Ne sont plus les auteurs de mes inquiétudes:
> Mon âme a vomi son poison,
> Et ses mauvaises habitudes
> N'ont plus d'intelligence avecque ma raison.

In *Autres Œuvres poétiques du Sr. Rotrou* (1631), p. 3. But obviously, Rotrou moves beyond such dark postulates—or more appropriately, returns to bright ones.

17. "A Minimal Definition of [French] Seventeenth-Century Tragedy," *French Studies*, X (1956), 306. For a "maximal" definition of tragedy, see my "Tragedy and the Tragic," *Arion*, II (1963), 86-95.

18. Stressing the "resurrection of the body" and reality as a "framework of promise and fulfillment," this theology is both Protestant and Catholic in expression. For a Protestant spokesman, see Carl E. Braaten, "Toward a Theology of Hope," *New Theology*, No. 5, pp. 90-111. For a Catholic spokesman, see Johannes B. Metz, "Creative Hope," ibid., pp. 130-41.

19. Quoted in the article on Rotrou in Liron, *Singularités historiques et littéraires*, I, 328-38.


*Appendix A*

1. *Le Théâtre du Marais*, I, 67-68.
2. *La Vie de Molière*, p. 52.
3. Pp. 1-134. The most controversial of these relations will perhaps always remain in shadow: those between Rotrou and Corneille during the famous Quarrel of *Le Cid*. The chief evidence of Rotrou's "championship" of Corneille is the letter signed "D. R.," "D'un Inconnu et véritable ami de Messieurs de Scudéry et Corneille" (see *La Querelle du Cid, pièces et pamphlets*, ed. Armand Gasté, pp. 154-57). This relatively early document in the Quarrel hardly corresponds in statement or tone to the "championship" of Corneille attributed to Rotrou by one critic after another. In his review of the question, Chardon recalls that, quite exceptionally, Jules Taschereau (*Histoire de la vie et des ouvrages de P. Corneille*, 1829) had found that the "unknown" author of the famous letter was obviously more pro-Scudéry than pro-Corneille. Chardon reads the document as conciliatory, laying blame and praise equally on Corneille and Scudéry in its call for an end to the quarreling. Chardon adds that this conciliatory attitude seems to reflect what little else we know of Rotrou personally (*La Vie de Rotrou mieux connue*, pp. 121 ff). However, in view of certain other evidence cited by Chardon himself, we might wonder how conciliatory Corneille would have considered

Rotrou in view of the latter's arrival, during the very peak of the battle, at the court of the Comte de Belin. Belin was Rotrou's patron, but he was also the patron of Mairet, Corneille's most virulent adversary in the Quarrel. The timing of Rotrou's visit might have given his friend and former pupil some cause for wonder. Again, Rotrou also dedicated his *Agésilan de Colchos* to Richelieu's niece, Mme de Combalet, during the Quarrel. But perhaps the visit to the "enemy camp" was, in fact, a mission of conciliation, just as the dedication was a gesture to show that, in favoring the Cardinal's literary enemy, Rotrou was not forgetting his loyalty to the Cardinal himself. Or were both gestures basically anti-Corneille? The answer to these questions may never be found in extrinsic evidence. However, if Rotrou's theater gives any clue to his probable attitude, the effort there to reconcile various antinomies suggests that Chardon's reading of Rotrou's role in the Quarrel is the correct one.

*Appendix B*

1. XIV, 1, col. 488.
2. Ibid., col. 485 ff. In reducing *sacramentum* to its etymological components, the *Oxford English Dictionary* notes that "the etymological sense of L. sacramentum would be either (1) a result of consecration, or (2) a means of consecrating, dedicating or securing by a religious sanction. The latter of these notions is that which seems to be present in the classical uses of the word: (1) the military oath, oath or solemn engagement in general; (2) the caution-money deposited by the parties to a lawsuit; hence (3) a civil suit or process. In Christian Latin from the 3rd century the word was the accepted rendering of Gr. μυσζήριοτ MYSTERY. This use is evidently not based on either of the specific applications just mentioned, but is the result of recourse to the etymological meaning." Obviously, the editors of the O.E.D. disagree with the theologian Michel on the influence of the classical applications upon Christian adaptations of the word. In *Principles of Sacramental Theology*, Bernard Leeming (S.J.) gives only the O.E.D.'s second interpretation of *mentum* in this context: "Hence, etymologically, the meaning is that by which something is made holy or sacrosanct." However, in the same passage, Leeming notes that the classical meaning of "solemn engagement or obligation assumed" did continue into the Christian tradition: "In Tertullian and Cyprian the meaning varies between that of an obligation assumed and that of a sacred mystery" (op. cit., pp. 560-61).
3. "St. Augustine's Rhetoric of Silence: Truth vs. Eloquence and Things vs. Signs" in his *Renaissance and Seventeenth-Century Studies*, p. 8. A strictly theological discussion of Augustine's sacramental theology is given at many points in Leeming, op. cit., but especially pp. 561-63.
4. Ibid.
5. *Dictionnaire de théologie catholique*, XIV, 1, col. 489.
6. "Figura" in *Scenes from the Drama of European Literature*, p. 37.
7. Ibid., p. 29.
8. Ibid., p. 37.
9. *Parole, église et sacrements*, p. 71.
10. "Figura," p. 61.
11. *Christian Rite and Christian Drama in the Middle Ages*, p. 284.
12. Ibid.

13. For a similar thesis, see my "Shakespeare: The Play as Mirror" in *Play within a Play*, pp. 11-35.

14. *A Natural Perspective: The Development of Shakespearean Comedy and Romance*, especially Chapter IV, pp. 118-59.

15. "The Search for a Dramatic Formula for the *auto sacramental*," *PMLA*, XLV (1950), 1196-97. Copyright © 1950 by the Modern Language Association of America. Reprinted by permission.

16. Ibid., 1197.

17. Ibid., 1207 (italics added in English passages).

18. Ibid., 1209.

19. XIV, 1, col. 693.

20. XIV, 1, col. 693. Furetière limits his definition of *sacrilège* to a strictly doctrinal sense (with examples). However, earlier in the century, in *A Dictionarie of the French and English Tongues* (London, 1611), Cotgrave reports both the doctrinal and extended senses: "*Sacrilege*: a sacrilegious person, church robber, stealer of holie or hallowed things; also sacrilege, or church robbing; *any hainous, or horrible offense or offender*" (italics added). On the other hand, Cotgrave gives only the strictly religious meaning of French *sacremens*: "Mysticall rites, or holie mysteries; and hence, the Sacraments of the Church."

21. *Don Juan: Une Etude sur le double*, p. 113. This French edition contains two separate essays: one on the theme of Don Juan and the other on the theme of the double. Much of the latter appears in English translation from the original German as "The Double as Immortal Self" in *Beyond Psychology*, pp. 62-101.

# Bibliography

Entries are arranged under the following categories: A. Original Editions of Rotrou's Plays; B. Critical Editions of Individual Plays of Rotrou; C. Other Works of Rotrou Cited, Including Collaborations; D. Collections of Rotrou's Plays; E. Adaptations of Certain Plays of Rotrou; F. Models and Sources of Rotrou's Plays; G. Dictionaries, Encyclopedias, and Similar Reference Works; H. Studies of Rotrou, Including Studies of Individual Works and Aspects of His Art and Life; I. Other References.

## A. Original Editions of Rotrou's Plays

*Agésilan de Colchos*, Tragi-comédie (Paris: Antoine de Sommaville, 1637).
*Amélie*, Tragi-comédie (Paris: Antoine de Sommaville, 1638).
*Antigone*, Tragédie (Paris: Toussaint Quinet, 1649).
*La Bague de l'oubli*, Comédie (Paris, F. Targa, 1635).
*Le Bélissaire*, Tragédie (Paris: Antoine de Sommaville & Augustin Courbé, 1644).
*La Belle Alphrède*, Comédie (Paris: Antoine de Sommaville & Toussaint Quinet, 1639).
*Les Captifs, ou les esclaves*, Comédie (Paris. Antoine de Sommaville, 1640).
*La Céliane*, Tragi-comédie (Paris: Toussaint Quint, 1637).
*Célie, ou le Viceroy de Naples*, Tragi-comédie (Paris: Toussaint Quinet, 1646).
*La Célimene*, Comédie (Paris: Quinet, 1637).
*La Célimene* Comédie (Paris: Antoine de Sommaville & Augustin Courbé, 1653).
*Clarice ou L'Amour constant*, Comédie (Paris: Toussaint Quinet, 1643).
*Clorinde*, Comédie (Paris: Antoine de Sommaville, 1637).
*Crisante*, Tragédie (Paris: Antoine de Sommaville & Toussaint Quinet, 1640).
*Les Deux Pucelles*, Tragi-comédie (Paris: Antoine de Sommaville & Toussaint Quinet, 1639).
*La Diane*, Comédie (Paris: François Targa, 1635).
*Dom Bernard de Cabrère*, Tragi-comédie (Paris: Antoine de Sommaville, 1647).
*Dom Lope de Cardone*, Tragi-comédie et dernier ouvrage de M. de Rotrou (Paris: Antoine de Sommaville, 1652).
*La Doristée*, Tragi-comédie (Paris: Antoine de Sommaville, 1635).
*Le Filandre*, Comédie (Paris: Antoine de Sommaville, 1637).
*La Florimonde*, Comédie (Paris: Antoine de Sommaville, 1655).

BIBLIOGRAPHY

*Hercule mourant*, Tragédie (Paris: Antoine de Sommaville, 1636).
*L'Heureuse Constance*, Tragi-comédie (Paris: Toussaint Quinet, 1636).
*L'Heureux Naufrage*, Tragi-comédie (Paris: Antoine de Sommaville, 1638).
*L'Hypocondriaque ou le mort amoureux*, Tragi-comédie (Paris: Toussaint du Bray, 1631).
*L'Innocente infidélité*, Tragi-comédie (Paris: Antoine de Sommaville, 1637).
*Iphigénie*, Tragédie (Paris: Toussaint Quinet, 1641).
*Laure persécutée*, Tragi-comédie (Paris: Antoine de Sommaville, 1639).
*Les Ménechmes*, Comédie (Paris: Toussaint Quinet, 1636).
*Les Occasions perdues*, Tragi-comédie (Paris: Toussaint Quinet, 1635).
*La Pelérine amoureuse*, Tragi-comédie (Paris: Antoine de Sommaville, 1637).
*La Sœur*, Comédie (Paris: Antoine de Sommaville, 1647).
*Les Sosies*, Comédie (Paris: Antoine de Sommaville, 1638).


B. *Critical Editions of Individual Plays of Rotrou*

Rotrou: "*Cosroès*," tragédie, édition critique, publiée par Jacques Schérer (Paris: Marcel Didier, 1950).
"Laure persécutée, tragi-comédie, édition critique," publiée par Jacques Morel. (Typescript, 1966).
*Jean Rotrou's "Saint Genest" and "Venceslas*," edited with Introduction and Notes by Thomas Frederick Crane (Boston, New York, Chicago, London: Ginn & Company, 1907).
Rotrou: "*Venceslas, tragi-comédie*," édition critique, éditée par W. Leiner (Schriften der Universität des Saarlandes: West-Ost-Verlag Saarbrücken GMBH., 1954).
*Le Véritable Saint Genest*, ed. R. W. Ladborough (London: Cambridge University Press, 1954).


C. *Other Works of Rotrou Cited, Including Collaborations*

*Autres Œuvres du même auteur* (Paris: F. Targa, 1635).
*Autres Œuvres poétiques du Sr. Rotrou* (Paris: Toussaint du Bray, 1631).
*L'Aveugle de Smyrne, Tragi-comédie*, par Les Cinq Autheurs (Paris: Augustin Courbe, 1638).
*La Comédie des Tuileries*, par Les Cinq Autheurs (Paris: Augustin Courbé, 1637).
*L'Illustre Amazone*, Anon. (attribué à Rotrou), published by Viollet-Le-Duc in Vol. 5 of his edition (see Section D, below).


D. *Collections of Rotrou's Plays*

*Œuvres de Jean Rotrou*, avec une notice sur la vie de Jean Rotrou et des notices historiques et littéraires par Viollet-le-Duc (5 vols.; Paris: Th. Desoer, 1820. Reprinted: Geneva: Slatkine Reprints, 1967).

BIBLIOGRAPHY

*Rotrou: Théâtre choisi*, avec une introduction et des notices par Félix Hémon (Paris: Classiques Garnier, s.d. Reprint of original: Paris: Laplace, Sanchez et Cie, 1883).

*Théâtre choisi de J. de Rotrou*, avec une étude par Louis de Ronchaud (2 vols.; Paris: Librairie des Bibliophiles, 1882).

E. *Adaptations of Certain Plays of Rotrou*

"*La Célimène*" *de M<sup>r</sup> de Rotrou*, accommodée au théâtre sous le nom d' "Amarillis, pastorale", par M<sup>r</sup> Tristan (Paris: chez Antoine de Sommaville et chez Augustin Courbé, 1653).

*Cosroès, tragédie*," *par feu M<sup>r</sup> de Rotrou*, nouvellement remise au théâtre (Paris: Pierre Ribou, 1705). Revision by Bernin de Valentiné, Sieur d'Ussé.

*Dessein du poème de la grande pièce des machines de "La Naissance d'Hercule", dernier ouvrage de Monsieur de Rotrou, représentée sur le théâtre du Marais, par les Comédiens du Roi* (Paris: René Baudry, 1650). Adaptation of *Les Sosies*.

"*Venceslas*," *tragédie de Rotrou, retouchée par M. Marmontel* (Paris: Sébastian Jorry, 1759).

F. *Models and Sources of Rotrou's Plays*

(For individual plays of authors listed in collections here, consult Index under name of author.)

Bargagli, Girolamo, *La Pellegrina, commedia* (Siena: Bonetti, 1589).
Cellotii, Lucovici. *Opera Poetica* (Paris: Cramoisy, 1630).
Cervantes, Miguel de (Cervantes Saavedra). "Las Dos Donzellas," *Novelas Exemplares*, ed. Rodolfo Schevill y Adolfo Bonilla (Madrid: Gráficas Reunidas, 1925), III, 5-68.
Corneille, Pierre. *Œuvres*, ed. Ch. Marty-Laveaux (12 vols.; Paris: Hachette, 1862-68).
Della Porta, Giambattista. *Le Commedie*, ed. Vincenzo Spampanato (2 vols.; Bara: Gius. Laterza & Figli, 1910-11).
Desfontaines, Nicolas-Marc. *Bélissaire* (Paris: Augustin Courbé, 1641).
———. *L'Illustre Comédien, ou le martyre de S. Genest, tragédie* (Paris: Cardin de Besogne, 1646).
Euripides. [Plays] in *The Complete Greek Drama*, ed Whitney J. Oates and Eugene O'Neill, Jr. (2 vols.; New York: Random House, 1938).
Mira de Améscua. *Teatro*, ed. Angel Valbuena Prat (2 vols.; Madrid: Ediciones de la "Lectura," 1926-28).
Oddi, Sforza. *L'Erofilomachia, overo il duello d'amore e d'amicitia, commedia* (Peruggia: Panizza, 1572).
Plautus. *Works*, with an English translation by Paul Nixon (5 vols.; Cambridge, Mass.: Harvard University Press, Loeb Classical Library, 1950-52).
Rojas Zorrilla, Don Francisco de. *No hay ser padre siendo rey* in *Comedias escogidas*, ed. Don Ramon de Mesonero Romanos (Madrid: Atlas, 1952).

## BIBLIOGRAPHY

(Biblioteca de autores españoles desde la formacion del lenguaje hasta nuestros días.)

*Seneca's Tragedies*, ed. and with an English translation by Frank Justus Miller (2 vols.; Cambridge, Mass.: Harvard University Press, Loeb Classical Library; London: William Heinemann Ltd., 1917).

Sorel, Ch. *Histoire amoureuse de Cléagenor et de Doristée. Contenant leurs diverses fortunes avec plusieurs autres estranges avantures arrivées de nostre temps disposées en quatre livres* (Paris: Du Bray, 1621).

Sophocles. [Plays] in *The Complete Greek Drama*, ed. Whitney J. Oates and Eugene O'Neil, Jr. (2 vols.; New York: Random House, 1938).

Urfé, Honoré d'. *L'Astrée*, ed. Hugues Vaganay (5 vols.; Lyon: Massen, 1925-28).

Vega (Carpio), Lope Felix de. *Obras escogidas*, ed. Federico Carlos Sainz de Robles (3 vols.; Madrid: M. Aguilar, 1946-55). (*Lo Fingido Verdadero, Villan de Xetafe*).

———. *Obras* publicados por la Real Academia Española (nueva edición), obras dramáticas, IX, 590-624 (13 vols.; Madrid: Tipografía de Archivos. Olózaga, I., 1916-30).

G  *Dictionaries, Encyclopedias, and Similar Reference Works*

Beauchamps, Pierre François Godard de. *Recherches sur les théâtres de France, depuis l'année onze cent soixante & un jusques à présent* (3 vols.; Paris: Prault père, 1735).

*Catholic Biblical Encyclopedia: New Testament*, ed. John E. Steinmueller and Kathryn Sullivan (New York: Joseph F. Wagner, 1950).

*Catholic Biblical Encyclopedia: Old Testament*, ed. John E. Steinmueller and Kathryn Sullivan (New York: Joseph F. Wagner, 1956).

Cayrou, Gaston, *Le Français classique: Lexique de la langue du dix-septième siècle, expliquant d'après les dictionnaires du temps et les remarques des grammariens le sens et l'usage des mots aujourd'hui vieillis ou différemment employés*, 6ᵉ édition revue et corrigée (Paris: Didier, 1948).

Chauffepié, Jacques G. de. *Nouveau Dictionnaire historique et critique pour servir de supplément ou de continuation au "Dictionnaire historique et critique" de Mr. Pierre Bayle* (4 vols.; Amsterdam: Chatelain; The Hague: de Hondt, 1750-56).

Cotgrave, Randle. *A Dictionarie of the French and English Tongues*, reproduced from the 1st edition, London (1611), with Introduction by W. S. Woods (Columbia: University of South Carolina Press, 1950).

*Dictionnaires des lettres françaises*, publié sous la direction du Cardinal Georges Grente: *Le Dix-septième Siècle* (Paris: Arthème Fayard, 1954).

*Dictionnaire de théologie catholique, contenant l'exposé des doctrines de la théologie catholique, leurs preuves et leur histoire*, ed. A. Vacant, E. Mangeot, and E. Amann (Paris: Letouzey et Ané, 1939), XIV, 1ᵉʳᵉ Partie.

*Dogmatic Canons and Decrees: Authorized Translations of the Dogmatic Decrees of The Council of Trent, The Decree on the Immaculate Conception, The Syllabus of Pope Pius IX, and The Decrees of the Vatican Council* (New York: The Devin-Adair Co., 1912).

# BIBLIOGRAPHY

Dupin, Louis Ellies (ed.). *Nouvelle Bibliothèque des auteurs ecclésiastiques, contenant l'histoire de leur vie, le catalogue, la critique, et la chronologie de leurs ouvrages, le sommaire de ce qu'ils contiennent, un jugement sur leur style et sur leur doctrine, et le dénombrement des différentes éditions de leurs œuvres* (8 vols.; Paris: Parlard; Amsterdam: Humbert, 1693-1715).

Furetière, Antoine. *Dictionnaire universel, contenant généralement tous les mots françois tant vieux que modernes et les termes des sciences et des arts*, 3⁰ édition rev. Basnage de Bauval (Rotterdam: Reinier Leers, 1708).

Godefroy, Frédéric (ed.). *Dictionnaire de l'ancienne langue française et de tous ses dialectes du IX⁰ au XV⁰ siècles, composés d'après le dépouillement de tous les importants documents, manuscrits ou imprimés, qui se trouvent dans les grands bibliothèques de la France et de l'Europe, et dans les principales archives départementales, municipales, hospitalières ou privées* (10 vols.; Paris: F. Vieweg, 1881-1902).

Larousse, Pierre (ed.). *Grand Dictionnaire universel du XIX⁰ siècle, français, historique, géographique, mytholgique, bibliographique, littéraire, artistique, scientifique, etc., etc.* (Paris: Administration du Grand Dictionnaire universel, s.d.).

Migne, Jacques Paul (ed.). *Encyclopédie théologique, ou série de dictionnaires sur toutes les parties de la science religieuse, offrant en français la plus claire, la plus commode, la plus variée et la plus complète des théologies* (50 vols.; Paris: chez l'éditeur, 1845).

———. *Nouvelle Encylopédie théologique, ou nouvelle série de dictionnaires sur toutes les parties de la science religieuse* (52 vols.; Paris: Petit-Montrouge, J.-P. Migne, 1851-1859).

———. *Troisième et dernière Encyclopédie théologique, ou troisième et dernière série de dictionnaires sur toutes les parties de la science religieuse, offrant en français et par ordre alphabétique la plus claire, la plus facile, la plus commode, la plus variée et la plus complète des théologies* (66 vols.; Paris: Petit-Montrouge, J.-P. Migne, 1855-66).

Moréri, Louis. *Le Grand Dictionnaire historique, ou le mélange curieux de l'histoire sacrée et profane*, 18⁰ édition revue, corrigée et augmentée (8 vols.; Amsterdam: Brunel, 1740).

*The Oxford Dictionary of the Christian Church*, ed. F. L. Cross (London: Oxford University Press, 1957).

*The Oxford English Dictionary, Being a Corrected Re-issue with an Introduction, Supplement and Bibliography of a New English Dictionary on Historical Principles, Founded Mainly on the Materials Collected by "The Philological Society,"* ed. James A. H. Murray, Henry Bradley, W. A. Craigie, and C. T. Onions (Oxford: The Clarendon Press, 1933), IX.

H. *Studies of Rotrou, Including Studies of Individual Works and Aspects of His Art and Life*

Alciatore, Jules C. "Stendhal, admirateur de Rotrou," *French Review*, XXXIII (January, 1960), 239-46.

Anonymous. "Lettre de Mʳ de . . . à M. de . . . sur la tragédie de *Venceslas*," *Mercure de France* (December, 1730), p. 2693.

Chardon, Henri. *La Vie de Rotrou mieux connue–documents inédits sur la* société polie de son temps et *La Querelle du Cid* (Paris: Alphouse Picard; Le Mans: Pellechat, 1884).

Curnier, Léonce. *Etude sur Jean Rotrou* (Paris: Typographie A. Hennuyer, 1885).

Fréron, Elie. "Venceslas" [Review article], *L'Année littéraire: 1759*, pp. 194-206.

Fries, Wilhelm. *Der Still der Theaterstücke Rotrous: Eine Untersuchung über Formprobleme des barocken Vostadiums der französischen Literatur des Klassizismus* (Würzburg: Buchdruckerei Richard Mayr, 1933).

Ganderax, Louis. "Revue dramatique: *Venceslas*," *Revue des deux mondes*, 50ᵉ année, 3ᵉ période (September 15, 1885), pp. 455-65. On the occasion of the reprise of *Venceslas* at the Odéon, August 30, 1885.

Garapon, Robert. "Rotrou et Corneille," *Revue d'histoire littéraire de la France*, L (1950), 385-94.

Gillot, Hubert. "Le Théâtre d'imagination au 17ᵉ siècle: Jean de Rotrou," *Revue des cours et conférences*, XXXIV (July 15, 1933), 577-90; (July 30, 1933), 674-87.

Hubert, Judd. "Le Réel et l'illusoire dans le théâtre de Corneille et dans celui de Rotrou," *Revue des sciences humaines*, XCV (July-September, 1958), 333-50.

Jarry, J. *Essai sur les œuvres dramatiques de Jean Rotrou*, thèse présentée à la Faculté des Lettres de Douai (Lille: L. Quarré; Paris: A. Durand, s.d.).

Knight, R. C. "*Cosroès* and *Nicomède*" in *The French Mind: Studies in Honor of Gustave Rudler*, ed. Will Moore, Rhoda Sutherland, and Enid Starkie (Oxford: The Clarendon Press, 1952), pp. 53-69.

Knutson, Harold C. *The Ironic Game: A Study of Rotrou's Comic Theater*, University of California Publications in Modern Philology, Vol. 79 (Berkeley and Los Angeles: University of California Press, 1966).

Laboullaye, Ferdinand Simon de, and Pierre-Etienne Piestre Cormon. *Corneille et Rotrou, comédie en un acte* (Paris: Marchant, s.d.). First played in 1845.

Lancaster, H. C. "The Source of *Britannicus*: II, 6," *Modern Language Notes*, XXVII (1912), 226-27.

La Pommeraye, Henri de. "*Venceslas*" [Review article] in *Recueil de pièces sur reprise du "Venceslas"* [at the Odéon, August 30, 1885]. (Holdings of Bibliothèque de l'Arsenal: Rf 7061).

Latouche, Hyacinthe J.-de. *La Mort de Rotrou* (Paris: Delaunay, 1811).

Lebègue, Raymond. "Rotrou: dramaturge baroque," *Revue d'histoire littéraire de la France*, L (1950), 379-84.

Leiner, W. *Etude stylistique et littéraire de "Venceslas," Tragi-comédie de Jean Rotrou* (dissertation, Saarlandes, 1955).

Le Menestrel, Ch. (ed.). *Jean Rotrou, dit "Le Grand": Ses Ancêtres et ces descendants, sa vie, coup d'œil sur l'art à son époque et sur ses œurves; chroniques extraites des manuscrits d'une des petites-nièces, La Comtesse Olympe de Lernay—compte-rendu de la solemnité du 30 juin 1867 pour l'inauguration de la statue du poète illustre, magistrat héroïque, à Dreux, sa patrie—Notice sur "Saint Genest" et "Venceslas"* (Dreux: Ch. Le Menestrel, 1869).

Liron, Abbé Dom. *Singularités historiques et littéraires* (Paris: Didot, 1738), I, 328-38.

BIBLIOGRAPHY

Maillier, Charles. *La Mort de Rotrou, pièce en vers en un acte et un épilogue* (Mesnil: Typographie Firmin-Didot, 1950).

Marmontel, Jean François. *Examen du Venceslas* in "Venceslas, tragédie," *Chefs-d'œuvres dramatiques, ou Recueil des meilleures pièces du théâtre françois. Tragique, comique et lyrique avec des discours préliminaires sur les trois genres et des remarques sur la langue et le goût par M. Marmontel* (Paris: Grangé, 1773).

———. "*Venceslas*" (Reply to Fréon's commentary). *L'Année littéraire: juin 1759*, pp. 117-30.

Millevoye, Charles-Hubert. *La Mort de Rotrou: Les Embellissements de Paris et autres poésies* (Paris: A. Bertrand, 1811).

Morel, Jacques. *Jean Rotrou: Dramaturge de l'ambiguité* (Paris: Armand Colin, 1968).

———. "Les Criminels de Rotrou en face de leurs actes" in *Le Théâtre tragique*, ed. Jean Jacquot (Paris: Editions du Centre National de la Recherche Scientifique, 1962), pp. 225-37.

———. "*L'Hercule sur l'Oeta* de Sénèque et les dramaturges français de l'époque de Louis XIII," in *Les Tragédies de Sénèque et le théâtre de la Renaissance*, ed. Jean Jacquot, (Paris: Editions du Centre National de la Recherche Scientifique, 1964), pp. 95-111.

———. "Le Mythe d'Antigone, de Garnier à Racine," *Revista de letras*, V (1964), 195-204.

———. "Les Stances dans la tragédie française du XVII° siècle," *XVII° Siècle*, Nos. 66-67 (Numéro spécial, 1965), 43-56.

Nelson, Robert J. "Rotrou: The Play as Miracle" in *Play Within a Play: The Dramatist's Conception of His Art—Shakespeare to Anouilh* (New Haven, Conn.: Yale University Press, 1958), 36-46.

Orlando, Francesco. *Rotrou: Dalla Tragicommedia alla tragedia*, Università di Pisa: Studi di Filologia Moderna, Nuova Serie, Vol. IV (Torino: Bottego d'Erasmo, 1963).

Person, Léonce. *Histoire du "Venceslas" de Rotrou, suivie des notes critiques et biographiques* (Paris: Léopold Cerf, 1882).

———. *Histoire du "Véritable Saint Genest" de Rotrou* (Paris: Léopold Cerf, 1882).

———. *Les Papiers de Pierre de Rotrou de Saudreville, secrétaire du Maréchal de Guébrant, commissaire des guerres à l'armée d'Allemagne, conseiller-secrétaire du roi, couronne de France, et de ses finances* (Paris: Léopold Cerf, 1883).

Peysonnié, Paul. *Cours d'appel d'Orléans. Audience de rentrée du 16 octobre 1899. Discours de M. l'avocat général Paysonnié: "Rotrou: magistrat et auteur dramatique"* (Orléans: Imprimerie Orléanaise, 1899).

Saint René-Taillandier. *Rotrou: Sa vie et ses œuvres* (Paris: Lahure, 1865).

Sarcey, Francisque. "*Venceslas*" (Review of reprise at Odéon, August 30, 1885) *Le Temps*, September 14, 1885. (Also contained in *Recueil de pièces sur reprise du "Venceslas"* in holdings of Bibliothèque de l'Arsenal: Rf 7061).

Schérer, Jacques. "Une scène inédite de 'Saint Genest'," *Revue d'histoire littéraire de la France*, L (1950), 394-403.

Steffens, Georg. *Rotrou-Studien: I—Jean de Rotrou als Nachamer Lope de Vegas* (Jean und Leipzig: Wilhelm Gronau, 1939).

# BIBLIOGRAPHY

Stiefel, Arthur Ludwig. "Jean Rotrous *Cosroès* und seine Quellen," *Zeitschrift für französische Sprache und Litteratur*, XXIII (1901), 69-188.

──. "Über die Chronologie von J. Rotrou's dramatischen Werken," *Zeitschrift für französische Sprache und Litteratur*, XVI (1894), 1-49.

──. "Über Jean Rotrous Spanische Quellen," *Zeitschrift für Französische Sprache und Litteratur*, XXIX (1907), 195-234.

──. "Unbekannte Italienische Quellen Jean Rotrou's," *Zeitschrift für Französische Sprache und Litteratur*, V. Supplement (Oppeln und Leipzig: Eugen Franck's Buchhandlung—Georg Maste—1891).

Valle Abad, Federico del. *Influencia española sobre la literatura francesa: Juan Rotrou (1609-1650)* (Avila: Senén Martin, 1946).

Van Baelen, Jacqueline. *Rotrou: Le Héros tragique et la révolte* (Paris. Nizet, 1965).


*I. Other References*

*Aristotle's "Theory of Poetry and Fine Art," with a Critical Text and Translation of "The Poetics,"* by S. H. Butcher, and with a Prefatory Essay, "Aristotelian Literary Criticism," by John Gassner (4th ed.; New York: Dover Publications, 1951).

Auerbach, Erich. "Figura" in *Scenes from the Drama of European Literature: Six Essays* (New York: Meridian Books, 1959), pp. 11-76.

Bady, René. *L'Homme et son "institution" de Montaigne à Bérulle*, Annales de l'Université de Lyon, 3ᵉ série, Fasc. 38 (Paris: Société d'Edition "Les Belles Lettres," 1964).

Baudelaire, Charles. "Mon Cœur mis à nu" in *Œuvres*, ed. Y.-G. Le Dantec (Paris: Bibliothèque de la Pléiade, 1951), pp. 1198-1229.

Bellarmin, Robert (Cardinal). *The Mind's Ascent to God by a Ladder of Created Things*, trans. Monialis (pseud.), with a Preface by P. N. Wagget (London: Mowbray; Milwaukee: Morehouse, 1925).

Bérulle, Pierre (Cardinal) de. *Œuvres complètes du Cardinal de Bérulle*, reproduction de l'édition princeps [1644] (2 vols.; Montsoult: Maison d'Institution de l'Oratoire, s.d.).

Boileau-Despréaux, Nicolas. *L'Art poétique* in *Œuvres complètes*, ed Charles-H. Boudhors (Paris: Les Belles Lettres, 1939), pp. 81-117.

Borgerhoff, E. B. O. *The Freedom of French Classicism* (Princeton, N. J.: Princeton University Press, 1950).

Bossuet, Jacques Bénigne. *Maximes et réflexions sur la comédie* in *L'Eglise et le théâtre: Bossuet—Maximes et reflexions sur la comédie, précédées d'une introduction historique et accompagnées de documents contemporains et de notes critiques*, ed. Ch. Urbain and E. Lévesque. (Paris: Grasset, 1930).

Bouyer, Louis. *Parole, église et sacrements dans le protestantisme et le catholicisme* (Bruges: Desclée de Brouwer, 1960).

Braaten, Carl E. "Toward A Theology of Hope," *New Theology*, No. 5, ed. Martin E. Marty and Dean G. Peerman (New York: Macmillan 1968), pp. 90-111.

Brasillach, Robert. *Pierre Corneille* (Paris: Arthème Fayard, 1938).

Bremond, Henri. *Histoire littéraire du sentiment religieux en France depuis des*

## BIBLIOGRAPHY

*guerres de religion jusqu'à nos jours* (Paris: Bloud et Gay, 1916-33). Here, especially, Vol. 1: *L' Humanisme dévot*.

Buffum, Imbrie. *Studies in the Baroque from Montaigne to Rotrou* (New Haven, Conn.: Yale University Press, 1957).

Butler, Phillip. *Classicisme et baroque dans l'œuvre de Racine* (Paris: Nizet, 1959).

Chambers, Edmund K. *The Mediaeval Stage* (2 vols.; London: Oxford University Press, 1903).

Chaunu, Pierre. *La Civilisation de l'Europe classique*, Collection Les Grandes Civilisations, dirigée par Raymond Bloch (Paris: Arthaud, 1966).

Cherpack, Clifton. *The Call of Blood in French Classical Tragedy* (Baltimore: The Johns Hopkins Press, 1958).

Craig, Hardin. *English Religious Drama of the Middle Ages* (Oxford: The Clarendon Press, 1955).

Dagens, Jean. *Bérulle et les origines de la restauration catholique (1575-1611)* (Paris: Desclée de Brouwer, 1952).

Deierkauf-Holsboer, S. Wilma. *Le Théâtre du Marais: I—La Période de gloire et de fortune 1634 (1629)-1648* (Paris: Nizet, 1954).

Descartes, René. *Œuvres et lettres*, ed. André Bridoux (Paris: Bibliothèque de la Pléiade, 1958).

Deschanel, Emile. *Le Romantisme des classiques: 1ère série: Corneille, Rotrou, Molière* (Paris: Calmann-Lévy, 1883).

Dewart, Leslie. *The Future of Belief: Theism in a World Come of Age* (New York: Herder & Herder, 1966).

Diderot, Denis. *Paradoxe sur le comédien* in *Œuvres complètes*, ed. J. Assézat (Paris: Garnier, 1875-77), VIII, 361-423.

Doubrovsky, Serge. "*La Princesse de Clèves:* une interprétation existentielle," *La Table Ronde*, No. 138 (June, 1959), 36-51.

Ehrmann, Jacques. *Un Paradis désespéré: L'Amour et l'Illusion dans l'Astrée* (New Haven, Conn.: Yale University Press; Paris: Presses Universitaires de France, 1963).

Fergusson, Francis. *The Idea of a Theater: A Study of Ten Plays—The Art of Drama in Changing Perspective* (Princeton, N. J.: Princeton University Press, 1949).

Fernandez, Ramon. *La Vie de Molière* (Paris: Gallimard, 1929).

Feugère, A. *Le Mouvement religieux dans la littérature du XVII⁵ siècle* (Paris: Boivin, 1938).

François de Sales, Saint. *Introduction à la vie dévote* (Paris: Nelson, s.d.).

Frye, Northrop. *A Natural Perspective: The Development of Shakespearean Comedy and Romance* (New York and London: Columbia University Press, 1965).

Gaquère, François. *Le Théâtre devant la conscience chrétienne (De Saint Jean Chrysostome à Pie XII et à Vatican II, de Bossuet au P. Carré* (Paris: Beauchesne, 1965).

Garnier, Robert. *Œuvres complètes: Théâtre et poésies*, ed. Lucien Pinvert (2 vols.; Paris: Garnier, 1923).

Gasté, Armand (ed.). *La Querelle du Cid: pièces et pamphlets publiés d'après les originaux.* (Paris: Welter, 1899).

## BIBLIOGRAPHY

Goldmann, Lucien. *Le Dieu caché: Etude sur la vision tragique dans les "Pensées" de Pascal et dans le théâtre de Racine* (Paris: Gallimard, 1955).

———. *Jean Racine: Dramaturge* (Paris: L'Arche, 1956).

Guizot, François Guillaume [with collaboration of Mme Guizot]. *Vie des poètes du siècle de Louis XIV* (Paris: F. Schoell, 1813).

Guthke, Karl. *Modern Tragicomedy: An Investigation into the Nature of the Genre* (New York: Random House, 1966).

Hardison, O. B., Jr. *Christian Rite and Christian Drama in the Middle Ages: Essays on the Origin and Early History of Modern Drama* (Baltimore: The Johns Hopkins Press, 1965).

Henry VIII, King of England. *Assertio Septem Sacramentorum or Defense of the Seven Sacraments,* ed. Louis O'Donovan. (New York: Benziger Brothers, 1908).

Herrick, Marvin T. *Tragicomedy: Its Origin and Development in Italy, France, and England,* Illinois Studies in Language and Literature, Vol. 39 (Urbana: The University of Illinois Press, 1955).

Hubert, Henri, et Marcel Mauss. "Essai sur la nature et la fonction du sacrifice," *L'Année sociologique,* II (1897-98), 29-138.

Kantorowicz, Ernst H. *The King's Two Bodies: A Study in Medieval Political Theology* (Princeton, N. J.: Princeton University Press, 1957).

Kitto, H. D. F. *Greek Tragedy: A Literary Study* (Paperbound edition, Garden City, N. Y.: Doubleday & Co., Inc., Anchor Books, 1954. First Published, 1939).

Knight, R. C. "A Minimal Definition of [French] Seventeenth-Century Tragedy," *French Studies,* X (1956), 297-308.

Lancaster, Henry Carrington. *A History of French Dramatic Literature in the Seventeenth Century* (9 vols.; Baltimore: The Johns Hopkins Press; London: Humphrey Milford; Oxford University Press; Paris: Les Belles Lettres, 1929-42).

———. *The French Tragicomedy: Its Origin and Development from 1552 to 1628* (Baltimore: J. H. Furst Co., 1907).

Lanson, Gustave. *Esquisse d'une histoire de la tragédie française,* (nouvelle édition revue et corrigée; Paris: Librairie Ancienne Honoré Champion, 1954).

Leeming, Bernard. *Principles of Sacramental Theology.* (Westminster, Md.: The Newman Press, 1956).

Lewis, C. S. *The Allegory of Love: A Study in Medieval Tradition* (Paperbound edition; New York: Oxford University Press, Galaxy Books, 1958. First published, 1936).

Loukovitch, Kosta. *L'Evolution de la tragédie religieuse classique en France* (Paris: Droz, 1933).

Mahelot, Laurent. *Le Mémoire de Mahelot, Laurent et d'autres décorateurs de l'Hôtel de Bourgogne et de la Comédie Française au XVII° siècle,* publié par Henry Carrington Lancaster (Paris: Champion, 1920).

Malinowski, Bronislaw. *"Magic, Science, and Religion" and Other Essays* (Paperbound edition; New York: Doubleday & Co., Anchor Books, 1954. First published: The Free Press, 1948).

Marsan, Jules. *La Pastorale dramatique en France à la fin du XVI° et au commencement du XVII° siècle* (Paris: Hachette, 1905).

## BIBLIOGRAPHY

Mazzeo, Joseph Anthony. *Renaissance and Seventeenth-Century Studies* (New York: Columbia University Press; London: Routledge & Kegan Paul, 1964).

McGowan, Margaret. *Le Ballet de cour en France: 1581-1643* (Paris: Editions du Centre National de la Recherche Scientifique, 1963).

Metz, Johannes B. "Creative Hope," *New Theology*, No. 5, ed. Martin E. Marty and Dean G. Peerman (New York: Macmillan, 1968), pp. 130-41.

Molière (pseudonym of Jean Baptiste Poquelin). *Œuvres*, ed. Eugène Despois et Paul Mesnard (13 vols.; Paris: Hachette, 1873-1900).

Moore, Will G. *French Classical Literature: An Essay* (London: Oxford University Press, 1961).

Morel, Jacques. *La Tragédie*, Collection "U": Serie "Lettres Françaises" sous la direction de Robert Mauzi (Paris: Armand Colin, 1964).

Nelson, Robert J. *Corneille, His Heroes and Their Worlds* (Philadelphia: University of Pennsylvania Press, 1963).

——. "Tragedy and the Tragic," *Arion*, II (1963), 86-95.

Niebuhr, Reinhold. *Beyond Tragedy: Essays on the Christian Interpretation of History* (New York: Charles Scribner's Sons, 1937).

O'Brien, Conor Cruise. "Burke and Marx," *New American Review*, No. 1 (New York and Toronto: The New American Library, 1967), 243-58.

Pascal, Blaise. *Pensées* in *Œuvres complètes*, ed. Léon Brunschvicg (Paris: Hachette, 1904), Vols. XII-XIV.

——. *Pensées sur la religion et sur quelques autres sujets*, ed. Louis Lafuma (3 vols.; Paris: Editions du Luxembourg, 1951).

Racine, Jean. *Œuvres*, ed. Paul Mesnard (10 vols.; Paris: Hachette, 1885).

Rank, Otto. *Don Juan: Une Etude sur le double*, trans. S. Lautman (Paris: Denoël et Steele, 1932).

——. "The Double as Immortal Self" in *Beyond Psychology* (New York: Dover Publications, 1941; Paperbound edition, 1958), pp. 62-101.

Rébelliau, Alfred. *Un Episode de l'histoire religieuse du XVII° siècle*, a series of articles in *Revue des deux mondes*, 5° période, as follows: "La Compagnie du Saint-Sacrement" (July 1, 1903), 49-82; "La Compagnie du Saint-Sacrement et la contre-reformation catholique" (August 1, 1903), 540-63; "La Compagnie du Saint-Sacrement et les protestants" (August 15, 1903), 103-35; "La Compagnie du Saint-Sacrement d'après des documents nouveaux" (August 15, 1908), 834-68; "Deux Ennemis de la Compagnie du Saint-Sacrement: Molière et Port Royal" (October 15, 1909), 892-923; "Le Rôle politique et les survivances de la Compagnie secrète du Saint-Sacrement" (November 1, 1909), 200-228.

Rieff, Philip. *The Triumph of the Therapeutic: Uses of Faith after Freud* (New York: Harper & Row, 1966).

Rousset, Jean. *La Littérature de l'âge baroque en France: Circé et le paon* (Paris: José Corti, 1954).

Sainte-Beuve, Ch.-A. *Port Royal*, ed. Maxime Leroy (3 vols.; Paris: Bibliothèque de la Pléiade, 1961).

Saint-Marc Girardin [pseudonym of François Auguste Marc Girardin]. "De la jalousie dans le théâtre français du XVII° siècle: Rotrou et Corneille" in his *Cours de littérature dramatique*, 10° édition (Paris: Charpentier, 1874), II, 340-73.

## BIBLIOGRAPHY

Sartre, Jean-Paul. *L'Existentialisme est un humanisme* (Paris: Nagel, 1946).

Schérer, Jacques. *La Dramaturgie classique en France* (Paris: Nizet, 1950).

Shakespeare, William. *The Yale Shapespeare*, ed. Wilbur L. Cross and Tucker Brooke (40 vols.; New Haven, Conn.: Yale University Press; London: Geoffrey Cumberlege; Oxford University Press, 1917-27).

Thomas Aquinas, Saint. *Basic Writings of Saint Thomas Aquinas*, ed. Anton C. Pegis (2 vols.; New York: Random House, 1945).

Trilling, Lionel. "The Sense of the Past" in *The Liberal Imagination* (London: Secker & Warburg, 1951), pp. 181-97.

———. *The Opposing Self: Nine Essays in Criticism* (London: Secker & Warburg, 1955).

Vahanian, Gabriel. *The Death of God: The Culture of Our Post-Christian Era* (New York: George Braziller, 1961).

———. *Wait Without Idols* (New York: George Braziller, 1964).

Vauquelin de la Fresnaye, Jean. *L'Art Poétique*, ed. Georges Pellisier (Paris: Garnier, 1855).

Voltaire [François-Marie Arouet de]. *Commentaires sur Corneille* in *Œuvres complètes*, ed. Louis Moland (Paris: Garnier, 1877-85), XXXI-XXXII.

Wardropper, Bruce W. "The Search for a Dramatic Formula for the *Auto Sacramental*," *PMLA*, LXV, No. 6 (1950), 1196-1211.

Williams, Charles. *The Descent of the Dove: A Short History of the Holy Spirit in the Church* (Paperbound edition; Grand Rapids, Mich.: William B. Eerdmans, n.d. First published, New York: Pellegrini & Cudahy, 1939).

Young, Karl. *The Drama of the Medieval Church* (Oxford: The Clarendon Press, 1933).

# Index

This Index is based on proper names: titles and characters of creative works; authors' names without titles for secondary references; movements (usually under the name of the personal founder); etc. Initial definite and indefinite articles in titles have been suppressed for ease of reference. Characters from creative works (including those of Rotrou) are listed throughout the Index. References to Rotrou's sources have been cross-indexed, with the works in question appearing both separately and under the name of author. References to Rotrou's plays as plays have been placed under his name, with italics indicating continuous discussion of a work.

Achille, 113-17, 119, 216 n. 20$^R$
Adam, 197, 204, 217 n. 27
Adraste, 215 n. 9$^R$
*Adrianus*, 26, 29
Adrian, 26
Adrien, 20-38, 100, 124, 143, 167, 180, 186, 202 n. 1$^R$
Agamemnon, 111-17, 216 n. 20$^R$
Agis, 70, 209 n. 27$^R$
Alcandre (*Bague de l'oubli*), 41, 46, 49, 205 n. 1$^R$
Alcandre (*Illusion comique*), 41
Alcide, 50
Alcmène (Molière), 84
Alcmène (*Hercule mourant*), 68, 80, 113, 209 n. 27$^R$
Alcmène (*Sosies*), 80-89, 211 n. 39$^R$
Alexandre (*Bague de l'oubli*), 42, 205 n. 1$^R$
Alexandre (*Venceslas*), 139-57, 164, 219 n. 3$^R$
Alexandre (*Véritable Saint Genest*), 44
Alfonce, 41-47, 73, 139, 205 n. 1$^R$
Aliaste, 203 n. 5
Alphrède, 127
Amintas, 216 n. 20$^R$
*Amores del alma*, 196
Amphitryon (Molière), 78, 82-83
Amphitryon (Molière), 82-84
*Amphitryon* (Plautus), 77
Amphitryon (*Sosies*), 80-85, 89, 211 n. 39$^R$

Andreas; *see* Cappellanus
Andromaque, 101, 158
Angélique, 49, 51, 206 n. 7$^R$
Anselme (*Clarice*), 218 n. 32
Anselme (*Sœur*), 133, 135, 136, 218 n. 1$^R$
Anthisme, 30
*Antigone* (Sophocles), 215 n. 10
Antigone (Sophocles), 106
Antigone (*Antigone*), 103-11, 153, 186, 214 n. 9$^R$
Antioche, 92-101, 213 n. 1$^R$
Antiochus, 140, 159
Antonie (*Bélissaire*), 120-22, 127, 217 n. 26$^R$
Aquinas, St. Thomas, 14, 119, 193, 207 n. 11, 214 n. 8, 219 n. 2
*Araucana*, 197
Arcas, 7, 65, 69, 72, 87, 153, 209 n. 27$^R$
Argie, 215 n. 9$^R$
Aricie, 171-72
Aristotle, 11, 21, 152, 221
Arnauld, 13
Artanasde, 162, 222 n. 21$^R$
*Art poétique*, 8, 10, 201 n. 17
*Astrée*, 3, 56, 58
*Athalie*, 11, 183, 223 n.6
Auerbach, Erich, 86, 88, 193-95
Auguste, 98, 99
Augustine, St., 6, 13, 38, 86, 88, 182, 185, 193, 194, 199 n. 1, 225 n. 3
Aurélie, 133-37, 218 n. 1$^R$

[239]

## INDEX

*Aveugle de Smyrne*, 16, 201 n. 24

Bady, René, 9, 200 n. 5
Bajazet, 121
*Bajazet*, 121
Bargagli (*Pellegrina*), 207 n. 14
Baronius, 10
Barroux, Robert, 200, n. 10
Baudelaire, 185, 186, 224 n. 16
Belin, 225
Bélissaire (also, Belisarius), 120-30, 134, 142, 143, 147, 165, 217
*Bélissaire* (Desfontaines), 119, 125
Bellarmin, 10, 75, 108
*Bérénice*, 10
Bérénice, 182
Bérulle, 86, 199, 213 n. 46
Blois, Robert de, 192
Boileau, 10, 201 n. 17
Bossuet, 8-11
*Bourgeois gentilhomme*, 133
Bouyer, Louis, 194
Bremond, 200
*Britannicus*, 121
Brunschvicg, 204 n. 13, 205 n. 19
Butler, Philip, 6, 104, 105, 109, 110, 181-83, 199 n. 2, 215 n. 15

Cadmus, 101, 109, 110
Caesar (also, César), 25, 34, 100, 104, 125, 180
Calchas, 112-16
Camille, 19, 20, 202 n. 1R
Camille (*Horace*), 99, 105
Capellanus, Andreas, 50, 207 n. 8
Cassandre (*Venceslas*), 139-59, 177, 219 n. 3R
Cassie, 92-100, 213 n. 1R
*Celestina*, 196
Céliante, 51, 52, 206 n. 7R
Célidore, 59, 61, 64, 208 n. 21R
Célie (*Pélerine amoureuse*), 49-52, 206 n. 7R
Célimène, 55
Cellot, 26, 29, 160; *Adrianus* 26, 29; *Chosroës* 160
Céphalie (*Sosies*), 212 n. 39R
Céphise, 58-64, 208 n. 21R
César; see Caesar

Chardon, Henri, 190, 224 n. 3
Charron, Pierre, 4, 10
Chaunu, Pierre, 12
Chekhov, 184
Cherpack, 222, 223
Chimène, 158, 159
*Chosroës*, 160
Christ, 9, 25, 98, 122, 192, 197, 207 n. 10, 219 n. 2
*Cid*, 151, 157-59, 211
Cinna, 98
Cinq Auteurs, 16
Clariane, 73, 74, 76, 210 n. 35R
Clarice, 218 n. 32
Clarimond, 211 n. 35R
Clarinde, 203 n. 5
Claudel, 182
Cléanthis, 82, 83
Cléopâtre, 74, 159, 168
*Cléopâtre captive*, 8
Cléodore (*Cristante*), 214
Cloridan, 203 n. 5
Clorimand, 51, 52
Clorinde, 214
Clytemnestre, 112, 113, 216
Combalet, Mme de, 225
*Comédie des Tuileries*, 16, 201
Compagnie d'Anger, 200
Compagnie de Paris, 200
Compagnie du Saint Sacrement, 10, 88, 200, 213
Constance (*Sœur*), 134, 148, 218 n. 1R
Corinthe, 92
Corman, 189
Corneille, 3, 4, 5, 8, 11, 23, 27, 41, 59, 72, 74, 97-99, 104, 106, 107, 109, 137-40, 156, 157, 159, 166, 168, 182, 183, 189, 199 n. 1, 200 n. 7, 202 n. 25, 208 n. 15, 225 n. 3
*Corneille et Rotrou*, 189
Cosroès, 160-77, 221 n. 21R
Crane, Thomas Frederick, 31, 137, 190, 203, 220, 221
Crates, 93, 99
Créon, 101-11, 152, 215 n. 9R
*Cresphontes*, 153
Crisante, 91-100, 158, 186, 213 n. 1R
Cyprian, 193, 197, 225 n. 2

[240]

# INDEX

Cyrus, 164

Dagens, Jean, 6
Damète, 209 n. 21[R]
Dante, 194
Décorateur (*Véritable Saint Genest*), 21
Deierkauf-Holsboer, 189
Déjanire (also, Deïanira), 64-70, 120, 209 n. 27[R]
Della Porta (*Sorella*), 133
Descartes, 25, 85, 204 n. 10
Deschanel, 26
Desfontaines, 22, 23, 26, 119, 120, 125, 204 n. 8
Dewart, Leslie, 214 n. 8
Diane (*Astrée*), 56
Diane (*Iphigénie*), 113, 116, 117, 216 n. 20[R]
Diane (*Pélerine amoureuse*), 53
Diderot, 24
Dioclétien (*Illustre comédien*), 23
Dioclétien (*Véritable Saint Genest*), 20, 100, 202 n. 1[R]
Dom Bernard, 142, 218
Dom Garcie, 218
Dom Pedre, 179, 180
Don Gayferos, 196
*Duc d'Ossone*, 207
Du Vair, 4

Edict of Nantes, 3, 8
Edict of Parlement of Paris, 7, 11
Ehrmann, Jacques, 56, 57, 208
*Ejemplo mayor de la desdicha*, 119
Ephyte, 107, 215 n. 9[R]
Erasme, 51, 206 n. 7[R]
Eraste, 132-37, 218 n. 1[R]
Ergaste, 132-37, 218 n. 1[R]
Eroxène, 132-37, 218 n. 1[R]
*Esther*, 11, 183
Etéocle (*Antigone*), 101-11, 114, 214 n. 9[R]
Etéocle (*Thébaïde*), 105
Euphorbe, 99
Euripides, 3, 111, 115, 118, 215 n. 10; *Iphigenia in Aulis* 111
Evandre, 73, 76, 77, 211 n. 35[R]
Eve, 88, 204 n. 14, 217 n. 27

Existentialism, 11

Fabrice, 40-48
Fédéric, 139-57, 164, 219 n. 3[R]
*Feint véritable*, 203 n. 8
Félismond, 72-77, 210 n. 35[R]
Felix, 97, 106
Fernandez, 190
Filandre (*Astrée*), 56
Filandre (*Célimène*), 56
Filandre (*Filandre*), 58-64, 208 n. 21[R]
Filène, 52, 206 n. 7[R]
Filidan, 49-54, 71, 207 n. 7[R]
*Fingido verdadero*, 22
Flavie, 34
Fouquet, Nicolas, 201 n. 24
Francis de Sales, Saint (also, François de Sales), 10, 14, 26, 31, 199 n. 1
Fréron, 137, 220 n. 5, 221 n. 11
Freud, 11
Frye, Northrup, 180, 181, 185, 195
Furietière, 10, 191, 226 n. 20.

Garapon, Robert, 208 n. 15
Garnier, Robert, 4, 8, 11
Gassendi, 9, 182, 200 n. 10
Genest (*Illustre comédien*), 22, 23
Genest (*Veritable Saint Genest*), 19-38, 47, 100, 124, 142, 147, 154, 163, 164, 180, 186, 202 n. 1[R]
Géronte, 132, 218 n. 1[R]
Gines (Lope de Vega), 22
Gnostic, 197
Godeau, Antoine de, 190
Godefroy, 191, 192
Goldmann, Lucien, 3, 181-83 passim, 223 n. 6
Guizet, François, 138

*Hamlet*, 159
Harnack, 185, 186, 201 n. 22
Hélène (also, Helen), 115-118
Hémon, 107, 110, 215 n. 9[R]
Henry VIII (King of England), 204 n. 12
*Héraclius*, 159, 222 n. 37
Hercule, 7-12, 37, 65-71, 86, 87, 113, 118, 155, 160, 209 n. 27[R]
Hercule (*Sosies*), 212 n. 39[R]

[241]

## INDEX

*Hercules furens*, 87
*Hercules Oetaeus*, 210 n. 32
Hermante, 73-77, 92, 111, 116, 121, 125, 129, 167, 168, 210 n. 35[R]
Hermes, 74
Hermione, 101, 121
Herrick, Marvin T., 183
Hippolyte, 171, 172, 182
Horace (Corneille), 99, 104, 105
Horace (*Sœur*), 218 n. 1[R]
Hormidaste, 162, 222 n. 21[R]
Hormisdas, 221 n. 21[R]
Hôtel de Bourgogne, 189
Hubert, Henri, 116, 117, 216 n. 22
Hubert, J., 203, 216 n. 22
Humanism, 6, 8, 11, 195

Ibsen, 184
*Illusion comique*, 208 n. 15
*Illustre amazone*, 16, 201 n. 24
*Illustre comédien*, 22, 119
Iole, 7, 65-72, 87, 209 n. 27[R]
Iphigenia, 115
*Iphigenia in Aulis*, 111
Iphigénie (*Iphigénie*), 7, 12, 111-18, 153, 186, 216 n. 20[R]
Isidore, 193, 194
Ismène, 110, 214 n. 9[R]

Jansenius (also, Jansenist, Jansenistic), 6, 9, 10, 13, 34, 35, 38, 81, 83, 88, 89, 132, 179, 180, 181, 182, 194, 204 n. 14
Jesuit, 20, 26, 28, 38, 132
Jocaste (also, Jocasta), 101-11, 214 n. 9[R]
Jodelle, 8
Joseph, Saint, 88
*Juifves*, 11
Jung, 197
Junie, 121
Juno, 87
Junon (*Hecule mourant*), 66, 68, 209
Junon (*Sosies*), 87, 211 n. 39[R]
Jupin, 68
Jupiter (*Amphitryon*), 82, 83, 84
Jupiter (*Hercule mourant*), 209 n. 27[R]
Jupiter (*Sosies*), 80, 86

Justinien (also, Justinian), 119, 120, 128

Kantorowicz, Ernst, 44, 156
Kitto, H. D., 109
Knight, R. C. 170, 186
Knutson, H. C., 17, 73, 140, 189, 202 n. 25

La Boullaye, 189
Ladborough, R. S., 204 n. 14
Ladislas, 40, 137-59, 162, 179, 219 n. 3[R], 221 n. 9
Lafuma, Louis, 204 n. 13, 205 n. 19
La Harpe, 137, 220 n. 5
La Mothe Le Vayer, 6
Lancaster, H. C., 15, 16, 17, 53, 55, 56, 60, 64, 69, 73, 77, 96, 101, 108, 121, 137, 159, 166, 170, 183, 190, 220 n. 6
Lanson, Gustave, 139, 181, 186
La Pinelière, 211 n. 35
La Pommeraye, Henri de, 221 n. 9
Léandre (*Bague de l'oubli*), 39-49, 205 n. 1[R]
Léandre (*Pélerine amoureuse*), 52, 206 n. 7[R]
Leiner, W., 139, 140
Lélie, 132-137, 218 n. 1[R]
Lentule, 31, 47
Léonie, 211 n. 35[R]
Léonor (*Bague de l'oubli*), 39, 40, 46-49, 205 n. 1[R]
Léonor (*Dom Bernard de Cabrère*), 140
Léonor (*Venceslas*), 140, 148
Léonse (*Bélisaire*), 123, 128, 162, 217 n. 26[R]
*Lettres provinciales*, 13, 88, 132, 179
Lewis, C. S., 49, 207 n. 8
Libertins (also, Libertinage), 6, 182
Liliane, 39-45, 205 n. 1[R]
Lope (*Dom Bernard de Cabrère*), 142, 218 n. 34
Lope (*Dom Lope de Cardone*), 179, 180, 218 n. 34
Loukovitch, Kosta, 8
Lucidor, 49-54, 71, 206 n. 7[R]
Lydie, 133-37, 219 n. 1[R]

[242]

# INDEX

Maillier, Charles, 189
Mairet, 207 n. 15, 210 n. 28, 225 n. 3
Malherbe, 53
Malinowski, Bronislaw, 41-42
Manichaeism, 54, 98, 120, 128, 217 n. 27
Manilie (*Crisante*), 97, 101, 213 n. 1[R]
*Marc Antoine*, 8
Marcella, 22
Marcelle, 24-30, 35, 202 n. 1[R]
Marcie, 92, 95-99, 214 n. 1[R]
Mardesane, 159-77, 221 n. 21[R]
Marmontel, J. F., 137, 138, 146, 158, 220 n. 5, 221 n. 11
Marot, 192
Marsan, 56
Marx, 11, 38, 198
Mauss, Marcel, 116, 117
Maximin, 20, 22, 26, 28, 29, 202 n. 1[R]
Mazzeo, Joseph, 193
McGowan, Margaret, 212 n. 40
*Médée*, 107
Mélite, 43
Menaechmi, 11
*Menaechmus Twins*, 78
Menalche, 209 n. 21[R]
Ménécée (*Antigone*), 108, 215 n. 9[R]
Ménechme-Soscicle, 142
Ménélas, 112-14, 216 n. 20[R]
Mercure (*Sosies*), 85, 211 n. 39[R]
Mérope, 153
Michel, A., 88, 193, 194, 210 n. 31, 214 n. 7
Millevoye, 189
Mira de Amescua (*Ejemplo mayor de la Desdicha*), 119
Molière, 13, 78, 81-86, 190, 213 n. 49, 218 n. 34
Morel, Jacques, 60, 61, 108, 146, 149, 189, 199 n. 1, 201 n. 18, 209 n. 22, 210 n. 32, 215 n. 19, 223 n. 7
*Mort de Rotrou*, 189

Narcissus, 192, 197
Narsée (*Cosroès*), 159, 161, 164, 168-72, 174, 177, 222 n. 21[R]
Narsès (*Bélissaire*), 123, 128, 162, 217 n. 26[R]
Natalie, 24-30, 167, 202 n. 1[R]

Naudé, 6, 182
Neoplatonism, 5, 42, 46, 55, 61, 197
Nérée, 58-64, 208 n. 21[R]
Néron, 121
Nesse, 70, 209 n. 27[R]
*Nicomède*, 159
Niebuhr, 110
*No hay ser padre siendo rey*, 137

C'Brien, Conor Cruise, 38
Octavio, 22
Œdipe (*Antigone*), 109, 214 n. 9[R]
Œdipe (Sophocles), 109
*Œdipe* (Corneille), 109
Oratoire, 10
Orgye, 135, 136, 218 n. 1[R]
Origen, 193, 194, 197
Orlando, Francesco, 21, 37, 77, 159, 160, 163, 166, 167, 189, 199 n. 2, 203 n. 2, 221 n. 16
Oronte, 203 n. 5

Palmyras, 163, 164, 166, 172-74, 221 n. 21[R]
Pamphile, 219 n. 1[R]
Pamphilie, 23
Paris, 115
Parthénie, 73-76, 210 n. 35[R]
Pascal, 9, 11, 13, 26, 34, 38, 41, 88, 111, 132, 176, 179, 181, 204 n. 14
Pauline, 27
Pelagius, 38, 200 n. 12
*Pellegrina*, 207 n. 14
Perside, 203 n. 5
Person, Léonce, 190
Peysonnié, 189
Phèdre, 74, 75, 121
*Phèdre*, 75, 171
Philippe (*Bélissaire*), 122, 123, 127, 128, 129, 217 n. 26[R]
Philoctète, 65-68, 209 n. 27[R]
*Phoenissae*, 215 n. 10
Pirandello, 21, 184, 203 n. 5
Plato, 5, 11, 194
Plautus, 3, 77, 78, 80; *Amphitryon* 77, 78, 80; *Menaechmus Twins* 78
Polidor, 218 n. 1[R]
*Polyeucte*, 8, 11, 23
Polyeucte, 27, 97, 106

[243]

# INDEX

Polynice (*Antigone*), 101-11, 114, 214 n. 9[R]
Polynice (*Thébaïde*), 105, 106
Pomoren; *see* Portmorand
Pompadour, Mme de, 138
Portmorand (also, Pomoren), 88
Pyrrhus, 121

*Querelle du Cid*, 224 n. 3

Racine, 3, 10, 11, 71, 74, 92, 101, 103, 104-6, 110, 121, 137, 138, 139, 159, 172, 181, 182, 183, 185, 186, 190, 199 n. 2, 202 n. 25, 223 n. 6
Raemond, Florimond de, 7, 9, 15, 72
Rank, Otto, 78, 79, 87, 197
Rébelliau, Alfred, 10, 200 n. 13
*Rescate del Alma*, 197
Richelieu, 74, 211 n. 37
Richeome, 9, 88, 200 n. 12
Rieff, Philip, 185
*Rodogune*, 74, 140, 159
Rojas, 137, 221 n. 6
Ronsard, 8
Rotrou: *Agésilan de Colchos*, 15, 225 n. 3 (Appendix A); *Amélie*, 14, 55, 207 n. 15; *Antigone*, 15, *101-11*, 114, 118, 139, 156, 160, 209 n. 22, 214 n. 9[R]; *Bague de l'oubli*, 14, *38-49*, 54, 58, 65, 73, 123, 139, 205 n. 1[R]; *Bélissaire*, 12-16 passim, 33, *119-30*, 132, 135, 140, 146, 160, 162, 165, 168, 184, 210 n. 29, 217 n. 26[R], 218 n. 30; *Belle Alphrède*, 15, 148, 151, 212 n. 40, 213 n. 49; *Captifs*, 15, 202 n. 25, 215 n. 19, 218 n. 30; *Céliane*, 14, 55, 56, 140, 206 n. 6; *Célie*, 15, 130, 216 n. 19, 218 n. 33; *Célimène*, 14, 55-57, 58, 61; *Clarice*, 15, 202 n. 25, 217 n. 25, 218 n. 32; *Clorinde*, 14, 212 n. 40, 214 n. 2; *Cosroès*, 15, *159-77*, 181-84, 218 n. 34, 221 n. 21[R]; *Crisante*, 15, 16, *91-101*, 108, 113, 146, 184, 212 n. 40, 213 n. 1[R], 214 nn. 2, 7; *Deux Pucelles*, 15, 212 n. 40; *Diane*, 14, 206 n. 6, 207 n. 14; *Dom Bernard de Cabrère*, 15, 91, 179, 202 n. 25, 216 n. 19, 218 n. 34; *Dom Lope de Cardone*, 15, 16, 179-81, 216 n. 19, 223 n. 3; *Doristée* (also, *Cléagenor et Doristée*), 14, 64, 210 nn. 28, 29; *Filandre*, 14, 58-64, 91, 208, n. 21[R], 210 n. 28; *Florimonde*, 15, 212 n. 40, 214 n. 2; *Hercule mourant*, 7, 13, 14, *64-72*, 87, 92, 98, 112, 153, 154, 155, 175, 209 n. n. 27[R], 212 n. 40; *Heureuse Constance*, 14, 210 n. 28; *Heureux Naufrage*, 14, 105; *Hypocondriaque, ou le mort amoureux*, 12, 14, 46, 54, 73, 203 n. 5, 205 n. 18; *Innocente Infidelité*, 12, 14, *72-77*, 92, 111, 116, 121, 129, 148, 167, 168, 210 n. 35[R], 212 n. 40; *Iphigénie*, 7, 15, *111-19*, 129, 160, 210 n. 29, 212 n. 40, 215 n. 19, 216 n. 20[R]; *Laure persecutée*, 15, 201 n. 18, 215 n. 19; *Ménechmes*, 14, 55, 78, 206 n. 6, 218 n. 30; *Occasions perdues*, 14, 210 n. 28; *Pélerine amoureuse*, 14, *49-55*, 71, 72, 130, 131, 147, 202 n. 25, 206 n. 6, 207 n. 14; *Sœur*, 12, 15, 16, 29, 33, 130, *131-37*, 148, 153, 163, 217 n. 25, 218 n. 1[R]; *Sosies*, 13, 15, 36, *77-89*, 91, 107, 117, 129, 130, 211 n. 39[R], 213 n. 49, 223 n. 3; *Venceslas*, 15, 77, *137-59*, 160, 163, 164, 175, 177, 179, 181, 183, 184, 190, 216 n. 19, 218 n. 34, 219 n. 3[R], 220 n. 5, 221 n. 9; *Véritable Saint Genest*, 3, 4, 11, 13, 16, *19-38*, 39, 46, 119, 124, 130, 132, 133, 135, 137, 145, 175, 190, 202 n. 1[R], 204 n. 14, 205 n. 18, 209 n. 22, 218 n. 33, 220 n. 6
Roxanne, 121
Rubens, 200

Sabine, 99
Saint Ange, 13
Saint Cyran, 9, 13, 74, 88, 211 n. 37
Sainte-Beuve, 23, 200 n. 12, 211 n. 37
Saint Germain, 159
Saint-Marc Girardin, 137, 150
Saint-René Taillandier, 189
Salamacis, 105
Sarcey, 150
Sardarigue, 162, 164, 166, 173, 177, 222 n. 21[R]
Sartre, 85, 212
Schérer, Jacques, 17, 24, 159, 160, 170, 171, 174, 202 n. 25
Séleucus, 140, 159
Seneca (also, Sénèque), 3, 7, 69, 72, 87, 210 n. 32; *Hercules furens* 87; *Hercules Oetaeus* 210
Sévère, 23

# INDEX

Shakespeare, 137, 180, 195
Sirmond, 10
Sophie, 132-37, 218 n. 1[R]
Sophocles, 3, 106, 108, 137, 215 n. 14; *Antigone* 215
Sophonisbe, 210
*Sorella*, 133
*Sortija del Olvido*, 206
Sosicle, 142
Sosie (*Amphitryon*), 82, 83
Sosie (*Sosies*), 84-87, 211 n. 39[R]
Steffens, George, 206 n. 5
Stiefel, Arthur L., 170, 206 n. 5, 207 n. 14
Stoicism, 11, 93, 100, 198
Strindberg, 184
Syra, 159, 161-77, 221 n. 21[R]
Syroès, 159-77, 221 n. 21[R], 223 n. 38

Tancrède, 41-44, 205 n. 1[R]
Taschereau, Jules, 224 n. 3
Teilhard de Chardin, 182
Tertullian, 193, 225 n. 2
Théane, 59-64, 208 n. 21[R]
Théandre, 210 n. 29
*Thébaïde*, 215 n. 10
*Théodore*, 11
Théodore (also, Theodora) (*Bélissaire*), 120-30, 140, 168, 217 n. 26[R]
Théodore (*Venceslas*), 140, 144-48, 150, 152, 155, 219 n. 3[R]
Thersandre, 211 n. 35[R]

Thimante, 59-64, 208 n. 21[R]
*T'imoléon*, 159
Tirésie, 107, 215, n. 9[R]
Trent, Council of, 8, 13, 36, 62, 63, 130
Tridentine; *see* Trent, Council of
Tristan L'Hermite, 56, 208 n. 21[R]

Ulysse, 112-17, 216 n. 20[R]
Urban IV, Pope, 196
Urfé, 56, 57

Vahanian, Gabriel, 12, 169, 183, 201 n. 19, 213
Valentine, Ussé de, 222 n. 37
Valérie, 19, 145, 202 n. 1[R]
Valdivielso, 197
Valle Abad, 190
Van Baelen, Jacqueline, 37, 94, 96, 112, 139, 147, 189, 210 n. 34
Vauquelin de la Fresnaye, 8-10
Vega (Lope de), 22, 26, 197; *Araucana* 197; *Fingido Verdadero* 22; *Sortija del Olvido* 206 n. 5
Venceslas (*Bague de l'oubli*), 40, 139
Venceslas (*Venceslas*), 40, 139-58, 162, 163, 175, 219 n. 3[R]
Viollet-le-Duc, 15, 126, 201 n. 24
Virgin Mary, 51
Voltaire, 137

Wardropper, Bruce W., 196, 197
Williams, Charles, 200

www.ingramcontent.com/pod-product-compliance
Lightning Source LLC
Chambersburg PA
CBHW030134240426
43672CB00005B/123